Tl

Th
on   This book must be roversial events and themes of
wo   in the present century.   Each book provides
sufficient narrative and explanation for the newcomer to the
subject while offering, for more advanced study, detailed source-
references and bibliographies, together with interpretation and
reassessment in the light of recent scholarship.

   In the choice of subjects there is a balance between breadth
in some spheres and detail in others; between the essentially
political and matters economic or social. The series cannot be
a comprehensive account of everything that has happened in
the twentieth century, but it provides a guide to recent research
and explains something of the times of extraordinary change
and complexity in which we live. It is directed in the main to
students of contemporary history and international relations,
but includes titles which are of direct relevance to courses in
economics, sociology, politics and geography.

The Making of the 20th Century

Series Editor: GEOFFREY WARNER

David Armstrong, *The Rise of the International Organisation:
A Short History*
S. R. Ashton, *In Search of Détente: The Politics of East–West Relations
since 1945*
V. R. Berghahn, *Germany and the Approach of War in 1914,* second edition
Raymond F. Betts, *France and Decolonisation, 1900–1960*
John Darwin, *Britain and Decolonisation: The Retreat from Empire in the
Post-War World*
John F. V. Keiger, *France and the Origins of the First World War*
Dominic Lieven, *Russia and the Origins of the First World War*
Sally Marks, *The Illusion of Peace: International Relations
in Europe, 1918–1933*
Philip Morgan, *Italian Fascism, 1919–1945*
A. J. Nicholls, *Weimar and the Rise of Hitler,* third edition
R. A. C. Parker, *Chamberlain and Appeasement: British Policy
and the Coming of the Second World War*
G. Roberts, *The Soviet Union and the Origins of the Second World War*
Alan Sharp, *The Versailles Settlement: Peacemaking in Paris, 1919*
Zara Steiner, *Britain and the Origins of the First World War*
Samuel R. Williamson, *Austria–Hungary and the Origins
of the First World War*

FORTHCOMING TITLES

Saki Dockrill, *Japan and the Origins of the Second World War*
J. E. Spence, *South Africa in International Society*
Glyn Stone, *Great Powers and the Iberian Peninsular 1931-1941*
Jonathan Wright, *Germany and the Origins of the Second World War*
R. Young, *France and the Origins of the Second World War*

Italian Fascism, 1919–1945

Philip Morgan

First published 1995 by
MACMILLAN PRESS LTD
Houndmills, Basingstoke, Hampshire RG21 6XS
and London
Companies and representatives
throughout the world

ISBN 0–333–53778–5 hardcover
ISBN 0–333–53779–3 paperback

A catalogue record for this book is available
from the British Library.

10   9   8   7   6   5   4   3
04   03   02   01   00   99   98

Printed in Malaysia

This book is dedicated to my father and to the memory of my mother, who was always asking when it was going to be finished.

Contents

Acknowledgement   ix

List of Abbreviations   x

Map of Modern Italy   xii

Part 1   The Conquest of Power, 1919–29   1

1   The Postwar Crisis and the Rise of Fascism, 1919–22   3
    Politics and society in post-unification Italy   3
    The war in Italy   6
    '1919-ism' and early Fascism   13
    The 1919 elections   16
    The *biennio rosso* and Fiume   21
    The Fascist reaction   34
    Giolitti and Fascism   40
    The transition from movement to party   43
    The March on Rome   52

2   Between 'Normalisation' and 'Revolution', 1922–5   60
    The various Fascisms   60
    Dictatorship by stealth   64
    The conquest of the South and the 1924 election   71
    The Matteotti crisis   75

3   The Construction of the 'Totalitarian' State, 1925–9   79
    'Totalitarianism'   79
    The party and the state   81
    Syndicates and corporations   88
    The Fascist constitution   92
    The conciliation with the Catholic Church   95
    The revaluation of the lira   97
    'Ruralism'   101

Part II The Fascist Regime, 1929–36   105

4   The Years of the Great Depression, 1929–34   107
     The party and the *inquadramento* of the nation   107
     The organisation of the young, welfare and free time   109
     The impact and limitations of 'totalitarian' control   116
     Corporativism and the Great Depression   124

5   The Creation of the Fascist Empire, 1935–6   131
     Imperialism, revisionism and the limits to Fascist foreign
        policy in the 1920s   131
     The 'totalitarian' state: internal policy as foreign policy
        and vice versa   136
     The Depression and Fascism's opportunity   138
     The invasion and conquest of Ethiopia   140

**Part III Fascist Expansionism at Home and Abroad,
1936–43**   145

6   The Axis Connection and the 'Fascistisation' of Italian
     Society, 1936–40   147
     The Axis with Germany   147
     Forcing the pace of 'fascistisation'   155
     Autarky and economic preparation for war   165
     'Non-belligerency' and war, 1939–40   169

7   Fascist Italy at War, 1940–3   173
     The collapse of Italy's parallel war   173
     The impact of war and the internal crisis of the regime   176
     The fall of Mussolini   180

Epilogue: The Italian Social Republic, 1943–5   183

Notes   189

Select Bibliography   193

Index   200

Acknowledgement

I am particularly grateful to Tony Mason, who offered to read the chapters as they were written, and did so speedily, giving not only comment and encouragement but also good advice on how to make the text more manageable and readable.

List of Abbreviations

CIL	*Confederazione Italiana del Lavoro* [Italian Confederation of Labour (Catholic trade union organization)]
CGL	*Confederazione Generale del Lavoro* [General Confederation of Labour (Socialist trade union organization)]
CLNAI	*Comitato di Liberazione Nazionale per Alta Italia* [Committee of National Liberation of Northern Italy (the organisation coordinating the political and military activities of the anti-Fascist Resistance)]
CONFAG	*Confederazione dell'Agricoltura* [Confederation of Agriculture (the umbrella organisation of landowners and farmers associations)]
CONFINDUSTRIA	*Confederazione dell'Industria Italiana* [Italian Industrialists Confederation]
EOA	*Ente Opere Assistenziali* [Agency for Welfare Activities (Fascist party social welfare organisation)]
ERR	*Ente Radio Rurale* [Rural Radio Agency]
FIOM	*Federazione Italiana Operai Metallurgici* [Italian Federation of Metalworkers (CGL-affiliated national metalworkers trade union)]
FISA	*Federazione Italiana Sindacati Agricoltori* [Italian Federation of Farmers' Syndicates (Fascist union of farmers)]
GIL	*Gioventù Italiana del Littorio* [Italian Youth of the Lictors (Fascist party youth organisation)]
GUF	*Gioventù Universitaria Fascista* [Fascist University Youth (Fascist students organisation)]
IRI	*Istituto per la Ricostruzione Industriale* [Institute for Industrial Reconstruction]
MVSN	*Milizia Volontaria per la Sicurezza Nazionale* [Voluntary Militia for National Security]

ONB	*Opera Nazionale Balilla* [National Balilla Organisation (Fascist children and youth organisation)]
OND	*Opera Nazionale Dopolavoro* [National Afterwork Organisation (Fascist leisure and recreational organisation)]
OVRA	*Organizzazione per la Vigilanza e la Repressione Antifascista* [Organisation for the Surveillance and Repression of Antifascism (the Interior Ministry's secret police branch)]
PCF	*Parti Communiste Français* [French Communist Party]
PFR	*Partito Fascista Repubblicano* [Republican Fascist Party]
PNF	*Partito Nazionale Fascista* [National Fascist Party]
PPI	*Partito Popolare Italiano* [Italian Popular Party (Catholic)]
PSI	*Partito Socialista Italiano* [Italian Socialist Party]
RSI	*Repubblica Sociale Italiana* [Italian Social Republic]

Modern Italy

Part I
The Conquest of Power, 1919–29

1 The Postwar Crisis and the Rise of Fascism, 1919–22

1. POLITICS AND SOCIETY IN POST-UNIFICATION ITALY

The national elections of November 1919 were the most significant in Italy since the political and territorial unification of the country in 1870. They were the first elections to take place under conditions approaching mass political democracy. All adult males had the vote. The electoral law of August 1919 introduced proportional representation with large multi-member constituencies replacing the prewar first-past-the-post, single-member constituency system.

These elections precipitated a crisis in the country's parliamentary system. Italy's first experience of mass democratic politics converged with a period of uninterrupted political, social and economic disturbances arising from the impact of an internally divisive war and a difficult transition from war to peace. Much of this opening chapter looks at how the elections provided the context for the emergence and rise of Fascism, initially an effect and then a cause of the political crisis they opened up.

The emergence of mass democracy was a dramatic challenge to the practice and management of oligarchic liberal parliamentary politics which had developed from unification to the eve of the First World War. From 1870 to the granting of near-universal adult male suffrage in 1912, national parliamentary institutions were raised on a narrow base of political participation. The electoral system reflected very real concerns among the country's rulers – the liberal nationalist minority drawn from the educated and propertied middle class and the liberal aristocracy – about the survival and cohesion of the newly-unified state. They faced initially endemic disorder and criminality in the south, which was worsened by the impact of unification. For the southern peasants and artisans, the new nation-state was a predatory one, imposing northern Piedmontese institutions and economic policies. These brought higher taxes, conscription and internal free trade, which destroyed previously protected southern industry. Banditry and crime in the south had always fed on peasant hostility to the exactions of the state. There was also the longer term problem of the Catholic church's official hostility to the Italian nation-state, based on the Papacy's claim that unified Italy had usurped its central Italian possessions, which were seen as the guarantee of the church's independence in the fulfilment of the universal mission to minister to all Catholics.

The evolution of parliamentary politics both mirrored and reinforced the mutual isolation of 'legal' Italy, the Italy of parliament, government and the state apparatus, and 'real' Italy of the mass of the population. 'Real' Italy was politically excluded by the limited franchise and the Pope's *non expedit* decree of 1874 banning Catholics from participating in national politics as either 'electors' or 'elected'. From the 1880s, governments were cobbled together through a process of *trasformismo*, which sprang from the practice of prime minister-designates co-opting their apparent political rivals into government and making in turn their parliamentary followings part of the new governmental majority. In blurring political differences, *trasformismo* at best represented a kind of liberal parliamentary consensus for the defence of liberal institutions and the political hegemony of the liberal political class against those forces, Catholic, democratic and socialist, which threatened the disintegration of the state. At worst, *trasformismo* perpetuated government by corrupt parliamentary oligarchies.

One of the essential lubricants and guarantors of *trasformismo* was the promise of ministerial office, which opened up patronage, favours and influence to parliamentary supporters of the government and their small electorate. The other was the political and electoral interference of the prefects, the most important state officials in the provinces, who essentially brokered the relationship of interest linking government, parliamentary deputy and electors. Single-member constituencies and a limited franchise obviously facilitated the operation of the system, which was particularly effective in delivering the southern vote. Deputies representing the south and the islands were the basic voting fodder for the parliamentary majorities of successive governments.

The workings of the parliamentary and electoral system became both cause and effect of the widening gap between the country and its formally liberal political institutions. *Trasformismo* certainly entrenched, if it did not create, the disparity between the political and economic development of northern and southern Italy. The price exacted by the southern deputies for their parliamentary support was that government should maintain and not challenge existing socio-economic structures and control of local government in the south, to which the deputy and his electors were inextricably linked. This effectively precluded any reform of the *latifundia*, the large, poorly farmed estates prevalent in many areas of the south. The backwardness of the south was essentially built into the functioning of Italy's parliament.

'Transformistic' practices also reduced parliament to a political cipher and helped to make the government and the state administration, rather than parliament, the focus of meaningful political activity. Managed elections and a largely docile parliamentary majority composed of southern deputies trading votes in parliament for government favours, made for 'bland parliamentary dictatorships'[1] and the relative absence of political conflict in parliament over *issues*. Such a situation similarly inhibited, by making unnecessary, the formation of party organisations among liberals at either the constituency or the parliamentary level. Since elections could be made and parliamentary majorities created so easily, liberal deputies had no need for party ties or support. They rather gathered themselves loosely in regionally based parliamentary groups and around leading politicians likely to be heads or members of governments.

Parliament, in other words, was not the centre of political activity of the country at large, but represented the interests of the liberal political class. An electoral and parliamentary system based on a limited suffrage, the fixing of elections and *trasformismo* could not reflect and represent divisions and conflicts within the nation as a whole. As a result oppositional movements to the left and right organised largely outside parliament and did not even really see parliament as a channel for the articulation and resolution of their interests and grievances. Catholic, socialist and later, nationalist programmes were systematically opposed to parliamentary forms of government and were alternatives to them. If there was an inherent 'crisis of the liberal state', then this was it: the problem, intensifying with the growth of socialism from the 1890s, of how to integrate popular forces into the political and parliamentary processes of the nation.

The issue was confronted by Giovanni Giolitti, Prime Minister at various points between 1903 and 1914. He attempted to narrow the growing alienation of parliament from country by harnessing or neutralising popular movements whose strength and interests were extra- and anti-parliamentary, without undermining the political hegemony of liberal élites. He encouraged a limited *de facto* abrogation of the papal veto on Catholic political participation by getting Catholics to vote with and for liberals against Socialists in 'clerico-moderate' electoral alliances. By introducing social reforms, and urging the prefects to soften the use of the wide discretionary powers given to the police in illiberal and repressive legislation, he sought to strengthen reformists against revolutionaries in the Socialist Party. To this end, Giolitti also adopted an unprecedented stance of governmental neutrality and mediation in labour disputes of an economic rather than political nature.

Giolitti's flexibility had its limits: his openness towards some Catholics and some Socialists was still a form of *trasformismo* and did not imply any fundamental changes in liberal parliamentary and electoral practice to accommodate new popular forces. Giolitti had a reformist strategy in the industrialising and developing north. This complemented and was made possible by the continuation of the customary methods of coercion, patronage and clientelism used to control southern politics and ensure the support of southern deputies for the government in office.

Characteristically, Giolitti's concession of near-universal adult male suffrage in 1912 was part of a package to co-opt reformist socialists into his government. Its democratising impact in the 1913 general elections was contained by the usual Giolittian holding operation: an anti-socialist electoral pact with the Catholics, and the clientelistic management of elections in the south. Giolitti's prewar reformism was finally broken and discredited by Socialist opposition to participation in government and to the Libyan War of 1911–12, which saw the revolutionary wing triumph over the reformists at the 1912 party congress. 'Red Week' in June 1914, marked by an antimilitarist general strike and a series of local popular insurrections, seemed to indicate the futility and danger of meeting social unrest and revolutionary agitation with Giolittian reformist methods.

2. THE WAR IN ITALY

The first democratic elections in Italy's history were held in an exceptional atmosphere, characterised by a generalised, diffuse but genuine popular mood of discontent and desire for profound change in Italian politics and society. The immediate postwar mood of *diciannovismo* or '1919ism' was generated by the experience of wartime mobilisation and its impact on a scarcely unified nation. It was this mood which the early Fascist movement, founded in March 1919, was intended to tap, targeting a particular constituency created by the war: radicalised ex-soldiers, the war veterans.

Most Italians, even by 1914, did not have much sense of identity with or attachment to the nation-state and its political institutions. This was the legacy of Italy's unification process which liberal parliamentary government had recognised, guarded against but failed to resolve. In this context, Italy's involvement in the First World War was the first great collective and national experience for literally millions of Italians, especially the largely peasant conscript army. But, partly because of imperfect nation forming since unification, and partly because of the way Italy entered the war in 1915 and the way that war was conducted, the Great War did not bring about national integration and unity. There was no *union sacrée*, no temporary national and political truce for the duration of the war. Italy's wartime experience was extremely divisive; it increased popular alienation from the liberal parliamentary state while heightening expectations of transforming it. Italy's national war was 'waged in an atmosphere of civil war'.[2]

The decision to renounce the Triple Alliance which bound Italy to Austria-Hungary and Germany, and enter the war in May 1915 on the side of France and Britain, was itself internally divisive. There was a heterogeneous majority in parliament made up of Giolittian liberals, Socialists and Catholics who wanted Italy to remain neutral and not intervene in the conflict, which seemed to match the mood in the country at large. Intervention was therefore a kind of coup against the will of parliament. Its neutralist majority was not only pressurised by the extra-parliamentary agitation of a vocal, equally heterogeneous coalition of interventionists. It was also obliged to endorse a *fait accompli* engineered by the right-wing liberal Prime Minister, Antonio Salandra, and the king which deprived parliament of a say in decision-making. Salandra had secretly negotiated the terms of the Treaty of London under which Italy was to enter the war without consulting parliament or Giolitti, leader of the largest group of deputies in the Chamber. The king as head of state had backed this up by circulating fellow heads of state in France and Britain on Italy's commitment to war.

This barely constitutional charade indicated how Italy's entry into the war was as much an act of domestic as foreign policy. This was the case not only for Salandra and the king but also for the unlikely combination of interventionists in 1914–15. The war, from their varying perspectives, was a chance to bury the Giolittian model of liberal reformism which had dominated Italian politics for much of the decade before 1915.

Salandra's royal coup was the conservative liberal option in action, enhancing the authority and powers of king and government as against parliament. The interventionist democratic left of Radicals, Republicans and Social Reformists wanted a war against Austria to complete national unification, but in a Mazzinian sense, as a contribution to a new international order premised on free, equal and democratically run nations. Such a stance linked Italy's legitimate territorial claims to the democratic renewal of Italy's political institutions. For the Nationalists, it was a war of expansion. An imperialist war necessitated a centralised, unitary organisation and mobilisation of human and material national resources, which approximated to and validated their own prewar vision of an anti-parliamentary and post-liberal authoritarian corporatist order.

Finally, the spectrum of interventionism took in groups on the revolutionary left. Some revolutionary syndicalists were joined in one of the interventionist organisations, the *fasci di azione rivoluzionaria*, by a small group of Socialists and ex-Socialists including Benito Mussolini. Their break with the Socialist Party was precipitated by its pacifist, internationalist and neutralist position, a unique stance when socialist movements elsewhere were rallying behind the national war effort.

The interventionist revolutionary syndicalists partly interpreted the war in a rather conventional way. They thought the Italian proletariat should join the struggle against German imperialism and militarism, whose victory would mean the end of those political freedoms making working-class organisation possible at all. They also shared with Mussolini the intuition that the war would be revolutionary in other less predictable ways, that *somehow* it would change things. As an important leader of the dominant revolutionary faction and editor of the party newspaper *Avanti!*, Mussolini was obliged to defend the PSI's strictly neutralist stance. What most appeared to gall Mussolini was that this position confined revolutionaries to the sidelines. It meant that Socialists did nothing except passively spectate on a general European conflagration which might well destroy existing political alignments and create revolutionary opportunities.

This kind of political adventurism was at least consistent with some aspects of Mussolini's individualistic and idiosyncratic conception of revolutionary socialism which he had revealed during his career as a Socialist organiser and propagandist up to 1914. Mussolini's socialism was a unique and personal cauldron of innate rebelliousness and anti-establishment feeling, opportunism and the attempt to assimilate Marxist class struggle with a reading of European and Italian critiques of rational culture and its political counterpoints in liberal democracy and reformist socialism. Blending Marx with Friedrich Nietzsche, Henri Bergson,

Georges Sorel and Gustave Le Bon produced a view of socialism at odds with the more deterministic and orthodox Marxism of even his fellow intransigents in the PSI. Mussolini saw the party as a dynamic revolutionary élite, whose main task was to form a revolutionary consciousness in the proletarian masses, to prepare them psychologically for revolution through propaganda and direct action. Mussolini's view of the party as a revolutionary élite, his instrumentalist conception of political ideals whose value lay in their ability to mobilise enthusiasm and commitment, and his emphasis on action and will shaping events, all testified to his exposure to the general European and Italian cultural and intellectual reaction against reason. They represented common ground in Mussolini's political and cultural development, and help to make intelligible his political journey from socialism through interventionism to Fascism.

The divisions opened up in the country by the way Italy went to war were widened at both the political and social level by the prolongation of the war. It was imperative that the government achieved some kind of lasting political and social truce in order to prosecute the war more effectively. Yet a lengthening war worked to destroy the conditions for such a truce. The PSI was the one party that remained officially committed to peace and neutrality throughout the war, a position defined rather ambiguously as 'neither support nor sabotage'. Such a formula in fact covered and rationalised both the party's anti-war stance and the reality of the party's and affiliated labour organisations' actual involvement in the war effort. Nevertheless, industrial labour was obviously crucial to sustaining greater production as the war continued, but its voluntary co-operation could not be guaranteed because of the PSI's stance. This contributed to a harsh factory regime being imposed on workers, who were put under military discipline in war-related industries. Food shortages in the industrial cities were accelerating inflation, eating away at the wages of even the highest-paid skilled workers in the engineering sectors. Food riots which erupted in Turin in summer 1917 had a definite anti-war edge.

In a war which accentuated rather than sublimated class and political divisions, military defeats fed back immediately and directly into internal political and social tensions. The military disaster at Caporetto in October–November 1917 left the Austrian and German armies occupying Italian territory. It was seen by the government, military and interventionists as not so much a defeat of the army as a failure of the nation to unite behind the war effort. Blaming Caporetto on internal pacifism, subversion and defeatism justified tighter government controls on the labour movement and the Socialist Party in the last year of the war. The PSI, then, was attracting simultaneously both greater government repression and popular support, arising from their opposition to the war and exploitation of discontent at its economic and social costs.

The party's maximalist revolutionary position was reinforced by the suggestive example and model of the 1917 revolutions in Russia, especially the October Bolshevik Revolution, which indicated that violent proletarian revolution was imminent, inevitable and would arise, as in Russia, from the war-induced crisis of the bourgeois capitalist state. 'Doing as in Russia'[3] confirmed the PSI in its fundamental hostility to the liberal state. The programme adopted in September 1918 called for the creation of a socialist republic and the dictatorship of the proletariat.

Caporetto and its aftermath heightened the isolation of the PSI from the nation. But the government's need to recover from the defeat and rally the home and fighting fronts to continue the war brought about significant changes in how it projected the war and war aims, particularly to the combatants in the trenches. The expectations of a better world which fuelled '1919ism' were in part the product of the social and national content which the government and military gave to the war in the period from Caporetto to the armistice in November 1918. 'The liberty of tomorrow is the discipline of today', according to the founder of the army's new education and propaganda units.[4] The soldiers' commitment and sacrifice for the nation in war was unambiguously linked to the rewards they could expect for that service in the postwar renewal of society.

The most tangible recognition of national service for peasant infantrymen was, of course, land. The government set up a special agency for ex-servicemen in January 1919, which aimed, among other things, to facilitate the transfer of land to returning soldiers. Without waiting for the government, the slogan 'land to the peasants' was translated directly into action in the postwar land occupations of the south, carried out by demobilised war veterans making good the wartime promises to them. In more general terms, the attempt throughout 1918 to make the war signify something to those who were fighting it, laid the basis of the myth of 'combatantism' (*combattentismo*). Several postwar movements, including Fascism, were to draw on this. Because soldiers had fought for the nation, they had won the right to remake the nation and become its new ruling class. In 1919 the interventionist democratic left revamped an old Republican idea for the calling of a popularly-elected Constituent

Assembly which would redraft the country's constitution and political system. This was exactly the kind of proposal inspired by the collective experience of war and indicated even in this legalist format how that experience had diffused the conviction that the country could not be governed as before. The government's own attempt to give a meaning to the war in 1918 had mortgaged the future of the liberal state and the liberal political class.

The last year of the conflict seemed to be bearing out the gamble behind revolutionary interventionism, that the war would become a 'revolutionary war'. The trajectory taken by the syndicalists during the war and particularly from 1917, completed their revision-cum-repudiation of Marxism. They had come to see Italy's problems as being nationally specific, which could not be addressed in the orthodox universal Marxist terms of capitalist crisis and class conflict. Italy's unique problems of economic underdevelopment and national disunity were brought into sharp focus by the country's mobilisation for war. The issue was not so much capitalism, as the chronic mutual alienation of state and society, which was both cause and effect of an unrepresentative parliamentary system and a corrupt and unproductive liberal political class. The syndicalist alternative to parliamentary democracy was a state in which a community of producers would participate in political life through their membership of economic organisations. Such a system would not only stimulate the greater production of national wealth to the benefit of all producers, including workers, but would also ensure a more meaningful and continuous form of political involvement because it was related to people's economic activity. The proletariat had failed to seize the 're-volutionary' opportunities of war, and the PSI had now adopted a Bolshevik-style socialist revolution which was irrelevant to the resolution of Italy's unique problems of economic growth and national integration. Hence, the anti-parliamentary revolution would be led by a new élite of ex-combatants, formed in and by the war.

Expelled from the PSI in late 1914 for rejecting neutrality, Mussolini's own definitive break with revolutionary socialism matured also in the period from Caporetto to the end of the war. Emblematic of Mussolini's position in 1918 and through into the Fascism of 1919, was the change in the masthead of his daily newspaper, *Il Popolo d'Italia*. He had started it in November 1914 with money from the French government and some Italian interventionist industrial concerns, who also saw the value of Mussolini's defection in dividing socialism. A 'socialist' daily up until the edition of 1 August 1918, thereafter it became the 'paper of combatants and producers'. These were all-inclusive and elastic categories which did not conform to the usual class and political divisions. Their use represented Mussolini's attempt to make something of the disruptive effects of war on existing political alignments and affiliations and of the experience of wartime mobilisation.

The personal and political opportunism was self-evident. Both Mussolini and the interventionist syndicalists had to accept that they had only managed to draw a small minority of workers into a 'revolutionary war'. Their conclusion that the proletariat was no longer the revolutionary class rationalised this failure. *Combattentismo* and 'productivism' were themes through which to appeal to new potential constituencies thrown up by the war. In December 1917 Mussolini had anticipated the emergence of a 'trenchocracy' (*trincerocrazia*) of worker-soldiers and peasant-soldiers, who because of their involvement in the wartime struggle to save the nation, could become the proponents of 'an antimarxist and . . . national socialism'.[5]

'Productivism' was similarly connected to the war experience. The maximisation of production in the national interest required the end to class conflict and the co-operation of organised groups of all producers, from workers to technicians and entrepreneurs. There would obviously be a place in the national community of producers for the worker-as-producer. But Mussolini's gloss on 'productivism' emphasised the creation rather than the distribution of wealth. This implied continuing social and economic inequality and an unavoidable 'natural' hierarchy among producers on the basis of experience, competence and responsibility, of the relative weight and importance of each producer to the productive process. 'Productivism' could be read as a charter for capitalist entrepreneurs. It certainly brought Mussolini closer to the Nationalist position and to the concerns of the war industrialists who were financing both the Nationalist press and *Il Popolo d'Italia*.

Mussolini's conversion to 'productivism' was also linked to the increasingly nationalistic and imperialist foreign policy stance that he adopted in the course of 1917–18. The muscle for a policy of national independence, let alone one of national expansion and grandeur, had to come from economic and particularly industrial growth. 'Productivism' also had an anti-political thrust. It confronted a parasitical political class with the superior national role of the producer, and intimated as an alternative to the liberal parliamentary state a syndicalist or corporative model of social and political organisation, capable of achieving the cross-class unity of producers.

3. '1919-ISM' AND EARLY FASCISM

The first *fascio di combattimento* (combat or fighting group) was formed at Milan in March 1919, just before a meeting called to launch the movement. By the summer, *fasci* had been set up in about seventy towns and cities, mainly in the north. There was no real break in continuity either in aims or personnel between the revolutionary interventionism of 1917–18 and the *fasci* of 1919. The movement quite consciously aimed to keep alive and exploit the wartime divisions between those who had wanted and fought the war and those who had not. The Fascist programme was put together by the summer of 1919 and broadly corresponded to the general tenor and content of Mussolini's speeches to the Milan meeting in March. It combined nationalism and patriotism and an anti-PSI stance with a collection of radical anti-clerical and democratic social and financial policies. These included proposals for a political system democratised by universal suffrage and proportional representation, and enhanced by a form of occupational corporate representation; an eight-hour day, minimum wage and social insurance legislation; and a heavy progressive tax on capital and confiscation of excessive war profits. A call for workers' control of industries and public services was tempered by 'productivist' concerns for efficient management.

Argument about whether this programme was tendentially to the left or right perhaps misses the point. The amalgamation of radical and nationalist ideas was determined by the perceived outlook and expectations of the constituencies it was meant to attract: left interventionists and ex-servicemen. The workers' demands in the programme addressed 'the workers who were returning from the trenches', a recognition of the 'rights of those who had fought in the war'.[6] Their rights, in other words, were due to them as combatants not as workers. Combatants included anybody and everybody who had been soldiers and could not be defined by the usual class and party loyalties. The Fascist programme attempted to catch the anti-establishment and subversive feel of '1919ism' and meet the aspirations of an unpredictable new 'class' formed in the war.

The adoption of the term *fascio* and Fascism's definition of itself as an anti-party movement were important in this respect. Denoting a repudiation of existing political structures and a discredited ruling class, *fascio* conveyed the idea of a loose grouping of people who whatever their background could act together to achieve common objectives. There was a transitoriness to this, because the movement could dissolve once its aims were realised. But being a movement rather than a party, the 'cauldron in which elements from all parties found a place',[7] was designed to encourage recruitment. It was common even after the formal constitution of a party in 1921 for Fascist members to be associated at the same time with other political organisations. Being a kind of pool for men of different backgrounds enabled the anti-party to pose as a national movement superior to and transcending other political and class loyalties – much the same effect which was sought by the claim to represent combatants and producers. As 'the church of all the heresies', the anti-party was permitted complete flexibility in tactics and programme and was not tied to the discipline and previously agreed principles of a party.

The *fasci* were therefore made for action, 'organs of creativity and agitation that will be ready to rush into the piazzas'.[8] Again in Mussolini's own words, the programme of the *fasci di combattimento* was in the name. They were combat organisations which would get things done pragmatically and resolve problems by acting decisively, and would not be inhibited from action by any ideological preconceptions. The war experience was the self-evident reference point for Fascism's activism and no-nonsense military approach, expressed most obviously in the recourse to violence as the way of settling political arguments.

The connection between the prewar anti-Giolittian 'revolt against reason', interventionism, the war and early Fascism's activist style could be seen most clearly in the high profile in the Milan *fascio* and some other *fasci* of the Futurists and their associates among the ex-servicemen, the *Arditi*. Modern cultural iconoclasts, the Futurists embraced violence and destruction as regenerative forces of change in both art and politics, were among the most vociferous of interventionists, volunteered for military service, and contributed much of the anti-establishment flavour of the 1919 Fascist programme. The *Arditi* or 'Daring Ones', some of them Futurists before the war, were specially trained and equipped wartime assault troops who undertook high-risk missions, often behind enemy lines. Very much an élite formation with their own *esprit* and mystique, they formed a separate ex-servicemen's organisation after the war which was subsidised and cultivated by Mussolini. Covered in a glamorised aura of violence by their much-publicised wartime exploits, they were the least likely of Italy's war veterans to take easily to demobilisation and civilian life.

Arditi became Mussolini's hired bodyguards on the formation of the Milan *fascio*, helped to organise armed units within the *fasci* in summer 1919 in support of Gabriele D'Annunzio's planned coup in Fiume, which many of them actually joined, and were used in the general squadrist militarisation of the Fascist movement from late 1920 and early 1921. Even though the Fascist movement became the Fascist Party in 1921, it retained throughout important characteristics of the anti-party of 1919, above all its activism and ideological relativism. These traits were embodied in squadrism in 1921–2, and its pretensions to be the only really national above-party political force.

Fascism claimed to represent the war generation but managed to attract only certain groups of it. The *Associazione Nazionale dei Combattenti* (National Servicemen's Association), founded in 1919, became the most important war veterans' organisation. It was particularly strong among the peasant conscripts and middle-class, lower-rank officers of the south and the islands, where its regional and local associations for a short period after the war tried to change the area's landholding and political structures in the name of the new men and new spirit formed in the trenches. The ANC shared with Fascism the anti-political and anti-system thrust of '1919-ism'. But certainly nationally and with some exceptions locally, it resisted both Fascist and Nationalist attempts to turn it in ultra-nationalistic and subversive directions. The mixed or separate ex-servicemen's electoral lists which stood in the 1919 elections usually had a democratic and reformist slant.

Instead, the Milan *fascio* and the early *fasci* recruited among the self-styled élite of ex-servicemen such as the *Arditi* and the volunteers, and among officers rather than men. In university and garrison towns and cities like Bologna, Padua and Florence, some young army officers resuming their studies while awaiting demobilisation founded or joined the first *fasci*. Elsewhere, Nationalist or Republican university and secondary students' associations were sometimes the nucleus of the *fasci* in northern provincial capitals, which for much of 1919 and 1920 only showed signs of life during the school and university terms.

Some revolutionary and democratic interventionists gravitated naturally into the *fasci*. The 1919 *fasci* in Venice and Cremona, for instance, practically re-created the local anti-PSI interventionist coalition of reformist ex-Socialists, Radicals and Republicans. The Milan *fascio* itself, which effectively assumed the leadership of the movement as a whole, included ex-socialists like Mussolini and revolutionary syndicalists like Michele Bianchi and Cesare Rossi, whose connections went back to the *fasci di azione rivoluzionaria*.

This rather motley collection of professional political activists and syndicalist organisers drawn from the interventionist and 'nationalised' left, and Futurist intellectuals and *Arditi*, together with some democratic

interventionists and a spattering of patriotic students and ex-army officers, made up most of the limited early constituency of Fascism. Mussolini's Fascist-Futurist list which stood in Milan in the November 1919
elections won barely 5000 votes of the 270 000 cast in the constituency.
This signified Fascism's failure to unify and represent even left interventionism. It marked the broader political failure of groups specifically
formed on the basis of the war experience and the aspirations of the ex-
servicemen to exploit the postwar mood for change.

4. THE 1919 ELECTIONS

It was clear from the 1919 election results summarised below that the
major beneficiaries of '1919ism' were the two postwar mass parties: the
PSI and the Catholic Popular Party or PPI (*Partito Popolare Italiano*). The
great majority of peasant and proletarian combatants had voted for these
parties as the radical alternatives to the 'old Italy'.

	Elections		
	1913	1919	1921
PSI	52	156	139 (includes 15 PCI)
PPI	(28 Catholic)	100	108
Liberals and allies	400	220	239 (includes 36 Fascists)

   The regional distribution of votes and parliamentary seats was extremely revealing. The PSI and PPI performed best in the north and
centre of the country. Only 10 of the PSI's 156 seats and 24 of the PPI's
100 seats were won in Italy south of Rome. The electoral strength of the
liberal groupings lay precisely and overwhelmingly in the south and the
islands. Ex-servicemen's candidates stood in most southern constituencies
as a self-declared regenerative force challenging the traditional clientelism
and jobbing of southern politics, and 15 of the 20 elected were in
southern seats. But veterans' associations were only politically significant
in Sardinia, and to a lesser extent in the Abruzzi and the Molise, where
they inspired democratic regional autonomy movements.

It was apparently one of the freest votes ever, since the Prime Minister in 1919, Francesco Nitti, had formally declared that there would be none of the usual governmental interference in the electoral process. The PSI and the PPI had made the most of the premium placed on party organisation and a party platform by a list and multi-member constituency form of proportional representation. In the prewar single-member and simple majority system, personalities without a party organisation could still win the day. This had happened again in the south and islands in 1919 even under the new electoral system, as clientelism persisted and the two mass parties were weaker and less organised there.

The parliament elected in 1919 was, therefore, a hybrid. Nearly half the Chamber of Deputies was made up of liberal groupings who had no permanent party organisation behind them and no precise and binding commitment to a party programme. The other half were deputies belonging to parties who were tied both to a party platform and an extraparliamentary party executive. The postwar Italian parliament was the meeting ground of modern party politics and the traditional liberal politics of personality, and the clash of two worlds played a part in the paralysis of parliamentary government between 1919 and 1922.

The electoral triumph of the PSI and the PPI in 1919 created a completely new parliamentary context for the resolution of political and social conflicts. Parties with mass constituencies had achieved levels of parliamentary representation proportional to their actual strength in the country. This destroyed the possibility of automatic liberal parliamentary majorities. As Charles Maier says, the 1919 elections marked the end of liberal parliamentary hegemony.[9] The 1919 election results and those of 1921, which showed a basically similar configuration of political forces, made coalition government essential. But it was difficult to achieve stable parliamentary majorities for governments in the period 1919–22.

To a great extent, this was due to the attitude of the largest single group in parliament, the PSI. Consistent with its revolutionary maximalist position, the PSI refused to participate positively in the workings of the parliamentary institutions of the bourgeois state which it was committed to overthrow, and would not collaborate in parliament or outside with bourgeois parties. Its role in parliament was a spoiling one. It would vote against governments because governmental instability hastened the bankruptcy of state institutions. But it would never be available itself as a partner or supporter of coalition governments. The Socialist parliamentary group contained a high proportion of reformists, probably about sixty deputies. But although the reformist Socialists disagreed with the party's maximalist stance, they were not prepared to break ranks out of a sense of party patriotism and unity. Only in August 1922 did the parliamentary reformist Socialists indicate their willingness to enter or support a coalition government, in circumstances that, as we shall see, made their gesture both futile and counter-productive.

The liberals were never a unified parliamentary bloc before or after the war. The decline in their position at least in northern and central Italy, reflected an inadequate electoral and party organisation for mass democratic politics, and political divisions opened up by the war, with neutralist liberals competing against interventionist liberals in many constituencies. Giolitti's alienation from right liberals over the war made agreement among liberals in parliament problematic, at least in 1919–20. By the time of the May 1921 elections, many of these war-derived divisions among liberals had been superseded by the need for unity against socialism, and ex-interventionist and ex-neutralist liberals stood together in Giolitti's governmental electoral lists. Nevertheless, even the establishment of the Liberal Party in October 1922 could not disguise the previous and continuing fragmentation of the liberal deputies in unstable parliamentary groupings based on personalities and regional affinity. Significantly, the main groupings of southern liberal deputies did not even join the Liberal Party.

The amorphousness of liberal parliamentary politics assumed real significance once it was clear after the 1919 elections that liberals could not govern alone and the PSI would not govern with any other party. Stable parliamentary majorities were possible only if liberals and the PPI could reach some workable and lasting accommodation. Such a situation gave the youngest and most inexperienced political movement, the PPI, the pivotal role in postwar parliamentary politics.

The foundation of the PPI in January 1919 marked the full integration of Catholics into the political life of the country. The Pope's revocation of the *non expedit* in 1918 decoupled Catholic participation in national politics from the issue of the loss of the papacy's temporal possessions in 1870, and from the exclusive identification of Catholics with the defence of the Church's interests. The PPI was to be independent of the Vatican and of the church's network of Catholic laypeople's organisations, Catholic Action: a 'party of Catholics', but not a 'Catholic party'. Unlike the PSI, the PPI was a legalist and constitutionalist party, though committed to political reform. Proportional representation had been one of the first demands of the PPI not only because it would secure the party more seats in parliament. In the conception of Luigi Sturzo, the Christian

Democrat Sicilian priest who led the party, proportional representation would help to clean up and modernise Italian politics by encouraging the formation of parties and open competition between them on the basis of programmes. In this way also, parliament could become the focal point of Italian political life, since under a reformed electoral system it would be truly representative of the popular will.

The PPI's progressive and reforming programme had a distinctively Catholic emphasis on decentralisation, freedom of association, small peasant proprietorship, class collaboration and corporate representation, and the vitality of those 'natural' institutions like the family linking the individual to society and the state. The party was formally aconfessional, but it was clearly inspired by Catholic principles: it was a Catholic democratic alternative to both liberalism and socialism. Sturzo's desire for the PPI to be independent of the church was genuine enough, though his own position was difficult, since he was a priest subject to ecclesiastical discipline. The party programme also included, if it did not highlight, a commitment to the freedom and independence of the church, in other words, the defence of the church's interests. Again, the church's parochial structure, although naturally enough not coinciding with constituency boundaries, was a ready-made way of bringing in the Catholic vote. Many parish priests in the north and centre were active supporters of the party, and anyway involved in the web of Catholic social and economic organisations which covered the catholic peasant heartland of Venetia and Lombardy. So, the PPI was not identified with the church, at least in its own eyes if not those of its political opponents. But it definitely had relations with the church and could not fail to be affected by the attitudes and priorities of the ecclesiastical hierarchy and the Vatican.

Despite aconfessionality, it was mainly a common religious affiliation which encouraged Catholics to vote for the PPI. Its appeal to Catholics across class differences, apparently one of the sources of its electoral strength, was at the same time its point of vulnerability. The party was, in fact, itself a coalition of wide-ranging and often incompatible interests with different conceptions of the party's role. At one extreme was a combative union organisation whose spokesmen, the PPI deputy and labour organiser, Guido Miglioli, saw the party as a class party representing the 'Christian proletariat'. At the other extreme were conservative Catholics, behind whom were important banking, industrial and landowning interests, who took a 'clerico-moderate' view of the party. They were open to right-wing political alliances, and concerned that the party should be unashamedly Catholic and confessional in its identification with and defence of the church.

As a cross-class party, the PPI would be particularly subject to centrifugal pressures at times of serious social and political conflict, which in fact existed for most of the period between 1919 and 1922. There were strong pressures from within the party and from the Vatican for the revival of 'clerico-moderate' electoral alliances against socialism, which Sturzo resisted to preserve the PPI's independence, but was unable to prevent in all cases. Equally, the PPI left was urging co-operation with even the PSI against Fascism in 1921 and 1922. But symptomatically, tentative discussions between the PPI leadership and the reformist Socialists were inconclusive, once the 'clerico-moderates' in the party declared their opposition to any such PPI–PSI understanding. Inactivity and procrastination bought party unity, but reconciling the PPI factions clearly inhibited the party's ability to be politically decisive and affected its availability for coalitions. Government crises were often confused and prolonged by the PPI struggling to come to terms with its own internal tensions. This was especially so in 1922, when the sheer exasperating inconclusiveness of the attempts to form governments undermined parliament's credibility and helped to ease the way for Fascism's entry into government.

The PPI was generally unwilling to take the responsibility for forming and leading coalition governments, because it was an inexperienced party and did not feel that its weight in parliament justified such action. However, the party's internal volatility meant that it could only with difficulty perform the pivotal stabilising role in parliament indicated by its commitment to parliamentary democracy and its electoral performance. Coalitions between the PPI and liberals were inherently fragile, contributing to the paralysis and inactivity of government. Behind this instability lay policy differences which intertwined with different approaches to parliamentary government, a measure of the sudden impact of political democracy and of the liberals' reluctance to adapt to the change.

Nitti, Prime Minister of three successive governments between June 1919 and June 1920, refused to adopt agrarian reform as a condition of PPI parliamentary support. His successor, Giolitti, Prime Minister between June 1920 and July 1921, whose government included PPI ministers, similarly reneged on promises of female suffrage, proportional representation in local elections and state recognition of Catholic schools, which were meant to guarantee PPI backing. Besides the anti-clericalism of many liberals, these land and democratic reforms were difficult to

accept, because they might damage liberals' electoral and political position, particularly in the south, even more the repository of liberal strength
after the 1919 elections.

Binding programmatic commitments were also anathema to the usual
liberal practice of the prime minister-designate cobbling together a coalition based on a loose alliance of parliamentary groupings, whose interests lay not so much in determining government policy as in gaining
access to office and the patronage accompanying it. In contrast, the PPI
insisted on prior agreement between prospective coalition partners for
governments with a clear legislative programme, whose composition
would be related to the parliamentary representation of each partner and
whose continuation would depend on the enactment of the agreed policies. This formal and rather inflexible stance directly related governments and their policies to the balance of parties in a popularly elected
parliament.

By bitter experience, the PPI could not help concluding that to enter a
government was to abandon its programme. This certainly influenced the
PPI's opposition to the mooted return to power of Giolitti in 1922, and
thereby prolonged the government crises of that year. The PPI and the
liberals never achieved a lasting accommodation because of this mis-
match between modern party politics and *trasformismo*. In this way,
postwar parliamentary politics reflected all too accurately the fundamental political, social and economic divide between the north and the
south of the country. The liberals had been defeated by the two mass
parties in 1919. But because of the PSI's indifference and hostility to
parliament, and the PPI's inability and reluctance to find a parliamentary
role, they still had to govern.

5.   THE *BIENNIO ROSSO* AND FIUME

The 1919 elections, then, destroyed the axiomatic liberal control of
parliament and dramatically ended the isolation of parliament from the
nation, though not necessarily in a way that strengthened parliamentary
institutions or facilitated stable parliamentary government. Italy anyway
faced a postwar crisis of such dimensions in the so-called *biennio rosso* or
'Red Two Years' of 1919–20 that it would have tested the resilience of
any political system.

The *biennio rosso* was a period of intense, widespread and almost continuous political, social and economic unrest in both town and country-

side from spring 1919 until late 1920, peaking during the spring to autumn of 1920. It was only from the autumn of 1920 that Fascism began to emerge as a mass movement, and the significance of this juncture can scarcely be overestimated.

The unrest of 1919–20 overlapped with and to an extent was caused by a postwar economic crisis, the effects of which were felt well into 1922. This crisis sprang from the economic strains imposed on a relatively poor country by the waging of a prolonged and expensive war which Italy quite literally could not afford to fight. As a result, the war was financed in ways which both mortgaged the country's economic future, postponing to the end of the war painful decisions about how its costs were to be met, and transferred national wealth unfairly. Government indebtedness increased to staggering proportions, both towards its own citizens who had loaned money to the government through wartime Treasury bonds, and towards the richer Allies, particularly the United States, who had supplied on credit the food, fuel and raw materials on which the country's economy relied also into the postwar period.

A production-at-any-cost mentality fuelled largely uncontrolled and ever-increasing expenditure of public funds on wartime economic mobilisation. The government paid for it by printing money, a characteristic device for financing growth without the means to do so. The inevitable outcome of expanding wartime demand and an increase in note circulation was an inflationary spiral which sustained a mainly artificial and speculative industrial boom. This favoured the rise to positions of prominence in the war economy of a few giant combines, Fiat, Ansaldo and Ilva. The war manufacturers' quick and high profits were speedily reinvested not only in new plant but also in buying shares in other companies, as they created unwieldy horizontal and vertical industrial empires covering mining, shipping and transportation, electricity generation, engineering and heavy industries.

The inflationary spiral continued through 1919 until mid to late 1920, fed by rising prices for postwar food and raw material imports and the declining value of the Italian currency abroad, as Allied war credits and support for the lira ended. Wartime and postwar inflation had mixed social effects. It certainly hit urban and rural property owners who lived from rent, especially when rental and leasing contracts were frozen for the duration of the war, and those with savings or fixed incomes, and all consumers. However, for those who owed money or wanted to borrow money – and this included the government of course – inflation constantly reduced the value of the debt. People who had given their savings as well as their sons to support the war effort undoubtedly resented the impact of inflation. It gave a cutting edge to the widespread sense of middle-class grievance at those who had apparently exploited their patriotic sacrifice, the 'sharks' and the 'shirkers'. These were the war profiteers and the industrial workers, perceived to be the beneficiaries of an economy of high prices and correspondingly high wages. This is perhaps the point to keep in mind when looking at the effect of postwar inflation on the discontent behind the 'Red Two Years'. A particularly sharp rise in food prices precipitated the strikes and popular demonstrations of July 1919. But generally, union agitation in 1919 and at least in the first half of 1920 for better pay, improved work conditions and fringe benefits was contained within the inflationary cycle, their costs passed on by the employers in higher prices.

Much of the agitation of 1919–20 was of such a conventionally reformist and defensive character, to put up hedges against inflation. But this was not necessarily how it was perceived by either side, because of the feverish climate of '1919ism', of great expectation of change generated by the war and European revolution. Economic disputes were often given a political and revolutionary aura, certainly by the Anarchists and Anarcho-syndicalists where they were influential in the labour movement in Liguria, Tuscany and the Marche, and also by the PSI, if only as a competitive reflex. Some of the major incidents of the *biennio rosso* had a definite though passing insurrectionary feel, such as the food riots of July 1919, the general strike in Turin and Piedmont in April 1920, and the June 1920 army mutiny in Ancona against transfer to Albania, which was supported by a general working-class mobilisation in the region reminiscent of 'Red Week' in 1914. Expectations were being raised beyond the demand for higher wages or the eight-hour day or social insurance schemes, all working-class gains of 1919–20, to the transformation of society. The aims and conduct as well as the revolutionary rhetoric of some of the agitation bore this out.

The unrest of the *biennio rosso* took different forms in the rural south and islands than it did in the industrial towns and cities and the countryside of northern and central Italy. In the south, it had a traditional shape: occupations of the *latifundia*. Spreading initially from Lazio in the spring to autumn of 1919, coinciding with the demobilisation of Italy's peasant army, land occupations resumed in spring 1920 and were particularly intense in the autumn of 1920, affecting parts of Sardinia, Sicily, Calabria, Campania and Apulia.

The Socialists, who were weak to non-existent in most of the south, did not usually lead or organise the occupations, except in Lazio and Apulia. Instead, the occupations were sometimes led by Catholic peasant leagues, and more often by men belonging to the local ex-servicemen's associations. They were recently demobilised peasants, taking action themselves to realise the wartime promises of land. The occupations of 1919–20 were rolled back or contained effectively enough by the combined repressive and mediating actions of the police and prefects. Their action was facilitated by the readiness to negotiate and compromise of the improvised veterans' co-operatives. This stance reflected the PPI's interclass approach and composition, and the continuing hold of the old clientelistic relationship between landlord and peasant. In general, land occupations in the south resulted in peasant co-operatives accepting rental and lease agreements rather than confiscation, division and ownership, and ironically contributed to the absorption of ex-servicemen's associations into the clientelistic fabric of local southern politics.

In the agricultural areas of the north and centre, and exceptionally in the southern region of Apulia, Socialist and sometimes also Catholic labour and peasant organisations led often extended and bitter campaigns against landowners and employers for better wages and tenancy agreements. The Catholic peasant leagues affiliated to the 'white' union federation, the CIL (*Confederazione Italiana del Lavoro*), founded in 1919, had 1.25 million members in 1920, recruiting mainly among waged workers on contract, sharecroppers, and small proprietors and tenant farmers of Liguria, Lombardy and Venetia. Even more dramatically, the socialist agricultural union federation, *Federterra*, had nearly doubled its prewar membership to almost half a million by Autumn 1919 and had 900 000 members in 1920. It expanded not only in its traditional areas of strength among the *braccianti* or landless labourers of Emilia and Apulia, but also attracted previously unorganised and quiescent rural groups, such as the *mezzadri* or sharecroppers in Tuscany and Umbria.

It is important to realise that the immediate postwar agrarian disputes were at their most intense in the areas of commercialised or capitalist farming in Apulia, the Po basin provinces of Lombardy, Venetia and Emilia, and central Tuscany. With the exception of Tuscany, the struggles of the *biennio rosso* were a culmination of nearly two decades of class conflict engaging entrepreneurial farmers and landowners and organised labour.

In Tuscany, the postwar outbreak of peasant discontent shocked landowners by its novelty and scale. The idealised cosy and co-operative relationship between landowner and *mezzadro*, harmoniously sharing both the costs and proceeds of the farm's production, had steadily disintegrated since the late nineteenth century. Landowners produced for the market and in the effort to maximise profits, strained the sharecropping system to its social and economic limits, by throwing more of the expenses of production onto their peasant tenants and by squeezing their share of the produce. The wartime and postwar promises of land and social justice completed the radicalisation of the sharecroppers: a massive agricultural strike ending in July 1920 and involving half a million of the 710 000 peasants in the region won a new *mezzadria* contract. This agreement gave an above half share of the proceeds to the tenant, and transferred a higher proportion of production costs onto the landlord, who felt that this destroyed the very viability of the commercialised sharecropping system. Worse still for the landowner, tenants' security of tenure and a voice in farm management could be construed as an erosion of his rights of ownership.

This was the real point at issue also in the prolonged and vicious labour disputes in the Po Valley provinces and Apulia, which again concluded in victories for the peasant leagues in the summer and autumn of 1920. Drainage and land reclamation schemes and high investment in the Po Valley from the 1880s had helped to create a productive capitalistic agriculture. This was, typically, medium-sized livestock and dairy lease-holding farms in Cremona and Mantua, and large estates leased or owned by commercial farmers, who employed an army of landless pro-letarians for the harvesting of wheat and increasingly important industrial crops such as hemp, tomatoes and sugar beet, in Ferrara, Bologna, Rovigo, Padua and parts of Brescia. The farming system of Bari and Foggia in Apulia was different in that it was monocultural and un-modernised, based on the extensive cultivation of wheat for market, which made even higher wages a direct threat to relatively low profit-ability. But otherwise, the working of the estates by landless agricultural labourers enrolled in combative socialist leagues, the only labour organ-isations of any substance in the south, gave the same pattern and tempo to class conflict here as in the Po Valley.

Employers in these commercialised farming zones were reluctantly prepared to concede higher wages and a shorter working day, at least as long as the inflationary spiral continued. But what they bitterly resisted and resented was *Federterra*'s demand to control the supply of labour and employment, and the Catholic leagues' call for peasant co-management of farms and even the right to buy out farmers. They saw these claims as an unacceptable challenge to property and management rights.

Control of labour was the key in the *braccianti* zones of the Po Valley, because there were always too many labourers chasing too little work. Rural overpopulation had created structural underemployment. A surplus of labour allowed employers to drive down wage levels and restrict workers to alternating periods of activity during sowing and harvest, and enforced idleness particularly during the winter months. The *braccianti* contracts, including the important Paglia–Caldo agreement concluded in Bologna in October 1920, invariably obliged employers to recognise the employment offices run by *Federterra* as the exclusive source of the supply of labour, and imposed year-round employment quotas on all farmers, large and small, the number of workers usually being related to farm size. The labour quotas not only guaranteed the allocation of work for the union's members. They were *Federterra*'s wedge into farm management, because the farmer's loss of control over the number of men he might want to employ and the duration of their employment affected other decisions about the amount of land to cultivate, the use of machinery, even the type of crop.

Federterra tried to organize a single peasant union, including sharecroppers and small tenant farmers as well as *braccianti*, and gained a much improved *mezzadria* contract also in 1920. But the interests of the agricultural proletariat remained the most important in the leagues. These were expressed not only in *Federterra*'s aim to 'socialise' land and have it worked on collective tenancies by co-operatives of agricultural labourers, but also in the shape of the unitary union organisation itself. An absolute labour monopoly was so crucial yet so precarious in the overpopulated countryside, that it could only be maintained by the discipline and control of the whole agricultural sector, including small peasants who had to be prevented from exchanging labour and thereby avoiding the quota. The system had to be watertight to function at all. This accounted for the coercive aspects of the leagues' attempt to secure and retain the labour monopoly, through fining, boycotting, and sabotaging the crops, livestock and property of those farmers employing non-union labour and those 'blackleg' workers who agreed to work for them.

The agricultural employers' economic defeats coincided and dovetailed with damaging setbacks in the autumn 1920 local elections, after which the PSI ran nearly one-third of all communal and almost a half of all provincial councils in Italy. Anti-Socialist coalitions won most of the major cities. But the real political damage was done in the provincial capitals and small towns of northern and central Italy, where the Socialist rural vote swept away the liberal and centrist politicians who usually represented landholding interests. In Siena province, 30 of 36 local councils went Socialist, as did 149 of 290 communes in Tuscany as a whole. In Emilia, the cradle of rural socialism, the PSI won control of a staggering 223 of 280 municipal councils, and in the province of Bologna alone, 54 out of 61.

The PSI had campaigned on a revolutionary platform, saying that they intended to take over the local sources of power of the bourgeois state and convert them into instruments of proletarian control, to enact a series of parochial revolutions. The Socialist town hall projected itself as a class administration waging the class war. The economic power of *Federterra* was now buttressed and complemented by the PSI's political control of the local seats of government. Socialist councils used their powers to raise taxes on wealth and property, increased spending on public services and works, favoured workers' co-operatives in municipal contracts, and sub-sidised consumer co-operatives to undercut the private retail and distribution trades. A whole swathe of middle-class interests in town and country, from farmers to manufacturers, builders, landlords, professional men, shopkeepers and tradesmen, felt under attack from these municipal 'dictatorships of the proletariat'. 'There are occasions when I don't know whether I'm in Russia or in Italy',[10] complained a large commercial farmer to his Bolognese agrarian association in spring 1920. In retrospect, such fears seemed exaggerated, and many historians have challenged the 'myth' that Fascism 'saved Italy from Bolshevism'. But in late 1920, after the propertied classes had suffered disastrous economic and political defeats in north and central Italy, this was exactly the perception of recent events. At a local and provincial level, the Socialist revolution was being inaugurated; it was already under way.

In the industrial centres, what alarmed employers most was the way working-class agitation sometimes went beyond wage demands to pose a challenge to ownership and managerial authority on the shop floor. By far the most significant and revolutionary development was the factory council movement in the mechanical and automobile plants of Turin. Building on the experience of wartime elective factory grievance com-mittees, the factory councils were elevated as the Italian equivalent of the soviets by the group of young Socialist (later Communist) intellectuals and labour organisers whose mouthpiece was Gramsci's review *L'Ordine Nuovo* (*New Order*). The councils were organs of factory democracy which wanted far more than a say in plant management. Sharing the revolutionary syndicalist belief that through organising themselves workers acquired discipline, expertise and responsibility, the councils were seen both as

executives of revolution and embryos of the post-revolutionary proletarian management of modern industry.

It was no wonder that industrialists resisted so intransigently the recognition of these factory councils, which was the real issue behind the
general strike in Piedmont in April 1920. The council movement explicitly rejected both the reformism of the union federation, the CGL, and
of the metallurgical workers' union, the FIOM, and the phony revolutionary position of the PSI maximalists, who in Gramsci's view were
failing to exploit the 'revolutionary situation' of the *biennio rosso*. The
councils operated at plant level, representing both union and non-un-
ionised workers, and challenged the writ of the FIOM as much as the
employers. This probably explained why the CGL and PSI leadership
isolated the movement by refusing to extend the regional strike into a
national one.

While workers' discontent touched the foundations of property and
management, the government's attitude to it sharpened employers' perception of a crisis *of* capitalism. Nitti had come to government in June
1919 with the intention of effecting the transition from war to peace as
rapidly as possible, and governing through a liberal reformism in the
prewar Giolittian mould. Bringing the war to a definite end linked both
domestic and foreign policy. The speedy conclusion of a peace settlement
would help to secure continuing economic aid from the other ex-Allied
powers, without which Nitti thought Italy could not survive economically,
let alone recover. It would also justify and make possible the quick demobilisation of the troops and of the war economy, relieving the state of
some of the enormous costs incurred in fighting the war.

Nitti inherited a disastrous international situation from the previous
liberal government led by Vittorio Emanuele Orlando and Salandra. At
the Versailles Peace Conference they had isolated Italy by adopting a
policy that was both contradictory and self-defeating. Effectively taking
up the Nationalist position on war aims, they demanded the fulfilment of
the terms of the Treaty of London and in addition the annexation to Italy
of the Adriatic industrial port of Fiume, which had a mixed Italian and
Croat population and was occupied by Italian troops at the end of the
war. By dubiously invoking the principle of national self-determination
for Fiume and simultaneously denying it in the name of national power
and expansion in the case of the Treaty of London, Italy alienated its
wartime Allies. France and Britain had signed the Treaty of London but
were not bound by the Italian claim to Fiume. The United States wanted
free city status for Fiume. It had not been party to a secret treaty which

bargained away other people's territory, and was just the kind of deal running counter to President Woodrow Wilson's projected new order based on open diplomacy, the recognition of nationality and internationalism.

The Italian delegation withdrew in protest from Versailles in April 1919 to a wave of patriotic feeling deliberately whipped up by the government, and as promptly squandered by its ignominious return to the Conference and continued failure to secure Fiume. This was a policy which created the sensation that Italy was losing the peace. Patriotic sentiment was transformed into nationalistic grievance at a victory in war now being 'mutilated' by Italy's Allies and by the government's inability to protect Italy's national interests.

Nitti was in an impossible position. But in his anxiety to settle the Fiume question in a fashion that restored good relations with the United States, he took little account of national feeling and the way it could now be directed against the government. His decision to evacuate the city and hand it over to inter-Allied military command precipitated the coup already being organised by the Nationalists. Led by D'Annunzio, the hypernationalist soldier-poet, a band of war veterans and mutinous soldiers occupied Fiume in September 1919, with the clear connivance of the army stationed in the border zones, to prevent the city passing out of Italian military control and to bring down Nitti's government.

It is arguable whether the occupation was the 'decisive step' in the 'crisis of the liberal state'.[11] Nitti did not fall and the coup did not spread beyond the border area, although Nitti's lack of action against it certainly showed that some sections of the armed forces were seditious and could not be trusted to uphold state authority. Embarrassingly for over a year D'Annunzio behaved as if Fiume was the model and inspiration and point of departure for the overthrow of the Italian state. But in retrospect, the Fiume spectacle probably had more importance for the development of Fascism than as a real threat to the integrity of parliamentary government.

For a time Fiume absorbed the energies of Mussolini and the Milanese leadership in fundraising and support, and emptied some provincial *fasci*, particularly in the north-east, as student and ex-officer members commuted to join in the great adventure. The Charter of Carnaro, the corporative constitution concocted for the city by D'Annunzio and his revolutionary syndicalist advisors, exercised a strong influence on many Fascists seeking an alternative blueprint to the liberal parliamentary order. For the Venetian Fascist leader, Pietro Marsich, D'Annunzionism *was* Fascism in action, both in its commitment to a violent coup against the parliamentary system and in its concrete implementation of a post-liberal corporative state. D'Annunzio's acclamatory and military style of personal government enacted in public spectacle and ritual, anticipated some aspects of the charismatic rapport between leader and masses idealised later in Mussolini's regime. More immediately, even though Mussolini's eventual ditching of D'Annunzio ruptured relations with the *Arditi* Association, many ex-*Arditi* stayed in or joined the *fasci*, and carried over into the Fascist squadrist campaigns of 1920–2 the violence, activist style and *braggadocio* they had displayed in the showcase of Fiume.

In a tacit political understanding with Giolitti, Nitti's successor as Prime Minister, Mussolini accepted or did not oppose the Italian–Yugoslav Treaty of Rapallo of November 1920 making Fiume a free city, and the government's forcible ejection of D'Annunzio and his followers from Fiume a month or so later. Giolitti's combined diplomatic and armed resolution of the Fiume question by late 1920 effectively liquidated war and postwar foreign policy issues as a source of internal political conflict and division. The PSI's opposition to the war and its postwar condemnation of the futility and irrelevance of Italy's national claims gave a patriotic edge to anti-socialism. But it was above all the domestic impact of the *biennio rosso* which was the crucial test of Italy's political system. Fascism was from the start nationalistic and imperialistic and stood for the revision of the peace settlement, a stance confirmed at the second Fascist congress of May 1920. But Mussolini's abandonment of D'Annunzio, which outraged many Fascists, neutralised a political rival operating on much the same ground, and at the same time recognised that Fascism's opening to national politics lay through exploiting the internal social conflicts of the *biennio rosso*.

That opportunity came because parliament reflected in its composition the divisions in the country and the mood for change, but was unable to channel and meet postwar agitation, whose resolution was as a result extra- and anti-parliamentary. The non-co-operation of the Socialists and the volatility of the liberal–PPI parliamentary accords meant that it was difficult for both the Nitti and Giolitti governments to sustain reform programmes, which in any case did not synchronise with popular expectations of radical change.

Nitti's sober and low-key injunction to 'produce more and consume less' might well have been the appropriate economic medicine for a poor country trying to recover from an expensive war. But it was singularly out of line with '1919ism'. Nitti's reforms never kept pace with the dynamic escalation of the disturbances of 1919–20. The Visocchi decree of late 1919 allowed the temporary occupation of uncultivated land, a provisional and expedient measure to contain the effects of land invasions already taking place. But while certainly alarming landowners, it hardly assuaged the land hunger behind the southern agitation and in fact encouraged new waves of occupations. Social welfare and eight-hour day legislation, and state-subsidised bread prices scarcely matched the scope of urban and agrarian working-class agitation which was questioning managerial and property rights on both farm and factory. State neutrality in labour disputes, whether a manifestation of the government's reformist tendencies or a rationalisation of the inadequacy of police resources in face of the scale of working-class agitation, led employers to believe that the government by its inaction was contributing to their defeats.

The perceived inability or unwillingness of government to defend property against revolutionary expropriation marked Giolitti's handling of the climactic events of the *biennio rosso*, the occupation of the factories in September 1920. It was initially a defensive measure in a dispute between the metalworkers' union, the FIOM, and industrialists over a new labour contract, designed to pre-empt a general employers' lockout. The occupations involved over half a million workers, mainly but not exclusively in the industrial triangle of Milan, Genoa and Turin, and were soon contesting rather more than better pay and conditions. Barricading themselves inside the occupied factories, workers led by factory councils attempted to manage the plants and continue production. Giolitti responded to what appeared to be a violation of property and managerial rights by re-enacting his prewar reformist policies and approach. He refused employers' demands to evict the workers by force, and followed up this initial neutrality with a government-mediated agreement between the FIOM, CGL and *Confindustria*, the national industrial employers' organisation. The agreement led to the workers' evacuation of the factories after nearly a month's occupation.

The problem was that this was 1920 not 1904 when Giolitti had used similar tactics in the first national general strike. For both sides to the original dispute, the occupation of the factories appeared to be a 're-volutionary' occasion. Employers had seen their factories taken over and operated by workers. The government had not only done nothing to reverse this usurpation of ownership and management. It had mediated an agreement to end the occupations which apparently recognised and would eventually legalise workers' control of production, even though the reformist FIOM and CGL saw such control as a union say in management rather than as a challenge to ownership, and the promised labour legislation was never passed through parliament. The government was perceived to be abetting and not resisting 'revolution'. The outcome of the occupations similarly disillusioned and demoralised the workers. For this reason they should be seen as the end point of the agitation of the *biennio rosso* and the summation of its failure.

The PSI had talked revolution both nationally and locally. Particularly in the provinces and communes of north and central Italy, it had even acted symbolically and substantially to suggest that a socialist revolution was not only imminent but actual. It draped the red flag from the town hall, and used its local government powers to 'expropriate' the propertied classes through high taxation and support of consumer and producer co-operatives. But the PSI leadership had no national strategy to achieve revolution and convert the party's local centres of power into the political control of the country as a whole, either by organising a coup or working through parliament, where it was still the largest single party after the 1921 elections.

In part, the party thought that it did not need a strategy to gain power, that it could deterministically wait on revolution while bourgeois society broke up from within under the impact of the postwar crisis. In part, also, the PSI lacked a strategy because the combination of revolutionary rhetoric and revolutionary inaction precariously bridged and disguised the very real tensions in the socialist movement. There was an unresolved conflict over aims and approach between the revolutionaries or 'maximalists' who were strong in the party executive and among party members, and the reformists who were strong in the PSI parliamentary group, the major unions and the CGL, and generally in the party-affiliated network of economic and social organisations. There was a sense in which the party leadership felt that it could not push for too drastic action without the backing of the mass of workers, who were organised and led by unions that were more interested in reform than revolution. The relationship was rather clumsily formalised in an agreement that the PSI would take the lead in agitation having a political direction or resonance, and that the unions would handle conflict of an economic character.

In practice this was another recipe for doing nothing. Some of the disturbances of the *biennio rosso* were both economic and political, or were economic disputes which developed a political, even 'revolutionary' significance. The factory occupations were a case in point, since at first they represented the escalation of an industrial dispute, and then raised fundamental issues of ownership and control of production which were to be resolved by government and parliament. In a mutual waiving of responsibility, the PSI leaders effectively let themselves be guided during the crisis by the union leaders who classed it as an economic dispute and precluded its extension under party direction, which would have given the occupations a definite insurrectionary edge. But even as a reform which stopped short of expropriating employers, a workers' control bill needed a PSI commitment to parliament and some kind of political relationship with government. This, of course, was exactly why Giolitti had proposed such an outcome as part of a typical 'transformistic' operation to the left. The self-fulfilling cycle of impotence was complete: a maximalist PSI would accept no favours from the bourgeois state it wanted to destroy, and would certainly not work to achieve reforms through parliament. The PSI's behaviour during the occupations, as during the *biennio rosso*, exactly matched Mussolini's own acute prediction of the party's dilemma, that it was incapable of carrying out reform or revolution.

Irrespective of whether a socialist revolution was a realistic proposition or not during the *biennio rosso*, the effects of the PSI achieving neither reform nor revolution were immense. The party's unwillingness or inability to translate talk of revolution into action disheartened workers who had lived through a repeating cycle of having their expectations of change raised and then disappointed; even the occupations of the factories had not led to revolution. Labour militancy ebbed after the end of the occupations, a decline in combativeness accelerated by the impact of the short but sharp deflationary economic recession which reached Italy in late 1920 and early 1921, and lasted throughout 1921. This was basically a crisis of overproduction. It was brought about by greater European and US competition, and falling internal demand arising from the demobilisation of the war economy, as government cut back on orders and credits to industry and in Giolitti's case, introduced taxes on excessive wartime profits and higher personal and corporate taxation. Prices and production fell as a consequence and employers met the costs of recession and Giolitti's fiscal policies by laying off workers and reducing wages.

If labour agitation fell away from late 1920, this did not shake the perception among both agricultural and industrial employers of a crisis of capitalism being reached at the same juncture. Converging in the autumn of 1920 were actual or imminent cuts in profitability threatened by government tax demands and the recently conceded high-wage labour contracts which no employer would want to respect as the recession started to bite; industrial and agricultural labour settlements won by mass union action, which as in the Bologna Paglia–Caldo pact and the factory occupations appeared to be direct attacks on property rights in the name of workers' control, and at the same time were spectacular demonstrations of the state's inability to protect property and order; and sweeping gains by Socialists in local government elections across the provincial capitals and agricultural towns if not the large cities of north and central Italy, which installed a string of self-styled municipal revolutionary 'republics'.

The negative achievement of the political and socio-economic gains of workers during the *biennio rosso* was to create a traumatic fear of 'Bolshevism' among groups which had most to lose in a socialist revolution. As Errico Malatesta, the Italian Anarchist, put it, 'if we do not go on to the end we shall pay with bloody tears for the fears we are now causing the bourgeoisie'.[12] Socialism provided the platform for the counter-reaction of Fascism. It created the fears on which Fascism grew, and almost literally set the stage for Fascism.

6. THE FASCIST REACTION

There were signs well before the autumn of 1920 that the Fascist movement would find its vocation as an anti-socialist reaction. The movement's national congress in May 1920 confirmed an opportunistic drift to the right, now that the PSI was clearly the major political beneficiary of '1919ism'. The new programme accentuated the inter-class appeal of corporate representation and of 'productivism'. The anti-clerical and republican thrust of 1919 Fascism was sufficiently diluted by the leadership to cause the departure of many of the Futurists and Republicans who had founded and joined the first *fasci*.

Also, in the spring and summer of 1920, the movement experienced its first real local political and organisational success in the border region of Venezia Giulia, and more particularly in the port of Trieste. Here the *fascio* was organising the city's Italian population against the 'Bolshevised' Slavs. Such a potent mix of nationalism and anti-socialism was never quite repeated elsewhere, but the Trieste experience anticipated much of what was to happen more generally from late 1920. Aided by the Italian military garrison occupying Trieste under the terms of the Armistice, the *fascio* had set up armed and mobile paramilitary squads which attacked the premises of Slav organisations in the city.

It was clear that from at least the summer of 1920 the Fascist leadership wanted to generalise the formation of militarised units in the *fasci*, and instructed their leaders to make this an organisational priority. Significantly in terms of timing and function, the first meaningful contact and collaboration between many *fasci* and the local political and socio-economic establishment coincided with the municipal elections of October–November 1920. Clearly anticipating services to be performed in the forthcoming elections, Leandro Arpinati reformed the Bologna city *fascio* in September on the basis of an approach for an anti-Bolshevik force of 300 men from the Association of Social Defence. This was a lobby of local industrialists, tradesmen and farmers, formed in April to protect property and order during the strikes and popular agitation of the *biennio rosso*. Similar arrangements were simultaneously being made in, for instance, Venice, Leghorn and Brescia, often accompanied by the reconstitution or indeed formation of *fasci*. Such was the case in Ferrara, where after several false starts the *fascio* was founded formally only in October 1920. Fascist activity in these local elections helped to make them credible as the virile activist vanguard of a broad middle-class front against socialism.

Again important in timing and purpose, the incidents which sparked off a more general anti-socialist reaction occurred as an immediate result of the Socialist victory in the elections. In a quite deliberate and premeditated repudiation of the election result, the Bologna *fascio* provoked violent incidents disrupting the official inauguration of the Socialist mayor and city council on 21 November 1920. As the Fascists hoped, the disorder eventually justified the suspension of the council and the nomination of a prefectural commissioner to administer the city. Similar incidents took place in neighbouring Ferrara in December and in both provinces made the *fascio* the focus of middle-class hostility to the socialist political and economic control of the town and its rural hinterland.

Fascism, then, emerged as a mass movement from the autumn of 1920 when it began to benefit from the class and patriotic reaction to socialism. The movement expanded above all in the towns and countryside of north and central Italy, especially in Tuscany, rural Piedmont and the Po Valley provinces of Emilia, Lombardy and Venetia, where the postwar social and political conflicts had been most bitter and intense and socialism appeared to be at its strongest. In much of the south and the islands Fascism was almost completely absent or insignificant before late 1922, except for Apulia, a part of eastern Sicily and some of the major cities like Naples and Bari, confirming the symbiosis between Fascism and socialism. Although the central committee had encouraged the militarisation of the *fasci* and thereby helped to equip Fascism for its anti-socialist role, the expansion of the movement from late 1920 occurred largely independently of the leadership in Milan. Fascism's growth was not the fruit of Mussolini's charismatic and dynamic leadership. It was financed, led and controlled locally, and the movement became an aggregate of provincial Fascisms shaped by their local settings. The provincialism and diversity of Fascism was important, but the movement developed with a broadly similar pattern and momentum, if at a varying tempo.

The crucible of Fascism in the northern countryside was the Po Valley, and the model of 'agrarian Fascism' was provided in Ferrara. Here, Fascism inserted itself into the long-standing and bitter class conflict exacerbated by the agitation of the *biennio rosso* between agricultural employers and landless labourers organised in *Federterra*. The nucleus of the squads formed within the *fascio* of the main town were ex-army officers and students, with both the taste for action and adventure and some experience and expertise in organised violence. They carried out the first reprisals in the surrounding countryside. These 'punitive expeditions' were effective because in planning and execution they combined mobility and concentration of armed force against largely unarmed and unknowing opponents. The squads leapfrogged from commune to commune, simultaneously attacking socialist organisations and founding rural *fasci*.

The Fascist squads were directly financed and equipped by local farmers' and business associations, which in some places actually founded *fasci* with a clear anti-socialist function and set up the sons and relatives of their members as squadrist commanders. They began a systematic campaign to destroy by violence and pressure the organisational fabric of socialism, physically smashing up party and union premises, intimidating and humiliating socialist organisers and leaders, importing and protecting 'blackleg' labour, enforcing tax boycotts against Socialist councils as a prelude to their dissolution by the prefect or imposed resignation. This was a campaign by landowners and commercial leaseholding farmers to put a definitive end to working-class agitation and organisations by force, and restore more congenial labour and contractural conditions. Cowed and intimidated *braccianti* were recruited into new syndicates, not formally Fascist even by name, but led by ex-revolutionary syndicalists in the *fascio* and clearly linked to it. The employers renegotiated with them, to the exclusion of Socialist and Catholic organisations, labour contracts which reversed or diluted the gains of 1920. This was a process with a built-in and accelerating momentum, as the pillars of socialist power in the countryside – the unions and the town halls – were brought to the point of disintegration by squadrist coercion and intimidation, and the sanction of unemployment. Unprotected in their persons or their jobs by the PSI and *Federterra*, the large number of day labourers pressurised into joining the new syndicates at least had immunity from violence and some prospect of employment.

The Fascists also won a rural lower-middle-class base in parts of Emilia, Lombardy and Venetia among sharecroppers, small tenant farmers and small peasant proprietors. Some of these had recently improved their position and extended their holdings or purchased land, by taking advantage of wartime demand for agricultural products and inflationary reductions in rent and mortgage payments, as well as the panic selling in 1919–20 by landowners fearing Socialist expropriation. Rural Socialism threatened these newly acquired gains, as it did the interests of those *mezzadri* and tenant farmers who were initially organised by *Federterra* in the successful campaign for the revision of rental contracts in 1920. The Socialist goal of a collectivised agriculture where everyone would be a landless worker, evidently sacrificed actual and aspiring peasant proprietors. More immediately, *Federterra*'s labour market monopoly was applied to large and small farmers alike and all had to employ their quota of *braccianti*. Fascist protection against the leagues under the slogan of 'the land to those who work it' was accompanied in some Po Valley areas, starting with Ferrara, by a modest but much-publicised redistribution through the agency of the *fascio* of land made available by the landowners for the settlement of *braccianti* on sharecropping contracts. Forcibly challenging the labour monopoly of *Federterra*, and ruthlessly exploiting the contradictions of the PSI's land policy and the heterogeneity of its rural coalition of 1920, the *fasci* had managed to bring together both large landowners and leaseholders and smaller farmers in an anti-socialist alliance.

The Fascists land policy of June 1921 would strain to reconcile the interests of large and small farmers and formalise the alliance under the slogans of 'agrarian democracy' and 'productivism'. It was regarded as socially desirable to make sharecroppers out of landless labourers and thereby build a fence against agrarian socialism. But no general redistribution of land was envisaged, and the commercial estates were inalienable and indivisible because efficient and productive. The policy basically reworked that of the Bolognese association of commercial farmers since 1919. It foreshadowed the formation in Bologna and other Po Valley provinces from late 1921 of the Fascist 'integral syndicate', a single organisation for all farmers and landworkers which located the 'productivist' larger farmers within a wider 'community' of 'producers'.

In a matter of four months the squadrist offensive in Ferrara led by Italo Balbo, the opportunistic young Republican ex-army officer in the pay of the agrarian association, had turned the province around by the spring of 1921. Most Socialist councils had been forced to resign, and the syndicates, which had no members in February 1921, were 40 000 strong in June. No other situation was reversed so rapidly or so dramatically. Bologna province counted six *fasci* in March 1921 when the large-scale squadrist attacks began, and forty-three by October with a membership of about 12 000; in Padua, the single city *fascio* existing in March had become sixteen *fasci* and over 5000 members in June, almost all located in the Po basin. The disproportionate size of the Bologna city *fascio*, about 5000 strong, indicated the importance of the initial impetus which the provincial capitals gave to the expansion of the movement.

Elsewhere the pace of growth was slower. This was in part because of the resilience and even resistance of workers' and peasants' organisations, in part because a less differentiated rural social structure did not allow the Fascists to recruit allies outside the big farmers against the Socialist leagues as effectively as in the Po Valley. The reliance on violence was correspondingly greater and the class interests it served all the more exposed. In central Tuscany, where *mezzadria* predominated, it was almost a straight fight between the *fasci* and squads sponsored by the agrarian association and the sharecroppers' organisation. In the wheat-growing areas of Apulia, the lack of any intermediate peasant groups meant that the action of the employer-backed squads against the *braccianti* leagues was not mitigated by any Fascist land policy, however demagogic, and even the syndicates had little weight. Generally outside Ferrara, agrarian Fascism finally broke the back of Socialist rural organisations during the winter to spring of 1921–2, often with the help of battle-hardened squads from neighbouring provinces and usually employing the methods of the Ferrara model: squadrism, syndicalism and the destabilisation of local government.

In what became the Fascist strongholds of the Po Valley and Tuscany, the violent defence of both urban and rural middle-class and propertied interests met in Fascism. Squadrism linked the Fascism of town and country in very obvious ways. It was usually the city *fascio* which first exported organised violence to the countryside. Any attempt to defeat socialism would have to confront the complementary urban and rural sources of its power in these areas, the agricultural unions and political control of the local council. Again, social and economic activities in town and country were inextricably interlinked. Many people had interests in both urban and rural areas, and much of local industry, trade, finance and the professions were concerned with servicing the needs of agriculture, or processing and refining agricultural products and employing peasant labour. Such connections evidently made industrialists and bankers as concerned as farmers about agricultural wage levels and general agricultural profitability and any threat to it.

The movement's counter-revolutionary alliance of threatened urban and rural interests therefore reflected this characteristic interpenetration between town and country. But even where this did not exist, Fascism took a basically similar form as an anti-socialist reaction, because industrial and agricultural employers faced the same kind of problems at broadly the same juncture and adopted the same violent solutions. Local industrialists founded Fascism in the small manufacturing towns and ports along the Ligurian coast and in the Tuscan mining and industrial towns, using the same complementary tactics of squadrist violence and syndicalism, and with the same motivation as 'agrarian Fascism'. So, the Carrara *fascio* was led and organised in the interests of the marble quarry owners and traders, but over 75 per cent of its 1600 members were workers, mainly blacklegs recruited to the squads by the local Fascist boss, Renato Ricci.

There were, however, more nuanced attitudes to Fascism among industrialists than was usually the case with farmers. Smaller-scale provincial industrialists and manufacturers funded and supported their local *fasci* at source. Some big industrialist concerns, particularly those that had expanded frenetically during the war like Ansaldo and Ilva, were consequently most exposed to the effects of the transition to a peacetime economy and Giolitti's confiscatory tax policies. They continued to fund Mussolini and *Il Popolo d'Italia*, as they had in fact done during the war and afterwards. Their connections to the Milanese leadership of Fascism rather than to the provincial movements might have reflected some concern over the apparently limited horizons and objectives of squadrism.

But this was a caveat scarcely worth making in Tuscany where industrialists large and small, including managers of the Ansaldo businesses in the region, enthusiastically backed Fascism. The reservations which existed were to be found more among the large entrepreneurs of the major industrial cities of Lombardy and Piedmont, including Gino Olivetti, Giovanni Agnelli and other Turin businessmen. For some of these industrialists the impact of the recession from late 1920 through 1921 was softening up labour without the need for recourse to Fascist squads. Their violent and crude methods of restoring industrial peace were anyway often seen as undermining the continuity of production and destructive of good relations with the workers and their unions in the factory. As a result the Fascist syndicates, elsewhere the appendages of squadrism, found it difficult to make much headway among workers of the big industrial centres, a situation that persisted long after Mussolini came to power in October 1922.

7. GIOLITTI AND FASCISM

The take-off of Fascism as a provincial mass movement coincided with what turned out to be the final government led by Giolitti. While it would be an exaggeration to say that his government directly supported or connived at Fascism's violent anti-socialist offensive, Giolitti certainly tried to extract political advantage from it. As was clear from his moderate tactics during the occupation of the factories in autumn 1920, Giolitti hoped to revive his prewar transformism to the left by bringing the PSI's non-revolutionary wing into the orbit of a reformist, centrist, liberal ministry. But at the PSI congress in January 1921 the party's reformists were not expelled nor did they leave the party, whose executive, however, remained in maximalist hands. As a result it was the extreme left factions that seceded to form the Communist Party. Nevertheless, in Giolitti's view the reformists might be induced to leave a weakened PSI, since its official but nominal revolutionary stance was simply drawing onto itself Fascism's counter-revolutionary violence.

Using Fascism as a kind of political stick to weaken socialism would soon prove to be an ambiguous and risky strategy. But it was consistent with Giolitti's parallel attempt to co-opt Fascism, by including it in a very broad anti-socialist electoral coalition to contest the general elections called for May 1921. The so-called National Bloc governmental electoral lists ranged from groups on the democratic left and centre, through centre and rightist liberals to the Nationalists and the Fascists. It was formed to bring about a centrist majority in the new parliament at the expense of the PSI and the PPI, which faithful to the Sturzo line, officially rejected any involvement in old-style electoral anti-socialist alliances between Catholics and liberals and generally stood on its own ticket. Giolitti expected to 'tame' Fascism and make it like any other political movement by getting it to participate in and thereby accept electoral and parliamentary politics. Parliamentary representation within a projected broad coalition of liberal interests would at least contain the level of squadrist violence and reduce the necessity for it, by indicating that there were alternative ways of resolving political conflict and exerting political influence.

Trasformismo was no more successful on the right than it was on the left. The 1921 elections produced no fundamental changes in the make-up of parliament. The vote of the two mass parties remained largely intact, though the PSI turnout fell dramatically in those areas of Tuscany and the Po Valley where squadrism was most active and Fascist intimidation made a mockery of free elections. The increased representation of groups likely to provide a parliamentary majority for a liberal government was largely accounted for by the Fascists winning thirty-six seats in the National Bloc. But almost immediately the newly elected Mussolini made it clear that the Fascist deputies would not be parliamentary fodder for liberal governments.

Fascist inclusion in the National Bloc exposed the equivocation and confusion of Giolitti's strategy. Their presence in the governmental coalition lists conditioned even more the attitude to Fascism and squadrist violence of the prefects and the police forces responsible to them. These were the very agencies of the state which were expected to respond and adapt to shifts in political opinion and influence in their provinces, and favour where they could the election of 'government' candidates. The considerable Fascist violence and intimidation during the election campaign was now legitimate in the eyes of the local state authorities when carried out by a movement which was a member of the governmental electoral slate. Connivance at continued Fascist violence could now be construed as official policy.

It was common enough during 1920–2 for civilian and military policemen (the *carabinieri*) to fail to prevent or repress Fascist crimes of violence. The effect, of course, was to give squadrists immunity from detection and prosecution and allow them to act outside the law with impunity, a situation that helps to explain the one-sidedness of the 'civil war' against 'Bolshevism'. In many cases the relationship between provincial squadrist Fascism and the local state authorities was something approaching complicity. In much of Tuscany, for example, policemen, *carabinieri* and regular army officers not only turned a blind eye to the depredations of the squads – which was common practice almost everywhere – but were also in some cases active in the squads, sometimes even joining them or planning joint operations and supplying intelligence, equipment and transport. What seemed to evolve was an undisguised rapport between Fascism and local state officials, from the prefect and police chief to the policemen on the ground, though generally complicity was more marked among the lower ranks of the police forces.

A shared class and patriotic hostility to the perceived threat of socialism goes some way to accounting for the sympathies Fascism could draw on among provincial state officials. The operational difficulties of policing during the *biennio rosso* also contributed to the effective immunity enjoyed by squadrism. Often apparently overwhelmed by the scale, scope and longevity of workers' agitation, and anyway enjoined by central government to be 'neutral' in labour disputes, Fascism appeared to an embattled force to be a legitimate and necessary civilian auxiliary which would help the police restore law and order. In these circumstances, Giolitti's quite explicit directives of April 1921 to the prefects of Tuscany and Emilia-Romagna, the storm-centres of squadrism, that violence should not be allowed to mar the election campaign, made a nonsense of his own decision to include Fascists in the National Bloc. As a result such contradictory orders were largely ignored on the ground. The prefects' failure to ensure the impartial application of the law against all law-breakers deprived the government of the conventional means to contain squadrism. This was because members of the state's own apparatus of coercion were accomplices or accessories to illegalities committed in the name of a patriotic reaction against socialism. In some areas the state had already lost the monopoly of force on which the rule of law depended to an armed faction dispensing its own form of justice.

Fascist inclusion in the National Bloc also enhanced Fascism's respectability and support among provincial liberals, traditionally the political representatives of local landowning and commercial interests in Tuscany and the Po Valley, at the point when the movement anyway was spearheading and benefiting from a general middle-class reaction to socialism. The National Bloc confirmed and strengthened the often close co-operation between the *fascio* and local liberal associations; many leading provincial Fascists and their influential sympathisers were simultaneously members of the liberal clubs. Giolitti's removal of the prefect of Padua for his inaction in the face of Fascist violence, was one of several instances of provincial state officials being disciplined for ignoring central directives on the maintenance of law and order. The prefect's justification was that the *fasci* contained too many important people in the province including liberals who led the agrarian association, for him to take action against them. This response laid bare the effects of an am-

biguous central government policy towards Fascism. So Giolitti had attempted to create at a national and parliamentary level a stable coalition
including Fascists which accommodated and neutralised the movement,
the classic 'transformistic' manoeuvre. But the effect was rather to accelerate the growth and increase the strength of the movement outside
parliament, through its alliance with provincial liberal leaders and its
collusion with the exponents of state authority.

The assumption behind Giolitti's effort to 'transform' Fascism in the
National Bloc and which continued to inform his attitude to it after the
May 1921 elections, was that Fascism was or could easily become a
normal political movement like any other. The Fascist agreement to end
violence, the so-called Pact of Pacification encouraged by Giolitti's successor as Prime Minister, Ivanoe Bonomi, in August 1921, and the
decision of the national Fascist congress in November to make the
movement into a party appeared to confirm Giolitti's prognosis. The
summer and autumn of 1921 saw the first great internal crisis of Fascism
and its resolution in fact made clear how different it was from the other
political parties.

8.   THE TRANSITION FROM MOVEMENT TO PARTY

The Pact of Pacification and the establishment of the Fascist Party were
interrelated aspects of the same crisis of identity over the political aims
and methods of Fascism. In the view of Mussolini and the Milanese
leadership of the movement, socialism was being defeated by squadrist
violence, which had served its purpose. It should therefore be contained
and run down as the 'Bolshevik' threat receded and before it became
politically counterproductive. Continuing and excessive violence would
make Fascism the cause of instability and disorder, alienating those
middle-class sympathies aroused by the battle against socialism and
perhaps precipitating the formation of an anti-Fascist coalition in parliament.

After the elections of May 1921, of course, the movement was represented in parliament and almost automatically had to give itself a
national political strategy. The creation of a party implied a centralised
and national organisational structure and the definition of long-term
political aims in a formal programme. Fascism would be thus equipped
for a more conventional phase of political activity in which it could
compete for power in a parliamentary framework and not simply exhaust

itself as a necessary but contingent anti-socialist reaction. Other related pressures were pushing Mussolini in the same direction, including the very rapid expansion of the movement, which grew from about 21 000 members in late 1920 to nearly 250 000 a year later. More crucially, the various provincial Fascisms were organisationally and financially independent of the movement's central organs. The transition from movement to party was Mussolini's attempt to control and organise provincial Fascism from the centre and make of it a national political force.

Mussolini's manoeuvre was only partially successful. Opposition to the pact and to the formation of the party came from the strongholds of squadrist Fascism in Emilia, Venetia, Tuscany and Piedmont. Eventually Mussolini and the provincial Fascist leaders were able to compromise by trading off repudiation of the pact against acceptance of the party. The pact pledged both Socialists and Fascists to put an end to violent reprisals and respect each other's economic organisations. One good reason for rejection was that it undermined the positions of local political and economic power being conquered by the movement and the employers who backed it through the squadrist offensive from late 1920. If violence was discontinued the squadrists would lose their reason for existence and their leaders the lever of control to dominate local affairs. The Fascists were intervening with violence in deeply divisive social conflict and employing it against one class in the interests of the opposing class, and this made control inherently precarious. A position acquired by force could only be maintained by force or the continued threat of force; coercion had its own momentum and rationale.

The pact, if acted on, would also reprieve Socialist unions. Once allowed to organise freely again, they would not only agitate to restore the labour and contractural conditions of 1920. They would also compete for a following with the Fascist syndicates, whose members had joined mainly unspontaneously because of the twinned pressures of intimidation and unemployment. For both employers and Fascists the pact threatened the disintegration of the syndicates, which by organising workers whom the squads had forced out of Socialist unions, were the way to make the squadrist defeat of socialism permanent and definitive.

Concern for the survival of the syndicates indicated that there was more at stake for Fascism than just the defence of class interests which undoubtedly lay behind squadrism. Many of the young provincial leaders of 'agrarian' Fascism, including Roberto Farinacci in Cremona, Balbo in Ferrara, Dino Grandi and Gino Baroncini in Bologna, and Augusto

Turati in Brescia, were syndicalists of varying degrees of conviction. They had been influenced by the ex-revolutionary syndicalist organisers and propagandists active in interventionism and early Fascism and by D'Annunzio's ephemeral corporative experiments in Fiume. The credibility of the Fascist syndicates was in many ways vitiated by their connections to squadrism and the favour of employers. But in 1922 and 1923, in for instance the provinces of Bologna, Cremona, Padua, Brescia and Siena, the squads took action against recalcitrant employers who were failing to observe labour and rental agreements made with the syndicates and to give precedence in employment to workers registered in the Fascist unions. The disciplining of employers as well as workers pointed to the evident need of the syndicates to hold their membership together by demonstrating they could stand up to the bosses.

It was also indicative of the Fascist syndicalist view that workers would have their interests defended in a projected national syndicalist order whose aim, in the words of Grandi, one of the major exponents of 'agrarian' Fascism opposing the pact in summer 1921, was 'making the masses adhere to the national state'.[13] The first essential step in the 'nationalisation' of the Italian proletariat was the destruction of the influence and organisations of the anti-national and unpatriotic PSI. This was to be followed by the re-education of workers in 'national' organisations like the syndicates and their subsequent integration into a national community of all producers through corporations of workers and employers. They would be the basis of a new system of economic and political relations which would be at once more productive and participatory. This national syndicalism with its Mazzinian overtones of 'making Italians' incorporated anti-socialism into a more ambitious formulation of a new state which would challenge and replace the existing liberal parliamentary system.

The whole anti-establishment and anti-parliamentary thrust of the Fascist movement was therefore contradicted by the pact and the party proposal, which aimed to redirect the movement's activities to more conventional political and parliamentary activity. To Marsich, the Venetian Fascist leader, a parliamentary route would destroy the essence of Fascism. It would involve the movement working through a system it regarded as corrupt and wanted to supersede, and compromising with the transformistic and timeserving liberal representatives of the bourgeoisie. Fascism would in such circumstances be no more than a conservative anti-socialist reaction. Characteristically Marsich's response to the pact was to mobilise the squads of Venetia for the occupation of the 'unfascistised' town of Treviso, which quite deliberately signalled squadrist Fascism's opposition to a parliamentary road as both means and end. Power should be achieved not through parliament but against it, by the squads carrying out a revolutionary coup.

The seriousness of the provincial Fascist opposition could not be lost on Mussolini when Balbo, Grandi and Marsich met D'Annunzio in August 1921. The approach proved to be inconclusive, but clearly demonstrated that even secession from the movement or the choice of a new leader with more congenial aims and methods were possibilities. In face of the public rejection of the Pact of Pacification by provincial Fascism, Mussolini resigned from the movement's Central Committee but not from the movement itself. It was really a case of 'reculer pour mieux sauter' and Mussolini clearly had to take some account of the nature of provincial Fascism if he was to establish himself as the movement's recognised national leader. At the Rome congress of early November 1921 the movement formally transformed itself into the National Fascist Party (*Partito Nazionale Fascista* or PNF), and adopted a new programme. Grandi and Mussolini put on a public display of reconciliation and unity, and the Pact of Pacification was officially buried shortly after.

The extent to which Mussolini was 'the leader who follows' was indicated in the first party statute of December 1921, a compromise between Mussolini's desire for centralisation and entrenched local Fascist positions. The executive organs of the new party were the Central and Management Committees, both elected by a national congress. These central agencies laid down the political and administrative policies which the provincial federations, *fasci* and squads were expected to follow. But the choice of squad commanders and provincial party leaders was a matter for local initiative and congresses.

The compromise between centre and periphery extended even further than this, because the Fascist Party retained important aspects of the anti-party movement it had apparently replaced. These made the PNF different from other parties and its co-option into a parliamentary framework unlikely. The PNF was certainly a political organisation which had a large following and a programme to match it. The snapshot of the social composition of the party provided by its own sample of about half the total membership in November 1921 can give a false impression. Nearly 50 per cent of members were agricultural labourers and industrial workers, certainly in the countryside largely the product of squadrist coercion. The party's unforced membership was a heterogeneous coalition of men drawn from the 'old' and 'new' middle classes, mainly living in the north and centre of the country. They were both the survivors and victims, and the beneficiaries and products of Italy's capitalist development from the late nineteenth century. Members included commercial farmers and industrialists; managers and technicians in agriculture and industry; state and private-sector white-collar employees and professionals like clerks, lawyers, soldiers, school and university teachers and their students; as well as artisans, shopkeepers and small farmers, whether peasant proprietors, sharecroppers or tenants. There is some evidence to suggest that Fascism was drawing into politics middle-class people who were new to or previously absent from political activity. Certainly, over 90 per cent of the party's national and provincial leaders were middle class, including men with a political past but also men who were entering politics as Fascists.

There was and is nothing unusual about political and party leaders being middle class in occupation and background. But the leadership of the PNF was distinguished by its relative youthfulness and, connected to this, its war service. There was some justification in the age profile of Fascism for the almost anthropomorphical vocabulary of the Fascist claim to represent new youthful national energies hardened in the war, which would sweep away the old corrupt political class and a discredited and redundant political system. The presence of so many young educated ex-junior rank army officers among the leaders of the party's military and political formations was presumably one of the reference points for the contention of Mussolini's biographer, De Felice, that the Fascism of the 1920s was a movement of 'rising' or 'emerging' middle classes, mobilised into political action by the war experience and the immediate postwar crisis.

This middle-class membership had, of course, come to Fascism in numbers only from late 1920. The motivation was the actual and perceived threat to their social and economic position posed not only by the wartime and immediate postwar conditions of inflation and high white-collar and intellectual unemployment, but also and primarily by the experience of the *biennio rosso*. The conjuncture of events of late 1920 and early 1921, and the social heterogeneity of the middle-class alliance brought together by Fascism in a common struggle against socialist revolution and the advance of proletarian organisations, might suggest that the movement was incapable of achieving a coherent and collective purpose and direction other than anti-socialism. Was this basically all that Fascism amounted to?

Fascism's anti-socialist offensive certainly grouped together men of different political outlooks. What linked them was the belief that Fascism at a time of crisis would best defend the class interests apparently threatened by a combination of proletarian militancy and government passivity in face of that militancy. While the priority remained the defeat of socialism, it was possible for right-wing liberals and *Popolari*, nationalists, syndicalists, republicans and monarchists to find a place in Fascism and to see it as a short- or long-term vehicle for their class and political aspirations. In this sense the rapid coalescing of middle-class people in Fascism justified and embodied the original conception of the *fasci*: a movement rather than a party, unashamedly eclectic, plagiarising men and ideas, whose unity came in action and from the pressure of extraordinary circumstances. Significantly the creation of the PNF and the hardening-up of the Fascist programme followed rather than preceded the great surge in the numerical and territorial expansion of the movement, inverting the usual progression from thought to action in a political organisation. This was a tribute to the movement's opportunism, or as the Fascists themselves saw it, to the way that action was shaping a new reality. However, the new party's programme, and especially its organisation and conduct, indicated that Fascism was rather more than an anti-socialist reflex.

The PNF's programme gave a productivist sheen to the defence and promotion of middle-class interests. A general commitment to private property and any policy likely to favour economic efficiency and maximise production was translated into specific proposals for the privatisation of public utilities, cut-backs in and tight control over government spending, and tax and fiscal reform to stimulate private enterprise. This was a rolling back of the state, in other words, in the interests of taxpayers and entrepreneurs. A productivist rationale was also given to the corporative and class collaborative aspects of the programme, which envisaged the legal recognition of professional and economic corporations and their inclusion in a system of joint parliamentary and corporative representation to cater for the individual as respectively citizen and producer. This partial diminution of parliamentary powers and functions in a corporative direction was admittedly a very insipid version of the national syndicalism enthusing some provincial Fascist leaders and labour organizers in the Po Valley. The *laissez-faire* economic perspective sat rather uneasily within the anti-liberal and statist framework given to the programme as a whole. The nation, the 'supreme synthesis of the material and immaterial values of the race', was the ultimate reference point for Fascism. The state as 'the legal incarnation of the nation' was therefore 'sovereign' and subordinated all other individual and collective rights and values. It was this primacy of the state over the individual as the custodian and promoter of the national will which justified the proposals for the greater nationalistic and militaristic content and tone to be given to elementary education. Such reforms would enable the school system together with military service and sport, to 'develop in the bodies and minds of citizens, from childhood on, an aptitude and habit for combat and sacrifice on behalf of the fatherland'.

Complementing the productivism of the party programme was the intention expressed in the party statutes to form *gruppi di competenza*, or technical study and consultancy groups, in each *fascio* if possible. These would be a pool of technical and professional expertise for the party to draw on for the reform and efficient management of the state administration, public services and the economy. The groups, which in practice did not get off the ground until late 1922 and early 1923, were meant to be a way of recruiting or co-opting to Fascism men of talent and ability, an embryonic new technocratic and managerial élite at the party's disposal. If nothing else, the *gruppi* indicated the party's intention to equip itself for the task of running the state after taking it over.

But as well as being a political organisation with a programme and apparatus geared to middle-class constituencies and aiming at the transformation of the liberal parliamentary system, the PNF remained very much a 'combat' organisation. Indeed, the political and military organisations and roles of the PNF were indistinguishable. This was becoming the case in organizational terms anyway. Increasingly in 1921 and 1922, the commanders of the squads were also the heads of the provincial party federations. The local Fascist bosses, who were called *ras* after the name for Ethiopian chieftains, combined in their own persons both military and political authority. The party's declaration in mid-December 1921 that all party members were to regard themselves as squadrists might well have been a tactic to pre-empt any government action to dissolve paramilitary organisations. No government would easily embark on the dismantling of a party of a quarter of a million members. But this position really only confirmed the formal shape that the party had assumed at the point of its creation: an armed militia claiming to represent and personify the nation and set on conquering the country and the state. As the November programme stated, concerning 'organisation for combat the PNF forms a single entity with its own squads, and these constitute a voluntary militia in the service of the nation-state, a living force embodying and defending the Fascist idea'.[14] Squadrism, in other words, was not to be sacrificed to the political tasks of the movement now that the squads were apparently winning the battle against socialism. Squadrism was essential to Fascism and helped to define it, shaping the ethos and practice of the movement and influencing both the route it took to power and its method of governing thereafter.

The squads were gangs of mainly middle-class young men, many of whom had served as lower-rank officers during the war. They were university and secondary school students, sons of the professional people, local traders, officials, businessmen and farmers who supported or sympathised with Fascism's drive against socialism. In some areas, like Florence, the squads had a plebeian element, drawing in the drifters and petty criminals of urban lowlife whose opportunism and lack of scruples were covered by their participation in a patriotic cause and the exceptional conditions of 1921-2. The squadrists' activities set them apart from the 'respectable' and propertied men who financed and backed them. As men of action and violence, they despised the 'bourgeois' attitude and mentality of their supporters who in their view were complacent, materialistic, playing safe. Adopting and acting out the daredevil slogans of the Fiume legionaries, 'I don't give a damn' and 'living dangerously', they self-consciously evoked the spirit of activism and dynamism of the generation who had fought in the war.

Action placed the squadrist above law, convention and morality because its demonstrable success was its own justification. They were achieving by doing, creating a new reality through action, removing apparently insurmountable obstacles by sheer acts of will. In a remarkable sublimation of the squadrists' actual links to employers and of the connivance of prefect and police which facilitated the success of their operations, violence acquired a kind of purity as action in its simplest, most straightforward form. It resolved complicated and intractable situations immediately and definitively, literally at a stroke. The cult of violence and action gave squadrists a special sense of being an heroic élite and vanguard, a cut above all politicians, including those in the Fascist movement itself, who talked rather than acted. Violence became a way of life for squadrists, at the same time the source and expression of a squadrist mentality and values.

Importantly then, violence was both means and end, and this was also in the logic of the initial use of force to settle class conflict. The squads from the city *fasci* who spread out into the surrounding countryside wanted to contest and then destroy the apparently impregnable economic and political strength of Socialist organisations. They saw themselves as an army operating in the enemy's own territory and behaved like an occupation force which had to dominate and subjugate a hostile population. In this kind of context violence could not be applied just once. It had to be applied continuously, or at least the threat of reprisal had to be always there, if opposition was not to revive. The squads effectively created a climate of terror, deterring resistance and dissent in both the present and the future. Imperceptibly, coercion and the retention of an apparatus of coercion justified itself not only as an instrument of conquest but also as a means of control. In this way, squadrism was beginning to outstrip the defence of the class interests of the farmers and businessmen who sponsored and benefited from the use of force against their workers.

The recourse to violence also marked the end to dialogue. Socialists were not to be negotiated with; they were enemies of the nation who had to be crushed, and permanently so, which was why the Fascists took over the role of organising the workers in 'national' syndicates. This was another good reason for the maintenance of coercive controls, since a proletariat barely 'liberated' from Socialism would have to be 'forced to be free'. The habitual use or threat of violence, 'legitimate' because exercised by a militia that claimed to personify the nation against those it identified as dividing the nation, demonstrated that the Fascists aspired to dominate affairs in an exclusive way, allowing no alternatives to exist. This in practice was how the rule of the *ras* operated in some northern and central provinces by the summer of 1922. Squadrism was creating the model of a single party system of rule, a kind of permanent terror, destroying its rivals by force and imposing an absolute control justified by its credentials as the national movement.

So the PNF was a political party which was unconventionally also a military organisation employing military methods of control. Its mode of action was incompatible with and subversive of the principles and conduct of democratic parliamentary politics. The belief of Giolitti and other liberals that the PNF could be successfully co-opted within the parliamentary system was illusory. They did not realise that violence was central to squadrist Fascism, rather than only a method of political struggle adopted temporarily and extraordinarily to defeat a perceived threat of proletarian revolution. The attempt by some provincial party organisations to make permanent squadrist methods of control, the intention to group in the party the managerial and administrative cadres for efficient government, and syndicalist-corporatist aspirations to create a new state, showed that Fascism was not reducible to a temporary antisocialist crusade. As we shall see, however, the tactics that Mussolini and

Fascism adopted to win power entailed a compromise rather than a complete break with Italy's political and economic establishment and parliamentary system. This perpetuated the confusion and illusions about Fascism's nature and function.

9. THE MARCH ON ROME

Giolitti's successor as Prime Minister, Bonomi, seemed to have some sense of the subversiveness of a political movement which imposed a single view through violence. His methods of handling Fascism were, however, basically no different from nor any more successful than those of Giolitti, at least up to his resignation in February 1922. The attempt to 'normalise' Fascism by negotiating an agreement to end violence through the Pact of Pacification had failed. Government directives like Bonomi's circular to the prefects in December 1921 telling them to disband all armed organisations, highlighted but did not confront the same problems of enforcement that had blighted Giolitti's orders to repress and punish illegality. This was the circular which the PNF had anticipated by proclaiming all PNF members squadrists. Mussolini correctly judged that the challenge would be evaded by the government, because it would involve dissolving a mass movement and recognising that violence was an endemic not incidental ingredient of Fascism which required special counter-measures. But as usual, the directive was not focused specifically on Fascist violence, and its implementation was left to the discretion and initiative of individual prefects. The result was that the prefects proceeded energetically against the *Arditi del Popolo*, left-wing anti-Fascist paramilitary groups set up in 1921 to combat squadrist violence. But they did or could do little to restrain Fascist coercion, reflecting the provincial party's dominance of local affairs, buttressed by the squads and the collusion of state authorities and the influential men of provincial society in Fascist violence. The prefects and police were being expected to exercise powers which effectively they no longer had.

During the spring, summer and autumn of 1922 organised Fascist violence took the form of province-wide and regional mobilisations of squads, a kind of creeping insurrection. These offensives aimed to extend Fascist control into areas where Fascism was weak or having difficulties and its political opponents were still strong. Their target and victim was also the authority of the state. In May 1922 Balbo called out the squads of the province to organise and marshal the occupation of Ferrara by thousands of landless labourers in the syndicates, in order to pressurise both the prefect and central government to concede public works. Relieving unemployment with public funds kept workers in the syndicates without rupturing relations between the party and the syndicates and their patrons among the agricultural employers. Farinacci, the Fascist boss of Cremona, would even argue that taking national power and thereby gaining access to ministries which dispersed public monies was vital to achieve by the start of the next winter if the party was to retain its mass following.

The holding of provincial power almost inevitably required Fascists to assume extra-provincial perspectives, though this basic political lesson was lost on the Socialists during the *biennio rosso*. Balbo realised that 'the local situations do not count if the life of the whole nation does not change . . . we must conquer the nation.'[15] His Ferrara squads then joined a general mobilisation and concentration of Emilian squadrists in Bologna in late May and early June, to force the transfer of the prefect, Cesare Mori, who was trying to enforce the law against Fascist illegality. Even more sensationally in September, the squads of Venetia occupied Trento and Bolzano, the main towns of the largely German-speaking South Tyrol, annexed in 1919 and bringing Italy's frontiers to their natural geographical limit of the Alps. The government-appointed civil commissioner was made to resign, because the Fascists objected to what they saw as the administration's lack of zeal in 'italianising' the region. Nowhere was it clearer that Fascism claimed to substitute itself for the state whenever the latter was seen to default in the defence of national interests.

But the turning point in the creeping insurrection came in the aftermath of incidents in Cremona in July, when Farinacci mobilised the provincial squads against the Socialist city council. In a general rampage Fascists entered and damaged the home of the PPI deputy and labour organizer, Miglioli. Mussolini had always feared that the uncontrolled extension of Fascist violence would eventually isolate the PNF politically and bring about an anti-Fascist government. This was one of the reasons why he preferred to work towards power through a parliamentary combination rather than risk everything on a putsch. Now these events finally provoked a parliamentary response to the Fascists' spring and summer offensives against their opponents, which was undermining the authority of the state. A vote of no confidence carried against the government led by the Giolittian deputy, Luigi Facta, who had only succeeded Bonomi in February 1922 because the PPI refused to support

Giolitti's return as Prime Minister, specifically cited the government's failure to repress Fascist disorder. A government crisis had been directly precipitated by the problem of Fascism, and in political and parliamentary logic it should have been resolved by the formation of an anti-Fascist coalition.

The breaking of the government crisis cut across discussions taking place since June between the PPI leadership and the reformists in the PSI, which were finally broaching the question of the reformist deputies participating in the formation of a government. Bonomi, one of several politicians invited by the king to try to form a government, attempted to cobble together an anti-Fascist centre-left coalition including the PPI, reformist Socialists and left liberals. Bonomi's soundings were torpedoed from all directions. The maximalist PSI leadership repudiated the possibility of Socialist collaboration with or in any government, keeping to the by now self-destructive line that worse was better and that the party should act to deepen rather than resolve the political crisis of the bourgeois state.

So as always since the 1919 elections, a parliamentary majority depended on an agreement between the PPI and the liberal groupings. Giolitti publicly ridiculed the idea of a coalition bringing together Socialists and Catholics, which made it clear that he and his group would not support the formation of any government against Fascism. If Fascism was the problem, then the answer was not an anti-Fascist government, which would risk civil war, but a government including Fascists. This familiar stance of Giolitti, that Fascism could be tamed by power, was in fact a capitulation to force and illegality. Fascism was only a problem because of its illegality. If Fascism was a normal political party, then with a parliamentary representation of only thirty-six seats there would be no question of it having to be in government. This was a necessity because of the illegal threat that Fascism posed. The right-wing Salandra liberals were at least less equivocal. They saw Fascism as a necessary and legitimate reaction against Socialist subversion, justified by the incapacity of government to resist revolution, and anticipated Fascists entering a strong anti-socialist ministry headed by Salandra.

The conservative Catholics in the PPI were also more anti-Socialist than anti-Fascist. Their opposition to a PPI–PSI agreement, which Miglioli had attempted to forge at a local level in Cremona in March 1922 to resist Farinacci's offensive against both Catholic and Socialist unions in the province, induced the PPI leaders to put party unity before the opening to the reformists. Some liberal and Catholic deputies were willing to accept Fascism in government, or at least were unwilling to accept the formation of an anti-Fascist government as the logical outcome of the July crisis. Their stance showed the extent to which the collusion of conservative circles with Fascism in the provinces was now bearing on parliamentary alignments at the centre.

The final tragic twist in the July 1922 political crisis came with the call of the so-called Alliance of Labour – an anti-Fascist grouping of some unions formed in February which had the support of Socialist, Communist and Republican parties and the Anarchists – for a 'legalitarian' general strike to restore political and union liberties. If this was a desperate attempt to influence the resolution of the parliamentary crisis and bring pressure to bear for the formation of an anti-Fascist ministry, then it was entirely counterproductive. The strike call created the situation it was meant to prevent. Not only did the strike compromise the outcome of the consultations for the formation of a new ministry, which had eventually once again been entrusted to Facta. It also provided Fascism with the pretext to stage massive mobilisations of the squads. Ostensibly to break the strike, which was anyway poorly organised and supported, the real aim was to extend Fascist control into other areas, including some of the major industrial cities where Fascism was struggling to make an impact. The removal of the Socialist city council in Milan and the breaking of the Socialist dockers' co-operatives in the port of Genoa were significant gains of the August mobilisations, which also took in Leghorn, Ancona and Bari. The Fascists had effectively pre-empted a government response to the strike, acting as if they alone were entitled to defend the nation's 'right to work'. They had again both usurped and demonstrated the impotence of state authority; the prefects and police were unable to prevent the concentrations of the squads or the violence which followed.

The events of July and August were important in two ways. First of all, they gave a measure of the extent to which Fascism had by the summer of 1922 already become the new state. The movement had taken off in late 1920 as a product of perceived government weakness in the face of Socialism; during 1921 and 1922, Fascism became the cause of government weakness. It was not simply that central government was unable to contain Fascist violence in large parts of the north and centre of Italy and in Apulia. Organised violence had become a system of control as well as conquest. As a consequence, *de facto* power had passed from constituted state authorities to the PNF, or rather to the provincial Fascist bosses, the *ras*, who presided over a kind of military occupation of some of the country. The provincial party executed law and order functions according to its own lights. It exercised an arbitrary terror against its opponents, and created a climate that made it difficult for prefect, police and judiciary to act independently and uphold the laws and dispense justice in an impartial way, even if they had wished to. Local government had been taken out of the hands of elected councillors· and given to nominated prefectural commissioners, who were usually Fascist followers or sympathisers or officials of the prefecture running 'technical' and non-political administrations. The party men arbitrated in labour disputes, and through the syndicates controlled the labour market.

Secondly, the July crisis, which was caused by Fascism, had not led to the formation of a government capable of resisting Fascism. It was increasingly unlikely that parliament would produce an anti-Fascist majority; in fact, quite the reverse. It was true that the reformist Socialists in parliament were by the summer of 1922 ready to enter or support an anti-Fascist government. But the PSI leadership's reiteration of its intransigent postwar position meant that the reformists could not carry the rest of the party's parliamentary group with it. They were later, in early October, formally expelled from the party for their willingness to collaborate with a bourgeois government. By the time some Socialist deputies were available for an anti-Fascist coalition, many liberals and right-wing Catholics were now themselves unavailable for such a solution, given the collusion with Fascism's anti-socialist offensive at the local level.

A mutually reinforcing cycle connected political developments at the centre and the periphery from late 1920 to late 1922, linking the weakness of parliamentary government and the growing extra-parliamentary strength of Fascism. What was seen as the failure of central government to resist Socialism in the provinces provoked the Fascist reaction as a kind of middle-class self-help. As a result state authority drained away in the provinces where the Socialist threat appeared greatest, with the Fascists substituting themselves for a defaulting state, and in particular breaking the state's monopoly of force. Parliamentary attempts to respond to the growing Fascist usurpation of provincial authority and co-opt Fascism into the Giolittian National Bloc only succeeded in accelerating the process of disintegrating authority in the provinces, by orientating local élites and state officials towards Fascism. This, in turn, heightened parliament's impotence at the centre. In 1922 it was impossible to form a coalition which would take a stand against Fascist violence, because many liberal and Catholic deputies were convinced that Fascism's action against Socialism was legitimate, and that the best way to contain Fascism was to give it a share in power.

If from the summer of 1922 it was difficult to see how Fascism would not soon enter government, what remained less clear was the way in which this would happen and the weight Fascists would have in a coalition government including them. As Mussolini put it in his speech to the PNF congress in Naples on 24 October, days before coming to power: 'legality or illegality? Victory by means of parliament, or through insurrection? Through what paths will Fascism become the State? For we mean to become the State!'[16] The question was rhetorical, and posing the problem in such an antithetical way was an intrinsic part of the strategy adopted by Mussolini and the central party leadership in the autumn of 1922. A meeting of Mussolini and PNF and militia leaders decided on 16 October to prepare for an insurrection, a 'March on Rome'. This was undoubtedly what the bulk of provincial squadrists and *ras* and some of the central leadership including the PNF Secretary, Bianchi, wanted and expected, since a violent taking of power would allow a decisive break with the parliamentary system. The squadrist mobilisations of the time and the efforts spearheaded by Balbo to make the squads into a national military organisation took on an even more sinister aspect as dry runs and preparation for an armed coup.

But preparing for a revolt was not incompatible with seeking power using a parliamentary and political route. As it turned out, the two paths to power were mutually reinforcing. Mussolini realised that the squads could not seize power for Fascism if the government ordered the army to resist. It was this fear of a coup failing which made Mussolini more hesitant than Bianchi or Balbo and more concerned to keep other political options open. By playing down the movement's republican tendencies and praising the armed forces to the skies as the great national institution, Mussolini aimed to neutralise any opposition to a Fascist takeover in military circles and from the king, commander-in-chief of the armed forces. In a speech at Udine in September Mussolini declared that 'the regime can be profoundly altered without touching the monarchy', though the statement was followed by the threat that if the king should oppose the 'Revolution', the monarchy would itself become a target.[17] Conciliation and threat operated in tandem: the existence of a private party army gave Mussolini enormous political leverage, because it allowed him to negotiate from a position of strength. The possibility of a squadrist rising was used as political blackmail, for if Fascism was not given power in a legal and constitutional way then it could threaten a coup. It was not incongruous then, for Mussolini and other PNF leaders to be negotiating with the most important liberal politicians for a stake in government and simultaneously planning and staging a coup. The latter was a way of bringing pressure to bear, to achieve the former on the most advantageous terms for Fascism.

This reading of Mussolini's twin-track strategy can be confirmed by the 'March on Rome', which as Adrian Lyttelton argues, was an exercise in successful 'psychological warfare'.[18] The first stage of the 'March' was to draw on Fascism's provincial strength, and required the seizure of government buildings in the provincial capitals in north and central Italy, before the convergence of three small squadrist armies on Rome itself. This first instalment was carried out successfully enough on the night of 27 and 28 October to induce a failure of will at the centre. As news of occupations of prefectures filtered in to the Ministry of the Interior overnight, it must have appeared as if the coup was succeeding and that state authority was collapsing. Certainly, applying the martial law decree decided on by Facta's government, which crucially was reactive not pre-emptive, would now involve rolling back these initial Fascist seizures. Doubts as to whether army garrisons, which had already shown tolerance or sympathy for Fascism in 1921–2, would be prepared to take sides in a civil war might well have influenced the king to rescind the martial law decree on October 28. It must have also struck the king as absurd to risk bloody civil conflict over Fascism and for him to take responsibility for it, when all the liberal leaders he had consulted were recommending or resigned to Mussolini's entry into government. The revocation of the emergency decree obviously meant that the army would not be employed against Fascism. That put Mussolini in a correspondingly strong position from which he could hold out for nomination as Prime Minister, not simply as a member of a Salandra-led government, which was apparently the king's preferred solution. This duly happened on 30 October, once Mussolini had arrived from Milan by train and not at the head of his stranded squadrist armies, who were permitted a triumphal march through Rome on the day after.

Was Mussolini's coming to power in these extraordinary circumstances to be regarded as the outcome of insurrection or as normal constitutional practice? The ambiguity lay in the fact that it was both and neither at the same time. The constitutional forms were respected; the king as head of state had officially invited Mussolini to form a government before the squads could get within firing distance of Rome. However, this was not a normal political crisis sparked by a no-confidence vote in parliament and nor was it resolved in a parliamentary way. The king acted under duress; the outcome was determined by the extra-parliamentary pressure and force exerted by a party militia. Paradoxically the 'March on Rome' could be taken by liberals as an indication of Fascism's accommodation in a parliamentary framework, and by Fascists as the start of their anti-parliamentary revolution. The ambiguity as to the parliamentary or revolutionary legitimacy of Mussolini's appointment as Prime Minister was to condition and cloud the early years of Fascist government.

2 Between 'Normalisation' and 'Revolution', 1922–5

1. THE VARIOUS FASCISMS

In retrospect the period from October 1922 to January 1925 marked the transition from the liberal parliamentary system to the Fascist state. Like many political transitions, it was an untidy and complicated process, a hybrid of elements of the old and new political order as one overlapped with and superseded the other. It seems difficult to establish precisely what were the intentions of Mussolini and the PNF. Were they intending all along to set up a single-party totalitarian dictatorship? Or were they aiming at something rather less drastic, a strong government certainly, but still one compatible with the existing parliamentary and constitutional framework, until driven off course by the fallout from an unpredictable event, the murder of the Socialist deputy, Giacomo Matteotti, in June 1924, which precipitated the definitive rupture with the parliamentary system?

One of the reasons for the confusion, illusion and uncertainty surrounding the direction that Fascism intended to take was that Mussolini's coming to power was as much parliamentary as insurrectionary and did not represent a clean and decisive break with the existing political system and its practitioners. Fascism's drive to power had subverted parliament but not eliminated it. If Mussolini's nomination as Prime Minister was the outcome of many liberals and the king capitulating to force or the threat of force, it was still the case that they had agreed to it happening within rather than outside and against parliament. A Mussolini government still needed to be endorsed by a parliamentary vote of confidence, and since the PNF had only thirty-odd seats in the Chamber of Deputies, a coalition was unavoidable. The question was how far and for how long Fascism would be conditioned by this compromise with the liberal political establishment and its parliamentary institutions. If Fascism intended to change things, then it would of necessity be a gradual and progressive matter, a process, in other words.

The other main reason for the lack of clarity about Fascism's eventual shape and orientation once in power was that it was a catch-all movement whose unifying myth was the nation and the national interest. It offered not one coherent vision of the future and a strategy of how to use power to realise such a vision, but several blueprints and strategies of varying degrees of coherence. Fascism was a disparate alliance and was internally divided over both ends and means. Very broadly, the basic tension was between the various forms of 'normalisation' desired by conservatives and moderates both within and outside the PNF, and the 'radicalisation' demanded by the squadrist and national syndicalist groups. Mussolini increasingly came to straddle these tensions and to some extent mediated between them, alternately and sometimes even simultaneously taking up conciliatory and intransigent positions. These tensions in part lay behind the dissidence and internal conflicts afflicting the PNF in 1923 and early 1924, though they also overlaid a jostling and competition for power among provincial party factions which otherwise were often agreed on objectives and methods.

The Fascist syndicalists had a reasonably articulated view of how the syndicates would be the building blocks of a new political order and system of popular representation. Their immediate concern after the 'March on Rome' was to extend the range of control of the syndicates over employers as well as workers, especially in industry where they had penetrated least. In the desire to widen Fascist control over economic and social groups and interests, they often had natural allies in the provincial *ras* and squadrists. Their conception of the 'revolution' came down to a crude 'fascistisation' of the personnel and practices of all organisations and institutions, putting Fascists at their head. Their ideal was to perfect and perpetuate the decentralized one-party tyrannies which had emerged from the squadrist offensives of 1921–2, with the PNF through the *ras* and a permanent squadrist terror exercising an absolute power and influence over all areas of life of the provincial community. Farinacci, the Fascist boss of Cremona and the spokesman and epitome of provincial 'intransigence', urged 'legalizing Fascist illegality',[1] which was perhaps not as self-defeating as it appeared. Getting the government to frame and enforce laws abolishing other parties and political and civil freedoms might well mean passing to state organs powers and functions at present arbitrarily wielded by the Party. But as with the 'intransigent' demand that the newly constituted Fascist Militia should be the Fascist state's political police, it could also mean the PNF becoming the state, assuming in this case the repressive function of government.

It was precisely this confusion or dualism of Party and state authority and function characterising *ras* rule and the early practice of the Fascists in central government, which offended the so-called 'revisionists' in the PNF. They were a small group centred on Massimo Rocca and Giuseppe Bottai relying on Mussolini's intermittent sympathy to compensate for their lack of a strong Party base. These were the 'normalisers' within Fascism, who argued that reform of the 'intransigent' Party should precede and make possible an orderly reform of the state. The violent, undisciplined, decentralised party of 1921–2 might have proved an agile combat organisation. But now that Fascism was in power its style, methods and leadership were inappropriate for the political tasks of government and running and reforming the state. The Party should become the organisation in which new Fascist managerial and technocratic élites circulated and were formed.

'Revisionist' hopes for a meritocratic Fascism focused on the *gruppi di competenza* or technical study groups, whose development had been the job given to Rocca in September 1922. National *gruppi* started up in 1923 to consider and propose reform in education and the state administration, and another was approved to deal with constitutional reform. They were envisaged not only as 'think-tanks', but also as the embodiment and vanguard of constitutional change, embryonic corporative bodies or National Technical Councils, the leading wedge of functional and economic representation in a modified but not transformed mixed corporative and traditional parliamentary system. This very much followed the lines of the 1921 PNF programme. Portraying the party as a prospective élite of competence who would efficiently manage a stronger executive, opened up the PNF to the collaboration of all experts, specialists and professionals. It was in this mood that the 'revisionists' could welcome the merger in 1923 of the PNF and the Nationalist Association with its membership and connections among the state's ministerial and judicial bureaucracy, as an injection of talent and expertise into Fascism's task of 'national' reconstruction. The 'intransigents' were against any such openness to non-Fascists in a spirit of national pacification and reconciliation. The 'rights of revolution', their participation in the combative and insurrectionary movement, gave them exclusive claim to be the new Fascist governing class. As a result the *gruppi* were obstructed and opposed by many in the party as a rival and unsound training ground of the Fascist élite.

Fascism's conservative 'fellow travellers' among right-wing liberals and catholics certainly expected Fascism to provide at least a period of strong government after the turbulence of the *biennio rosso*. To this end they voted in parliament to give Mussolini emergency decree powers in economic, fiscal and administrative matters for a year from December 1922. Some, like Salandra, echoing the coup against parliament in 1915, wanted to go beyond this temporary suspension of parliamentary control of the executive and strengthen the power of the king and government at the expense of the legislature. If the Fascist government did this, it would still be acting within the bounds of constitutional 'normality', as long as it also put an end to continuing party and squadrist illegality and revamped the authority of state organs by freeing them from party interference. Some 'normalisers' even anticipated the PNF's dissolution, now its anti-socialist crusade was completed and Fascism was in power, and Fascism's merging into a broad political alliance of the conservative right.

Such views on party–state relations were shared by conservative 'normalising' dissidents in the PNF, like Alfredo Misuri in Perugia, Dino Perrone-Compagni in Florence, and Ottavio Corgini in Reggio Emilia. These were men who significantly were linked to agrarian associations now resisting the corporatist controls being pushed by party and syndicates in agriculture. The Nationalists were close enough to Fascism politically to be both rivals and allies, and after the merger became the 'official' Fascist right wing. They had a relatively coherent view of an authoritarian corporatist political and social order which was to shape much of the Fascist state created after 1925. They were less bothered than Salandra and other liberals about preserving a parliamentary system in some form. But they were monarchist, and as believers in state authority and orderly institutional change were another of the 'normalising' pressures on the Fascist coalition government to end party violence and its chaotic and improvised domination of provincial affairs.

Many of Fascism's non-Fascist political supporters, and interest group organisations, including *Confindustria*, looked to Mussolini rather than Fascism for the limited political reform and strong, stable government which they thought necessary. Mussolini was willing enough to be taken as a 'normaliser' like them, and the only one who as leader of Fascism and head of government could restrain and control the Fascist movement. Mussolini used the pose of mediator between the Fascist movement and its so-called 'flankers' as a means of extending their political support for his government: whatever he did was a lesser evil compared to the greater evil of an unchecked, party-led revolution.

2. DICTATORSHIP BY STEALTH

After October 1922, then, a confused and confusing political situation
was created by Fascism's coming to power through compromise with the
country's existing political institutions and liberal political class, and by
apparently unresolved arguments within and outside the PNF over Fascism's objectives and methods. It is, however, still possible to say that the
hopes and expectations of 'normalisation' were misplaced in the period
1922–4. Fascism was perceptibly moving towards a one-party state or a
progressive monopolisation of power in a process of creeping dictatorship,
or to paraphrase Mussolini, 'plucking the chicken one feather at a time'.[2]

This process was evident in Mussolini's speeches and actions and in
those of the Fascist government and party, and started as soon as the
government had been formed. In the first place, new party organs were
created and the government embarked on drastic constitutional reform.
The Fascist Grand Council, which met first in December 1922, was an
assembly initially of Fascist leaders in the top party, syndicate and state
positions. It gathered frequently in the early years of the Fascist government to discuss and formulate the main lines of Fascist policy. It was
Mussolini's creature, in the sense that he called and presided at the
meetings, set the agenda and could co-opt people as members. The
Council spent much time dealing with the PNF's internal crises and
organisation, and in October 1923 formally put itself in charge of the
party, becoming an important mechanism of centralized control of the
movement under Mussolini's leadership.

Mussolini portrayed the Grand Council as a consultative body co-
ordinating the action of the PNF and the government. This was hardly
reassuring to 'normalisers' wanting to end party interference in government and the state. The Council, an exclusively Fascist organ which only
Fascist ministers in the coalition government attended, met to align
government policy to that of Fascism and hence extend Fascist power.
The Council had no legal or quasi-constitutional status until 1928, and
was basically an alternative Fascist cabinet existing alongside and pre-
empting the actual cabinet or Council of Ministers. The Grand Council's
position as a *de facto* party organ parallel to and superseding its government equivalent, matched at the centre the party–state dualism between
provincial PNF secretaries and prefects in the localities. It indicated the
way that the balance was swinging towards the party. The Council took
unconstitutional decisions, in its first meeting passing to Mussolini the
king's prerogative to choose the date of elections. It also made coalition

government meaningless by diminishing the standing of the Council of Ministers, which was sometimes asked to endorse measures decided beforehand by the party assembly. The route followed to enact one of the government's early major innovations was instructive. The decision to create the Fascist Militia, or MVSN, was taken at the first improvised meeting of the Grand Council in December 1922, then approved by the Council of Ministers and embodied in a decree law of January 1923.

The foundation of the Militia was seen in some quarters as an important act of 'normalisation', in that it regularised the position of the Fascist squads by incorporating them into a national paramilitary organisation which would presumably ensure they acted in a more disciplined way. Certainly, one of the aims of the reform was to improve Mussolini's hold over the party and bring it under greater centralised control by breaking the local links between the *ras* and the squads. Many squadrists were reluctant to join the MVSN in 1923, a diffidence encouraged by the party bosses precisely because of the threat to local control of the squads on which their provincial tyrannies rested.

However, the formation of the Militia was an obstacle to 'normalisation'. Its job was to maintain internal public order – in other words, to defend Fascism against its political opponents – and to impart the warlike spirit of the combatants and squadrists to the nation's youth in premilitary training. Its political function was clear: at the orders of Mussolini not the king, the MVSN was a now legal private army to keep Fascism in power at public expense; no other political party could legally give itself a paramilitary arm. Until the Matteotti crisis Mussolini always resisted calls for the suppression of the Militia or its transformation into a military force integrated into the army's command structures. This attachment to the Militia as the armed bodyguard of Fascism showed that Mussolini ultimately staked his retention of power on the extra-parliamentary coercion of a party army. It was the clearest possible indication that Fascism repudiated free and equal political competition between parties, because nothing short of force would make Fascism give up power.

One of the very first issues discussed by the Grand Council was electoral reform. It was the only matter of political significance put to parliament during the period of the government's temporary emergency decree powers, and in approving it parliament effectively destroyed the principle of parliamentary government.

The so-called Acerbo law was a hybrid of majority and proportional representation electoral systems. The electoral list which gained the largest number of votes, provided this exceeded a quarter of the total votes cast, received two-thirds of the seats in the Chamber of Deputies; the remaining third of seats would be allocated proportionally among the other lists. The measure, transparently designed to give Fascism the opportunity of securing an unassailable majority in parliament, was so drastic as to be 'constitutional reform'.[3] A party winning barely 25 per cent of the popular vote would find a Chamber packed with its own supporters and could form a government that would enjoy such automatic and unbeatable parliamentary support as to make recourse to parliament superfluous. The Acerbo law undermined the principles of one man's vote being equal to another, of governments being ultimately accountable to the choice of the electorate and responsible to an elected parliament. The effect of the law was to transfer choice and decision from the electorate to the selection and composition of the governmental electoral list. This was to be a very important lever in the government's erosion of political pluralism.

It appears staggering at the time and in retrospect that this bill should have passed through parliament on the votes of liberal deputies, even though most of them certainly hated the postwar proportional system which had destroyed the axiomatic prewar liberal parliamentary majorities. Their acceptance of the Acerbo bill must presumably be related to the continuing misperception that Fascism could be 'normalised'. Salandra argued that electoral reform would constitutionalise and legalise Fascism. He seemed to be assuming that with a secure parliamentary majority, Mussolini would accept that his mandate to govern came from parliament, removing the dependence on a violent and revolutionary Fascist movement.

But party violence was an essential component of the 'double-track' tactics which Mussolini and Fascism had applied in 1922 before and during the 'March on Rome' and which they continued to use up to the general election of April 1924. Blending conciliation and the threat and actual use of violence, Fascism unravelled the democratic parliamentary system within which the government appeared to be working. Squadrist intimidation continued after October 1922, not only to preserve entrenched party positions in that self-justifying cycle of coercion, but also taking in 'unfascistised' areas of political and economic activity. The attacks on the working-class neighbourhoods of Turin and Parma, and the *ras* Turati's mobilization of the provincial squads against the PPI and Catholic organisations and town councils in Brescia, all in late 1922, were typical incursions into enemy territory. Responsibility for organised political violence lay also now with the state and the government, following the formation of the Militia as a state organ, and of a unit in Mussolini's press office to harass and intimidate prominent opponents of Fascism as well as PNF dissidents.

Party pressure on political opponents and non-Fascist organisations worked in tandem with the actions of state authorities. Not only were the prefects generally tolerant of the coercive methods of the governing party; they also applied administrative measures of their own, using the wide discretionary powers they had under existing legislation in order to dissolve local elected councils and disband unions, co-operatives and Chambers of Labour for alleged irregularities, their assets passing to the Fascist syndicates.

The combined and cumulative action of party and state authority was never so effective or necessary as in the syndical sphere. Edmondo Rossoni, the head of the national confederation of Fascist syndicates, was pushing the idea of 'integral syndicalism' both before and after the 'March on Rome'. This meant the formation of 'mixed syndicates' or corporations, with employers and workers in the same legally recognised organisation and exclusive rights of representation. 'Integral syndicalism' clearly embodied Fascism's class collaborative and productivist objectives. But is also resolved a practical dilemma facing Fascist syndicalism. In agriculture, the syndicates struggled to reconcile their links with squadrism and the big farmers, without which they would barely have existed at all, and the need to keep together their initially coerced worker members by getting farmers to respect labour agreements guaranteeing employment. This lay behind the repetition in the summer of 1923 of the conflict between syndicates and agrarian associations in many of the Po Valley provinces, which intertwined with factional rivalry within the local PNF.

The dilemma was similar in much of industry, though here the syndicates had to do something to improve their relatively low membership among industrial workers. Taking action on behalf of workers against employers was obviously one option, but this as obviously alienated employers when the control of labour was what recommended Fascism to them. 'Integral syndicalism' was a way out of the impasse, because the 'mixed syndicate' would incorporate employers and allow them to be disciplined and controlled as well as workers in an embryonic 'community of producers'.

Rossoni's concept could only be realised with party and government support, not only on the ground but also from the centre. The Grand Council endorsed 'integral syndicalism' in March 1923, and in November recognised as the sole 'official' organ of farmers, FISA, the Fascist farmers' union set up a year before in competition with the existing national organisation, CONFAG. 'Integral syndicalism' and the loss of organisational autonomy it apparently entailed met strong resistance from *Confindustria*. As a result the Palazzo Chigi agreement brokered by Mussolini in December 1923 acknowledged that industrial employers and workers should organise separately, but that each side – *Confindustria* and the Fascist syndicates – should co-operate to the implicit exclusion of other organisations. This was a step towards the union monopoly of the industrial syndicates, which was definitely negotiated in the Palazzo Vidoni pact in October 1925 and built into the regime's labour and corporative legislation of 1926. 'Integral syndicalism' prevailed in agriculture after the imposed merger of FISA with CONFAG in 1924. This guaranteed a voice for the southern landowners strongly represented in the latter without undermining the hold in the old and enlarged FISA of the commercial and 'productivist' entrepreneurial farmers of the Po Valley.

It should be clear that between 1922 and 1924 organised economic interest groups were being brought into the Fascist orbit. This was happening more rapidly and comprehensively in agriculture than in industry, cutting out the liberal politicians and lobbyists who had traditionally mediated between these groups and government. The aim of the Fascist bodies involved in this process and of the Fascist syndicates was to gain the exclusive right to organise in the economic and union arena. The means used to achieve this combined simultaneous party and state action at the centre and the periphery, ranging from squadrist violence and biased prefectural intervention against non-Fascist organisations, to national agreements. As was evident in the self-perpetuating cycle of violence and intolerance of squadrist Fascism, a monopoly of organisation and representation was ultimately the only way the Fascist syndicates could survive. In a competitive situation workers would and could join other organisations. This was demonstrably still the case in industry, and was the perpetual fear in agriculture if control of the labour force loosened. Complete and permanent control was the answer; the only safeguard of the syndicates' existence was to prevent their rivals from existing. In the economic and labour as in the political sphere, the Fascist Party and government were working to erode the bases of a pluralist society.

Practically all of Mussolini's speeches in 1923, to party or non-party audiences alike, were alternately menacing and conciliatory and could plausibly be read either way. His first and notorious speech to the

Chamber of Deputies as Prime Minister in November 1922 set the tone for the approach he would follow towards other politicians and parties over the next eighteen months. 'I could have transformed this drab, silent hall into a bivouac for my squads . . . I could have barred the doors of parliament and formed a government exclusively of fascists', he declared, adding, 'but I chose not to, at least for the present'. He had formed a coalition government not in order to secure a parliamentary majority, 'which I can now get along very well without', but to rally 'all those who, regardless of nuances of party, wish to save this nation'.[4] The speech explicitly rejected the notion that his government was legitimate because it was accountable to parliament, but simultaneously held out the poisoned chalice of co-operation with Fascism.

It soon became clear that collaboration was possible only on Fascism's terms, and that co-operation could not be genuine and mutual as between equals, but more like the relationship of a blackmailer with his victims. The government's conservative 'flankers' were constantly confronted with the threat of a Fascist 'second wave' unleashed by the party and militia unless they backed its policies. Nowhere was this more evident than during the parliamentary debate on the Acerbo bill in July 1923. In a Chamber ringed with armed squadrists and militiamen, which gave a tangible feeling of physical intimidation to the Deputies, Mussolini rephrased once again the message of the 'bivouac' speech, saying effectively that if the Deputies did not vote for a gerrymandered parliament, there would be no parliament.

The collaboration which was no collaboration at all was offered across the spectrum of organisations and parties. Mussolini made two overtures to the leaders of the main union confederation, the CGL, in November 1922 and July 1923, offering them a post in government and suggesting a merger of the syndicates and non-Fascist unions. Here was an attempt to remedy the weakness of the Fascist industrial syndicates and tie workers' organisations to the government while detaching them from the Socialist Party. Significantly, the initiative came to nothing, and not only because of PNF and syndicate opposition to the deal. The CGL put an unacceptable condition on the possibility of co-operation, union freedom of organisation, which would require the government, PNF and syndicates to lift their pressure on non-Fascist unions and live by the give and take of a free and pluralist society.

It was significant that the apparently conciliatory call for patriotic co-operation in the 'bivouac' speech was directed not at parties but at men 'regardless of the nuances of party'. As was evident in the approach to the

CGL, Mussolini's real target was the PSI and its reformist working-class base. He wanted to divide, fragment and disintegrate the anti-Fascist and non-Fascist movements and parties, again employing the characteristic blend of force and concession. This tactic was applied to the PPI, Fascism's main political and democratic rival after October 1922.

The PPI was itself internally divided in its attitude to Mussolini's government. The PPI parliamentary group had decided to vote confidence to the new government and *Popolari* were ministers in the coalition, in the hope that their presence would keep the government to a constitutional and legal path and deflect Fascist attacks on Catholic organisations. The party's conservative grouping were willing to enter a formal 'clerico-moderate' parliamentary alliance with Fascism and right liberals, but much of the rest of the party were moving towards an anti-Fascist stance. Sturzo was able to prevent the PPI from splitting into pro-Fascist and anti-Fascist wings at the party's congress in April 1923, which decided that they would continue to support the government on condition that it kept within the bounds of constitutional and legal 'normality'. Significantly, Mussolini was not prepared to accept conditional support of this kind, and he dismissed the PPI ministers from the government.

Mussolini skilfully involved the Vatican in his attempts to destabilise the PPI. Fascism's anti-Bolshevism, even its anti-liberalism, were certainly congenial to the Vatican.. But the government made important concessions to the Catholic religion in its 1923 educational measures, and held out the prospect of further gains in a more general settlement of church–state relations. All of this was to demonstrate that the Vatican could deal directly with government, and that the PPI was redundant as the party ostensibly defending the church's interests. Such a view suggested a limited perception of the role of the PPI. But it would have struck a chord with Pope Pius XI, who believed that Concordats, formal bilateral agreements between the Vatican and national governments, and a Catholic laity organised in bodies directly dependent on the ecclesiastical hierarchy, were a surer way of preserving and extending the church's influence in society.

Mussolini's overtures had made the PPI one of the obstacles to a possible church–state understanding. Continuing squadrist violence against the PPI also served to make the PPI rather than Fascism a problem for the Vatican. There were signs that Fascist violence was turning on the clergy and church organisations as well as the party. The threat of the church being drawn into a generalised anti-clerical campaign because of the PPI's anti-Fascism was precisely the reason given for Sturzo's resignation as party leader in June 1923. Fascism's unsubtle blackmailing of the Vatican, which aimed at weakening the PPI, came deliberately at the point of parliament's consideration of the Acerbo bill. The passing of the bill depended on the PPI's support or abstention, but it was also the lever to break up the party. In order to cover their divisions the PPI parliamentary group decided to abstain, only for some right-wing Catholic deputies to vote for the bill at the last moment. The party lost about one in five of its deputies and practically all of its senators in the expulsions and departures which followed the vote. Some of these pro-Fascist Catholics were included as candidates in the governmental *listone* or 'big list' which stood in the 1924 elections. Once it was clear that the PPI would not give unconditional support to the government, Mussolini had successfully prevented the party from defending parliamentary de-mocracy by widening its internal divisions. The PPI's conservative wing had been detached and brought into the Fascist orbit. The centre and left had been neutralised both by the need to preserve a precarious party unity, and by the Vatican's distancing from the PPI under the pressure of Fascist violence and blandishment.

3. THE CONQUEST OF THE SOUTH AND THE 1924 ELECTION

The merger of the Nationalist Association with the PNF in March 1923 was part of Fascism's absorption of pro-Fascist groups which were initially either independent organisations or belonged to other political parties and groupings. This process of co-option culminated in the formation of the *listone* for the 1924 elections. The recruitment of the Nationalists helped Fascism to extend its political control to the south and the islands. The price it had to pay was the sacrifice of the PNF's radical pretensions in the area to the 'transformistic' and clientelistic politics of the south.

The rider to the fusion with the Nationalists was the dismissal in May 1923 of Aurelio Padovani, the PNF leader in Naples and zonal MVSN commander, whose 'intransigent' republican and anti-clientelistic Fascism was the model for a string of young party bosses throughout Campania. This kind of southern Fascism resembled that of the northern *fasci* of 1919, both in its ex-junior army officer and university student base, and its lack of political weight. Padovani and some of his acolytes in Cam-pania had built up a relatively combative party and union organisation. But in most southern *fasci*, where they existed at all before October 1922, the few young men who saw Fascism as the new ex-combatant élite regenerating a corrupt politics and society had locked the PNF into self-perpetuating political isolation.

Southern politics revolved around personality and municipality: control of the local council was the source of favours which kept the electors sweet; who you were and what your connections were mattered above all in the murky exchange of patronage for votes which passed as political activity. The youthful parvenus running the *fasci* were nobodies who promised nothing. They remained so, while they continued in their well-meaning but naïve crusade against the old men and the old ways to exclude from the PNF the local worthies and their factional followings. So in Campania, as a reaction to and refuge from Padovanian 'intransigence' in the PNF, the dominant local clienteles drew closer to the Nationalists. They expanded in many other parts of the south following the 'March on Rome', as the usual factional in-fighting over municipal power took on the appropriate political labels of the time. An Interior Ministry report on the Basilicata in early 1923 spoke volumes for the shallow and opportunistic roots of Fascism in many Southern regions: 'Where there is a mayor, a communal administration supported by the old clienteles, camouflaged as Nationalists, there arises Fascism, or better, the other opposition clienteles dress themselves as Fascists and the Fascist section is created.'[5]

The *en bloc* entry of the Nationalists into the PNF made a partner out of a rival in the south and inserted their clienteles within the party. Fascism co-opted the southern liberal politicians and their local and regional followings in the same way, using the fact that it was now the party of central government to overcome the PNF's absence or weakness on the ground before October 1922. Liberals in the south were government supporters before they were liberals, because what interested them was access to the patronage and resources of the state. It was no wonder that Mussolini in his coalition government continued the liberal government tradition of appointing prominent southern politicians to head the Ministries of Posts and Telegraphs and Public Works, which payrolled thousands of real and phantom jobs in the south.

All that was needed was to convince the local notables who delivered the votes that the PNF now represented the best line of connection to central government. The prefects of the southern provinces worked hard to make Fascism known and accepted locally. They made use of the time-honoured levers of prefectural interference in provincial affairs on behalf of the central government, control over public spending and public sector employment and the power to dissolve municipal councils, to cajole and co-opt the local men of substance into the party. In places like Avellino and Benevento, the prefect was the architect and arbiter of the provincial PNF. The 'ministerialism' of southern politics also worked against those few prominent liberal leaders – Nitti in the Basilicata and Giovanni Amendola in Salerno – who resisted co-option by Fascism and became a kind of 'constitutional opposition' before, during and after the 1924 elections. As the 'outs' of local and national politics, they had no channel to the government favours and funds previously sustaining their own clientelistic followings, which were steadily 'transformed' into backers of the government party.

The formation of the *listone* was the other way of making the PNF the indispensable conduit of political influence in the south. In line with the kind of co-operation first offered in the 'bivouac' speech and reiterated in Mussolini's speech of January 1924 after the dissolution of parliament for the forthcoming elections, the *listone* was put together on the basis of 'men, not parties'. Since the Acerbo law weighted the allocation of seats so much, the sure way of being elected was to be included on the government list of candidates. This was inducement enough for southern politicians and outgoing deputies to join the PNF. Once the major personalities of the southern liberal parliamentary grouping were on the *listone*, their followers and factions came too.

The *listone* then, marked the absorption into Fascism of its 'flankers' among rightist and southern liberals, Nationalists, conservative *Popolari* and others. The process had gone furthest in the south: whereas about a quarter of candidates on the *listone* in Venetia, Emilia and Tuscany were 'flankers', 60 per cent of government candidates in Sicily were liberals. The election results reflected the vote-gathering rewards of southern *trasformismo*. The *listone* nationally won nearly 65 per cent of the vote and 374 seats, but did not have a majority over the other electoral lists in Piedmont, Liguria, Lombardy and Venetia. It gained majorities in the heartlands of squadrist Fascism, Emilia and Tuscany, where particularly in rural districts, the squads had ensured the vote – 100 per cent for the *listone* in some areas of Ferrara; and in the south and the islands, 68 per cent of votes cast in Sicily going to the *listone*, including blocs of votes delivered by liberals whom the 'intransigent' party leader in Palermo, Alfredo Cucco, had previously excluded from the PNF as *mafiosi*. Of the 374 elected, about 60 per cent were Fascists; the rest were the 'fellow travellers' now adopting the Fascist label.

This pattern of results would not have been out of place in prewar

Giolittian Italy, where the bank of government supporters in parliament were southern liberals. The 1924 elections could be seen as the culmination of a vast exercise in *trasformismo*, with Mussolini as 'super-transformer'. It might appear that Fascism was the victim as much as the beneficiary of *trasformismo*. This was especially so in Sicily where the PNF was sucked into the world of clientelism in 1924 and never re-emerged. The central party leadership was alternately bemused and exasperated by their inability to make sense of and affect the island's personalised and parish-pump politics. More generally, Mussolini's government had given southern Fascism a conservative cast as a result of its basic decision to ditch Padovani and his anti-clientelistic party and syndicates. By accepting rather than challenging the usual southern mode of politics and co-opting its practitioners, Fascism had preserved the traditional landholding system behind clientelism. Fascism's conquest of the south appeared to mean the south's conquest of Fascism, with Mussolini basically renewing the Giolittian deal whereby the south's political representatives supported the government in return for government's non-interference in the region's socio-economic structures.

But Mussolini's *trasformismo* was different because it was permanent. Co-operation on the basis of 'men, not parties' aimed at the disaggregation or disintegration of existing non-Fascist parties; the Fascist 'normality' was for there to be no other parties, no position independent of Fascism. In the 1924 elections the parties remaining as independent political formations were the two Socialist parties, the Communists, the Republicans, the PPI and the southern liberal opposition of Amendola and Nitti. They had to stand outside the *listone* and accept inevitable political defeat, competing only for a third of parliamentary seats. Even the non-oppositional 'flanker' lists, like the Giolittian liberals in Piedmont, were in the same position as Fascism's declared political opponents because they insisted on standing separately and did not join their fellow liberals in the *listone*. The 'flankers' in the *listone* had lost their political independence; they ran as Fascists not liberal allies of Fascism. They were not members of an electoral coalition, like the one the Fascists had themselves joined in 1921, but incorporated into a one-party bloc.

In this light, the practice of the Fascist Party and government, the creation of Fascist institutions which operated alongside and against the existing framework of parliamentary democracy, and electoral reform, indicated that what Mussolini and Fascism were aiming at between 1922 and 1924 was a gradual change to a more authoritarian political order, where the PNF would effectively monopolise political power. It was not yet formally a one-party state or dictatorship, at least in a legal and institutional sense. But the situation was approaching that in fact, and it was certainly not 'normalisation'.

4. THE MATTEOTTI CRISIS

If this is a correct reading of the actions and intentions of Mussolini's government, then the political crisis caused by the abduction and murder of the reformist Socialist Deputy, Matteotti, in June 1924, was not such a clear watershed between the periods of liberal parliamentary and Fascist systems of government. However, it did in the end mark the final and definitive point of rupture with the old system and fatally expose the illusions of 'normalising' Fascism. Matteotti's speech to the new Chamber of Deputies on 30 May catalogued the violence and coercion of the Fascist election campaign, and denied that a government whose parliamentary majority was contrived by fraud and intimidation had the right to govern. The speech was itself a serious blow to the 'normalisers'. The anti-Fascist opposition was refusing to accept the validity of its political defeat, at the very point that both 'flankers' like Salandra and 'revisionist' Fascists like Rocca were saying that Fascist power was legitimised by its electoral victory and hence PNF violence should end and national pacification begin.

The revenge promised and meted out to Matteotti, who was kidnapped and beaten to death by a group of Fascists on 10 June, was nothing less than might have been expected of a movement and government which was intolerant of opposition. The body was discovered in mid-August. But Matteotti's disappearance was immediately critical because even though Mussolini's direct responsibility could not be proven, the gang making the attack were assumed to be linked to his press office and acting on orders from his closest entourage. The assault could not be passed off as the regrettable unauthorised action of provincial squadrism; it originated in government circles.

About 150 PPI, Socialist, Communist, Republican and Amendolian liberal deputies withdrew from parliament in protest at the end of June. Adopting their name from a famous political protest against tyranny during the Ancient Roman Republic, the so-called 'Aventine Secession' was as much a response to the elections as to Matteotti's seizure: they declared that they alone represented the nation and were determined to overthrow the Fascist government. Their anti-Fascism kept to the high

moral, legal and constitutional ground; only the Communists contemplated some form of popular protest to topple the government. The
Aventine clearly expected the king to withdraw his confidence from a
Prime Minister implicated in criminal activity and sanction the formation
of a government that would repress PNF illegality and violence. In retrospect, abandoning parliament was probably a mistake, because the
king's inaction could be justified on the constitutional ground apparently
occupied by the Aventine. Since neither parliament nor the Council of
Ministers moved against Mussolini, the king could pretend that there was
no government crisis which demanded his intervention.

In fact, the Matteotti crisis, by raising the possibility of an anti-Fascist
government, seemed to clarify for the king and other important institutions and interest groups why Mussolini's government was preferable, if
only as a lesser evil. The king might well have been struck by the return of
the dilemma confronting him at the time of the 'March on Rome', and
which Mussolini constantly raised in his two years of power in order to
bend Fascism's conservative 'flankers' to his political will. If the Fascist
government fell, even on a parliamentary vote of no confidence, the fear
was that the Fascist movement would resist by force. Six Militia legions
were mobilized in June and given arms on request by the army. The
MVSN was carrying out precisely the role for which it had been created:
a private party army at Mussolini's orders to defend the 'Revolution'.

Similar fears of a civil war arising from Fascism's likely refusal to go
peacefully emerged in the Pope's public intervention in September 1924
to scotch talks within the Aventine on the possibility of PPI and Socialist
participation in an anti-Fascist coalition to succeed Mussolini. Shades of
July 1922: co-operation between Catholics and Socialists, even reformist
Socialists, was clearly unthinkable, especially when it involved bringing
down Fascism which had saved the country from Bolshevism.

Confindustria did not take a public stance as an organisation on the crisis,
but its leaders confirmed the Mussolinian, if not Fascist, position of the
previous two years in a private communication to Mussolini in September. 'We are government supporters by definition', the head of FIAT,
Agnelli, had declared after the 'March on Rome'.[6] This particular government had been the businessmen's friend. It had ended the rampant
union power of the *biennio rosso*, removed high tax Socialist local councils,
and repealed postwar social legislation. It had generally combined implementation of the PNF's *laissez-faire*, privatising and productivist programme of 1921 with a not so hands-off state salvage of banks and firms
hit by the 1921–2 recession. Now in 1924, the criminal acts of Fascism

seemed to be the cause of instability. But the secret memorandum's answer was not the fall of the government, which would be Socialism's opportunity, but a 'normalising' Mussolini-led government.

It is difficult to suppress the feeling that one has been this way before. The common and consistent elements in these conservative responses to what appeared to be the crisis of Fascism were the fear of the alternatives to Fascism, and the corrosive effect of Fascism's essentially violent and coercive character. If the overturning of the government would provoke violent Fascist resistance, then it would be better not to try; if Fascism had brought about its own crisis, then the crisis, by opening up alternatives, only made its continuation appear all the more necessary. In this light, Mussolini showed a sure political touch when he attempted to recast his government, apparently shorn of its illegality, in June and July. The men suspected or accused of involvement in the attack, Aldo Finzi, Giovanni Marinelli, Rossi and Emilio De Bono, were dismissed from their party and government posts. In the most significant and symbolic change, Mussolini gave up the titular headship of the Interior Ministry to the ex-Nationalist, Luigi Federzoni. In an even more indicative move, a government decree law in August threatened to take away the Militia as Fascism's exclusive armed guard. The MVSN was to be integrated into the armed forces: it would swear an oath of loyalty to the king, and be officered by retired army men rather than by ex-squadrist commanders, making it a national and not a party formation.

The Matteotti crisis was an opportunity to 'normalise'. But it was equally an opportunity to carry forward the 'intransigent' Fascist revolution by finally destroying and replacing the liberal state, and ending the 'transformistic' compromises with the old men and the old order which blocked the path to power of the exponents of provincial Fascism. In the 'intransigent' view, only the continued existence of the vestiges of parliamentary government and of conditions of freedom made the Matteotti case into a political crisis of Fascism. Fascism had always ultimately rejected the legitimacy of parliament, and the Militia was on hand to show that Fascism could only be ejected by force. The party 'intransigents' argued with some logic that it was absurd for the government to go on behaving as if its survival depended on the king and a parliamentary majority. Liberty would have to disappear once it meant the right to criticise and overturn the Fascist government. The argument seemed to have been won when a meeting in August of the PNF National Council, a body composed of Grand Council members and all the provincial Party leaders, decided to review the constitution and bring into being a Fascist state, setting up a special commission for the purpose.

The new Militia regulations came hard on the heels of the PNF's crucial decision, and appeared to contradict it. The problem for Mussolini was that he was finding it increasingly difficult to straddle 'normalisation' and 'revolution' in this way. In December a definitive choice had to be made after the publication in Amendola's newspaper of Rossi's deposition implicating Mussolini in Matteotti's murder. Giolitti had earlier gone into opposition in parliament. With these new revelations it appeared that even the *listone* majority was crumbling at the edges as two Salandran liberals looked likely to resign from the government. On the other hand, a MVSN conspiracy which had been brewing in the 'intransigent' party strongholds of Emilia and Tuscany literally erupted on Mussolini's doorstep on 31 December. Angry and exasperated Militia consuls, whose immediate concern was the effect of the MVSN reforms on their own positions of command, threatened to Mussolini's face that they would take action against Fascism's opponents, with or without him. The situation clarified, in his famous speech to parliament on 3 January 1925 Mussolini assumed responsibility for all that had happened since taking office and promised decisive action within two days, which would, in fact, inaugurate the dictatorship.

3 The Construction of the 'Totalitarian' State, 1925–9

1. 'TOTALITARIANISM'

Mussolini first used the term 'totalitarian' publicly in his speech to the PNF's national congress in June 1925. He spoke of Fascism applying its 'ferocious totalitarian will' to the remnants of opposition, and to the 'fascistisation' of the nation so that 'tomorrow Italian and Fascist, rather like Italian and catholic, mean the same thing.'[1] This usage corresponded to the earlier coining of the term by anti-Fascists lamenting Fascism's desire not only to defeat but to destroy its opponents and monopolise power. It hence referred also to the explicitly 'totalitarian' drift of provincial squadrism and syndicates from 1921–2 to eliminate all political opposition and ensure party control of all aspects of life. The operation of party rule under the *ras* was 'totalitarian' even before the term was officially formulated. As we shall see, the provincial party extremists revived all the themes of 1923 'intransigence' during 1925, when they attempted to generalise and formalise their experience as the basis of the new Fascist system.

Mussolini's connection of 'totalitarian' to a process of 'fascistisation' also echoed the description of Fascism as a 'total conception of life'[2] in March 1925 by Giovanni Gentile, the Hegelian philosopher and pedagogue who was Minister of Education from October 1922 until July 1924. His speeches and writings provided, at least until the 1930s, one of the most important and publicised ideological rationalisations of the Fascist phenomenon. Gentile's use of the term 'total' conveyed Fascism's claim to ubiquity and a comprehensive, all-encompassing outlook on life, like a religious faith inspiring all facets of existence. Individuals only found full self-realisation through unity and identification with the state, which was not a neutral umpire of society but an 'ethical' authority embodying moral values and inculcating them in society. Such a vision subordinated individuals to the state and imposed no limits on the activity of the state, which educated and moralised them in conformity with its values and purposes so as to achieve the unity of the two.

The definition of 'totalitarian' given the widest currency was Mussolini's formulation of October 1925: 'everything within the state, nothing outside the state, nothing against the state'.[3] This rationalisation owed most to Alfredo Rocco, the ex-Nationalist jurist and ideologue. He was one of the most enthusiastic advocates of the merger with the PNF in 1923, precisely because he believed that Fascism in power was the vehicle for the realisation of already well-developed plans for the reorganisation of the state. Obviously impressed by the bleak rationality and coherence of Rocco's blueprint, Mussolini appointed him Minister of Justice in January 1925, and he was responsible for drafting the major legislation which transformed the state between 1925 and 1928.

Rocco drew on an idealised model of the government's wartime mobilisation to project a view of a sovereign and all-powerful state which regulated and co-ordinated all the organised groups in modern society, from the industrial cartel to the trades union. Once again, as for Gentile, all the boundaries between society and state disappeared. Social and economic organisations, in liberal Italy operating as competitive private and sectional interest groups and hence always at cross-purposes with the national good, were to be absorbed into the state. They would become legally recognised organs of state exercising control over their members in the national interest as defined by and embodied in the state. The Nationalist outlook characteristically blended the nation-state's internal and foreign policies. Such a concentration and disciplining of national energies and resources through the state would alone empower the Italian nation to engage successfully in the only struggle which counted, the inevitable imperialistic conflict for power and primacy between competing states.

Mussolini's adoption of a statist idea of 'totalitarian' was significant. It differed subtly from the 'intransigent' party's view of the Fascist movement progressively encroaching on and controlling the functions and activities of all organisations and institutions. It would justify the subordinate incorporation of every body, including the PNF, under the indivisible authority of the state.

Mussolini's public statement of the 'totalitarian' nature of Fascism in 1925 was the first time the term had been used to define a political regime in the making. It was deliberately meant to mark the point of rupture with the previous system heralded by the 3rd of January speech. Although the Fascist 'Revolution' was usually later backdated to 28 October 1922, 'totalitarianism' was both the definition and justification of the new Fascist state.

The construction of this state was real enough, and it did represent a fundamental change. But all along, the measures taken to create the new system of government reflected a symbiotic balance and a series of compromises between institutions and political and economic forces, which had been revealed during the Matteotti crisis and its resolution in Mussolini's 3rd of January speech. That speech was precipitated by an ultimatum from the Fascist Party and the Militia, the hard core of the government's support throughout the crisis, that if Mussolini did not launch the 'second wave' of the Fascist revolution, then they would do so without him. The other reason for Mussolini's survival was that the ex-Nationalist and military ministers did not resign from the government, even during the dramatic coda to the crisis in November–December 1924. Their stance confirmed the king's decision not to dismiss him. Mussolini had to respect this balance in paying off his political debts after January. The presence of ex-Nationalists in the government was strengthened. Rocco was appointed to the Justice ministry, while in February Farinacci, the *ras* of Cremona and the epitome and spokesman of provincial 'intransigence', was made national head of the PNF. The outcome of the Matteotti crisis was the decision to destroy the liberal state, but still in play was the form the new Fascist state would take. In particular, the way the issues of party–state relations and worker–employer relations were resolved was to have a crucial bearing on the orientation of the Fascist regime.

2. THE PARTY AND THE STATE

As national PNF Secretary Farinacci started to reorganise and unify the party around the methods and goals of provincial 'intransigence'. By his appointments and exhortation, he extended the practices of *ras* rule from its Emilian and Tuscan strongholds to Liguria, Venezia Giulia and the big cities of the south and Sicily. He intended to realise full power to Fascism by unleashing a fresh wave of violence, coercion and pressure, where party control was once again linked to the action of the squads in a crude and unchecked 'fascistisation' of state and society. In the spring and summer of 1925, encouraged and directed from the centre, the provincial party instituted a kind of terror. Its physical and verbal offensive took in the remaining known opponents of Fascism, the leaders and members of Catholic organisations, bankers and industrialists, and as a particular target, the civil service, including the least 'fascistised' personnel of the ministerial bureaucracies in Rome. The campaign involved not only anti-Fascists but also the non-Fascists, the uncommitted, the 'enemies within', including those 'opportunistic' members who had joined the winning side after October 1922. Farinacci decided to close the party to new members in November 1925. Although reversed by the Grand Council a few months later, it was clearly the signal for a purge of membership and a sign of his commitment to a 'revolutionary' vanguard party restricted to the political élite who had participated in the movement's squadrist and insurrectionary origins.   .

The campaign ignored Federzoni's insistence from the Interior Ministry that law and order should be enforced by state organs, the police and prefects, who would soon be equipped with new and wider repressive powers in government bills now going through parliament. It could do so with impunity, because the party boss backed by the squads could still rely on that subordination and connivance of provincial state authorities which had facilitated the original squadrist offensives of 1921–2. Indeed, the party was stimulated not restrained by the impending legislative action of the government. The bill to limit the right of association was to include a retroactive ban on state military and civilian employees belonging to secret societies, wide enough to outlaw any association but probably aimed at Masonry. It was introduced in January and became law in November, and its parliamentary passage was accompanied by the party's attempt to implement the measure *de facto*. Many civil servants were Freemasons, and the campaign against Masonry was a wedge for the party's intended 'fascistisation' of the state bureaucracy, the professions and business.

From this sprawling party attack emerged a sense of the PNF's understanding of its 'totalitarian' status and role. It was aiming at what Farinacci later called 'the strictest dictatorship of the Party in the Nation'.[4] It saw itself as the élite guardian of the Revolution, standing outside the government and state, the better to 'fascistise' them. It was the carrier of 'permanent revolution' or at least permanent terror, since only the party's control exercised indefinitely and without restriction could ensure that society and institutions became and remained Fascist. There was a clear contrast between this version of 'totalitarianism', which saw the party as independent of and superior to the state, and the vision behind Rocco's drafting of the legislation of 1925–6. That made the state the source of all power and authority, emanating through the enactment and application of laws by the permanent organs of the state, the executive and the judiciary.

Between November 1925 and April 1926 and during November 1926, in two swathes of lawmaking whose timing found a pretext in the first and last of four attempts on Mussolini's life, Fascism legislated itself into permanent existence. Some of these laws and decrees formally eliminated all existing opposition and made illegal any possible anti-Fascist activity, creating a vast machinery of legal repression and effectively installing a one-party and police state.

It is certainly possible to connect these measures to some of the illiberal practices of liberal governments preceding Fascism. In the liberal state, the independence of the judiciary from the executive branch of government was often honoured more in principle than in reality, and the prefects and police had and used discretionary legal powers to restrict individual and collective freedoms. But this scarcely justifies the conclusion that there was no break in continuity between the liberal and the Fascist state system, as if Fascism was more of the same, only worse. The context of repression was qualitatively different, because these so-called 'exceptional laws' changed the relationship of state to individual. The latter was deprived in both principle and practice of any rights, even the right of redress, against the state and its agents whose actions were therefore unaccountable. This emerged most clearly in the decree of Public Security of November 1926, where a provincial commission run by the prefect could put under police sanction and surveillance 'whoever are singled out by public rumour as being dangerous to the national order of the state'.[5] The Special Tribunal set up by the law for the Defence of the State, also of November 1926, quite literally applied the summary justice of the military court martial to the judgement of civilians charged with political crimes. In both cases, the state administered its own justice without recourse to the normal courts of law. The prefects and police had an almost unlimited remit to penalise and restrain individuals whom they only had to suspect of being 'dangerous'. The definition of 'public order' was widened to include the defence of institutions and policies of the Fascist state, extending the areas of life in which the police could intervene.

Mussolini's patience with the party's 'revolution from below' finally broke in October 1925 when Fascists in Florence went on a public rampage against Freemasons. He vigorously denounced illegal party methods in the Grand Council, which decided to dissolve the squads and purge the Florentine *fascio*, one of the most 'intransigent' in Italy. The party had itself demanded the framing of the repressive measures to defend the Revolution and 'legalise Fascist illegality'. But the imminent passing of these into law gave the prefects and police the means to maintain Fascist rule and devalued the functions of political and social control exercised informally and arbitrarily by the party. Once order could be ensured through state organs applying Fascist laws, coercion by the party, which alienated public sympathies and destabilised the state administration, became increasingly redundant.

It was with this realisation and from this perspective that Mussolini replaced Farinacci as Party Secretary in March 1926. His successor, the Fascist boss of Brescia, Turati, restructured the provincial extremist party which had brought Mussolini to power. He integrated the PNF into the Fascist state in a way which conformed with the statist conception of 'totalitarianism' adopted by Mussolini. This view was reiterated in Mussolini's famous circular to the prefects in January 1927, which insisted that the party, 'simply the instrument of the state's will', must 'collaborate in a subordinate fashion' with the prefect, 'the highest authority of the state in the province'.[6] Here was an unequivocal repudiation of party control in the provinces, where it had overlapped with and superseded governmental authority.

The revamping of state authority would remain a statement of principle as long as the provincial party was unreconstructed. The new Party Statute of October 1926 abolished the election of all party posts, ending the acclamatory legitimation of the provincial party leader in local assemblies which was what internal party democracy amounted to in most areas. The hierarchical nomination of party posts from above anticipated Turati's concerted campaign between 1926 and 1929 to dismantle the substance and style of the 'intransigent' party. On an organisational level, Turati demanded that provincial party federations conform to centrally defined bureaucratic and financial procedures. This broke with the cavalier and unaccountable administrative practices which masked the arbitrary, personalised and often corrupt way in which the local *ras* ran his province.

Turati's more direct challenge to the 'intransigent' party struck at the source of its power to arbitrate provincial affairs, which lay in the squads. In a purge continuing into 1928–9, probably about 60 000 ex-squadrists and early Fascists were expelled or defected from the party. Pro-Farinacci 'intransigent' provincial leaders were replaced or domesticated. Other party bosses were removed, sometimes spectacularly, as in the case of the disgrace of Mario Giampaoli in Milan in 1929, whose dismissal unravelled a seedy network of squadrist protection rackets in suburban food markets. Hand in hand with the expulsion of squadrists went the recruitment to the party in 1926 of more passive members. These lay among white-collar public employees of an 'unfascistised' state administration and various fellow-travelling groups – the very opportunistic latecomers whom Farinacci felt had no place in the party. That the purge and recruitment policies were complementary could be gauged from what happened in some parts of the south, where the increase in number of public officials joining the party was most marked. In Sicily, the removal of the young parvenu provincial party leaders patronised by Farinacci, like Cucco in Palermo and Damiano Lipani in Caltanissetta, allowed in the old liberal politicians whom the 'intransigents' had kept out as men of clientelism and the mafia.

Having lost the battle for party supremacy over the state, Farinacci imaginatively proposed the merger of party and state positions in a kind of supercharged 'political prefect'. Given its source, the idea never got off the ground, but a real point had been made. The PNF's subordination to the state would not necessarily have liquidated its political role and influence if party leaders occupied state positions. The fusion of both state and party authority, combining party and state office in the same person, in fact only occurred at the top and the bottom. Mussolini was Head of Government and *Duce* of Fascism. Sometimes, the Political Secretary of the *fascio* was also the *Podestà*, the term given to the municipal state office which replaced the previously elected mayor and council in the laws of February and September 1926 reforming local government. But this was hardly the preferred situation, and prefects probably resorted to it as an expedient to compensate for the shortage of leadership material in small communes.

Fascists certainly became prefects, and PNF pressure on the service grew once prefectural powers were restored and extended in the Fascist state from 1926. But the influx of party men to the Interior Ministry was controlled. 'Fascist prefects', meaning those with a genuine Party background and pedigree who came from outside the career administration, rather than state officials who had taken out PNF membership, counted for about one-fifth of all prefects in office in 1928, one-quarter in 1934 and a third in 1937. The government thus continued to rely on the career service for about two-thirds of its prefects, confirmed by a 1937 decree which stipulated that at least 60 per cent of prefects should be drawn from the Interior's own ranks. As far as one can gauge this, whether an official had a philofascist, anti-Fascist or non-Fascist record of service made no difference to his being appointed as prefect and remaining in the service. These conditions reflected the inability of the PNF to throw up cadres of sufficient quality for such a key position in the state apparatus. They also showed the Fascist government's conciliation of the state bureaucracy, and willingness to work through career officials who were competent and satisfied the broad tests of political loyalty established in the measures of 1925–6.

In some important ways this situation probably inhibited the 'fascistisation' of provincial society. The prefect appointed or recommended the appointment of a large number of local public and official posts, including the *Podestà*. The Interior Ministry recognised that the prefect should consult the local party on nominations to such positions, and in most cases this happened. But the Party's opinion was not binding, and in making appointments the prefect often placed criteria of competence and general acceptability before the date of party membership or record of past services to Fascism.

This generally seemed to be the case with the *Podestà* appointed by the prefects. While it remained an unpaid post, it was likely to be filled by the local worthies or in some cases by reputable and neutral candidates such as retired military and policemen. Unsurprisingly, in the north and centre, rural communes and major towns in mainly agricultural provinces were run by local landowners, many of them also aristocrats in Tuscany. These men were returning to positions of municipal leadership they had lost to the Socialist mayors and councils in 1920. Many of these were certainly Fascists or sympathisers from the days of provincial squadrism, but they were not usually the archetypal Fascist young ex-officer professional men who had led the squads, or the squadrists themselves. However, the increasing number of paid *Podestà* during the 1930s did suggest a shift towards officeholders of an urban middle-class white-collar or professional background.

Like the prefects, the police forces of the Interior Ministry remained a largely career service, the Chief of Police from 1926 to 1940 being a career prefect, Arturo Bocchini. The Militia set up its own political investigation units in 1926, but these never became a party political police. Indeed, operationally responsible to the prefect, they specialised in reporting *on* PNF affairs, and were never more than auxiliaries to the state police.

Although important, perhaps too much can be made of the relative immunity of the Interior Ministry and its officials from the PNF's methods and personnel. Career prefects still had to oversee and implement the Fascist government's policies in the provinces, and the police enforce Fascist laws. There was no party terror or police terror to replace it, as a result of the PNF's subordination to the state from the late 1920s. But the police's preventive and repressive powers were now so extensive and pervasive as to create a real climate of fear and repression. Police harassment and surveillance became habitual and continuous, affecting even the most mundane areas of daily life, especially in working-class districts. In the early 1930s the political police alone were taking about 20 000 actions weekly, leading to hundreds of arrests, detentions and sequestrations. There grew up a vast network of informants and agents acting for the political police, particularly the notorious OVRA, the special inspectorate initially created to investigate and combat anti-Fascist activity. Policing increasingly came to involve information-gathering and comment on practically everything that talked or moved. In the enforced absence of any real public opinion in a repressive system, police reports constituted the regime's and historians' only regular if compromised account of shifts of the popular mood. Repressiveness was not the most distinctive feature of the Fascist 'totalitarian' system, but it was an essential and inescapable component of it. As we shall see, the regime's organisations and initiatives, which aimed at generating support and 'consent', operated in the context of a repressive atmosphere that gave a sense of compulsion to any involvement in activities sponsored by the regime.

Turati regarded his party reforms as preliminaries to the PNF undertaking new functions within the Fascist state. The party could not now expect to direct political matters and decision-making, certainly not at the centre of government where Mussolini was supreme, and less so in the provinces, where the prefect's authority to run affairs was usually respected after 1927. Its transformation into a 'civil and voluntary force at the orders of the State' carried a change of function as the executor rather than the framer of the state's will. It was 'the capillary organization of the regime',[7] conveying the state's will to the people by organising and indoctrinating them. This gave the PNF a wider social and controlling role, to reform the Italian character and mentality so as to secure a positive commitment to the Fascist state. Turati's Secretaryship saw the steady growth of 'capillary' organisations, extending the party's interests in youth activities, leisure, culture, sport, social welfare and syndical affairs, a trend accelerated under his successors.

3. SYNDICATES AND CORPORATIONS

The Matteotti affair and the 3rd of January speech encouraged the Fascist syndicates to be more militant in their continuing circular pursuit of the industrial working-class support which would oblige employers to take them seriously as workers' representatives in contractural negotiations and labour disputes. During the general crisis of confidence in Mussolini's government in late 1924, there were signs and fears of revived working-class agitation, stimulated as well by rising inflation which fed into higher wages demands in early 1925. Anti-employer militancy was also fuelled by the party's offensive under Farinacci against Fascism's lukewarm and opportunistic fellow-travellers, including businessmen unsympathetic to dealing with the syndicates.

Both Farinacci and Rossoni initially supported the metallurgical workers' strike for higher wages and union recognition rather improbably called by the Fascist syndicates in Brescia under the guidance of the provincial *ras*, Turati, in March 1925. The spread of the strikes throughout the industry brutally revealed the dilemma of the Fascist syndicates' position. The strike took hold only because the CGL-affiliated metalworkers union, FIOM, called out the bulk of men who remained loyal to their non-Fascist unions. What Mussolini called 'the race to be the reddest'[8] exposed the persisting isolation of Fascist syndicates among workers, and was contributing to the resurgence of labour agitation led by the old unions. The strikes were the final and fatal demonstration that the syndicates could not capture industrial workers or impress employers, using trade-union tactics in a normal competitive situation. They depended on the support of the party and state authorities to achieve the monopoly of labour representation they wanted.

The strike's settlement by PNF and state mediation, pointedly excluding the FIOM, anticipated in microcosm the general arrangement between the Fascist syndicates confederation and *Confindustria* in October 1925. The so-called Palazzo Vidoni pact made explicit what had been intimated in the 1923 Palazzo Chigi agreement. The industrial employers recognised the Fascist syndicates as the sole representatives of labour. The workers' elective factory councils, which had socialist and communist majorities as late as 1925, were abolished. Significantly, the employers would not agree to them being replaced by the syndicates' own *fiduciari di fabbrica*, factory 'trustees' or agents. This meant that the syndicates had no presence beyond the factory gates, and managerial authority in the factories was preserved.

The agreement was effectively written into the institutional structures of the Fascist state. Rocco's April 1926 law on the judicial regulation of labour relations stipulated that only the single organisations legally recognised by the state could negotiate collective labour contracts binding on the relevant branch of production as a whole. These, of course, in industry were *Confindustria* and the Fascist industrial syndicates. The syndicates' minority position on the ground had been transformed into a legal monopoly of workers' representation. Other organisations could exist as *de facto* bodies under Rocco's law, but deprived of the legal right to negotiate labour contracts they simply atrophied. Both the CGL and the CIL dissolved themselves in 1927. Catholic Action kept alive a semblance of Catholic labour organisation under the guise of training and welfare, while allowing Catholics to join the syndicates. The Rocco law also made illegal strikes and lockouts, the normal levers of pressure for workers and employers in a liberal economy. Instead the law created labour courts as the final stage of a process of compulsory arbitration of labour disputes.

The Rocco law and the way it was implemented, reflected the balance between various social and economic forces being incorporated into the framework of the Fascist state and, in particular, the power of the industrialists' interest group, *Confindustria*. Since as a result of the Matteotti crisis a Fascist 'totalitarian' dictatorship was being created, *Confindustria* recognised that they would have to enter some formal, institutional relationship with the Fascist state. Their aim was to safeguard their interests within the new structures. This meant consolidating definitively the gains arising from the Fascist defeat of the Socialist Party and labour movement, and also maintaining their organisational independence against 'integral syndicalism'. Industrialists were as much afraid of the syndicates' reliance on party and state support as their reviving labour militancy in 1925. State intervention in and regulation of labour relations and economic matters might threaten the autonomy of private enterprise and the freedom of business to make its own decisions about production.

The syndical law and what followed indicated the extent to which Mussolini's concern to secure industry's support and co-operation with the government compromised the corporatist drift of Fascism. The gradual and piecemeal evolution of the corporative system, rather than its systematic, once-and-for-all establishment, was itself a mark of *Confindustria*'s successful resistance to the realisation of the corporative idea. Rocco's law actually dealt with labour relations and the negotiation of collective contracts between separate organisations of workers and employers in each area of production. It was not really a full-fledged corporative reform, with 'mixed syndicates' or corporations, unitary bodies bringing together under a single hierarchy all the people involved in production, employers, workers and technical-managerial staff, and actually organising and planning production. The law allowed but did not oblige the setting up of fledgling corporations as 'organs of coordination' of the syndical associations. This was perhaps enough to suggest that a corporative system was in the making. But the facility to form corporations was never actually exercised nor contemplated by industrial employers, before the legal creation of corporations in 1934.

Corporative hopes were rather vested in the new Ministry of Corporations, set up in July 1926. This was meant to supervise the legally recognised syndical bodies and facilitate the stipulation of collective labour contracts. The nominal Minister was Mussolini, and the Under-Secretary between November 1926 and September 1929, when he was made Minister, was the ex-revisionist, Bottai. He intended to make the Ministry the state's central economic planning and co-ordinating body, managing a corporatively organised economy staffed by Fascism's new technocratic and administrative élite. Predictably enough, Bottai's parvenu and predatory Ministry was obstructed and ostracised by the existing Economics Ministry. He found it difficult to take the Ministry's activity beyond the bureaucratic regulation of the syndical bodies' affairs and the conciliation of labour disputes, while the corporations had no legal standing or existence. Between 1926 and 1934 there was a Ministry of Corporations with no actual corporations to direct.

Bottai was given the job of producing the 'Charter of Labour', defining Fascism's social principles. But the final draft approved and publicised by the Grand Council in 1927 was Rocco's work. It once again mirrored that balance in favour of employers limiting the scope of the syndical law. The Charter spoke of corporations organising production as if they already existed; recognised private enterprise as the most efficient way of production; and outlined some workers' rights in terms of employment and social insurance and welfare provision. Far from meeting Rossoni's demands for a full and definitive statement of legally binding workers' rights, the Charter was a general indication of intent, having the force of suggestion rather than the force of law.

Bottai, however, with the support of the PNF and *Confindustria*, was instrumental in bringing about the *sbloccamento* or dismantling of Rossoni's national confederation of workers' syndicates in November 1928. This was fragmented into a number of separate confederations covering workers in the various branches of the economy. From Bottai's perspective, it was a 'corporative' reform, since it broke up a large labour confederation of nearly three million members still organised on class lines and with a class mentality. Forming several workers' associations which were exactly symmetrical to employers' organisations in industry, agriculture and the services, would apparently facilitate inter-class co-operation and the co-ordination of the different sectors of production under the state control of the Ministry of Corporations. This was a profound miscalculation, later regretted by Bottai. He assumed that corporative planning under the state's auspices would involve the state's direction of *both* employers and labour. But the *sbloccamento* clearly weakened the political and economic muscle of labour organisations with respect to the employers. Most immediately, it deprived the workers' syndicates of the full weight of a unitary confederation in settling labour contracts and disputes. It contributed more generally to the imbalance in favour of employers which would mark the composition and operation of the corporations, when they arrived.

The Rocco law quite deliberately attempted to draw the sting of class conflict by transferring labour issues from the factory, where employers and workers actually confronted each other, to another plane, that of the law and legally recognised organisations. These were susceptible to state and political pressure for the harmonisation of capital and labour in the interests of national production. Wage agreements and the settlement of disputes arising from them were increasingly brokered by the party or the Ministry of Corporations, or a combination of both: the outcome of a bureaucratic exchange rather than the competitive interaction of employer and workforce.

There was an underlying 'productivist' rationale to the legal subordination of class-based and interest group organisations to the overriding will of the state. This inevitably skewed labour relations in favour of employers and to the detriment of workers. The main criterion was always what was best for or most likely to maximise production, and hence the economic strength of the nation. It was the production rather than the distribution of wealth that really mattered. Employers could argue that wage cuts or the introduction of different and more exploitative work practices were necessary to maintain efficient and continuous production. Italy's industrial base was probably not strong enough for a high-production, high-wage economy on the American 'Fordist' model. But anyway, Rocco's law was first enacted during the government's revaluation of the lira in 1926–7, introducing almost a decade of deflationary economic policy straddling the Great Depression.

Almost the first acts of the newly legalised workers' syndicates were to endorse wage reductions in both agriculture and industry, so that production costs could be accommodated to the new value of the currency while retaining competitiveness.

The government's refusal early in 1929 to countenance an attempt by the workers' syndicates to relaunch the *fiduciari di fabbrica*, came after *Confindustria*'s successful lobbying of Mussolini. Only a direct syndicate presence on the shopfloor could ensure that an employer was keeping to the terms of the collective labour contract governing pay and conditions in his industry. But the industrialists said that any challenge to or restraint on the employers' absolute authority to manage their firms would risk damaging production. Again almost without exception, the same 'productivist' criteria were applied in the party and government mediation of labour disputes, and in the decisions of the labour courts on the relatively rare occasions when a dispute actually reached that advanced stage of the arbitration process. Class collaboration in a 'productivist' framework invariably involved one-way collaboration.

4. THE FASCIST CONSTITUTION

The other 'most Fascist' laws which marked the formation of the Fascist state system were more properly constitutional measures, since they affected the relations of government to parliament and to the king. The law of December 1925 invented a new position of Head of Government, replacing the previous designation of President of the Council of Ministers or Prime Minister of the cabinet. As Head of Government, Mussolini was accountable not to parliament for government policy but to the king, who alone could dismiss him. Since the Head of Government also decided what parliament could and could not discuss, the law effectively negated the principle of responsible parliamentary government and removed from parliament the right to initiate legislation. From January 1926 the Head of Government could issue laws by decree. Even though such decrees required eventual retrospective parliamentary ratification, executive and legislative powers were now practically combined in the same position and person.

A law of May 1928 formally reshaped parliament in a quasi-corporative direction. The Senate, whose members were appointed for life by the king, was unchanged. But the Chamber of Deputies was to be made up of 400 deputies, chosen by the Grand Council from 1000 candidates nominated by the national syndical confederations and other public bodies. The one list of candidates was simply approved *en bloc* by the voters in a form of plebiscitary election. This arrangement was another halfway house. It was far from genuine corporative representation, with parliament as a corporative lawmaking assembly of producers. The PNF and government controlled the syndical bodies making the nominations, and the Grand Council sifted the nominations. This was yet another demonstration that the real point of corporative reform was to extend state control over the organised economic forces of the country.

With Rocco's law of December 1928 the Grand Council became a legal organ of state. It was to deliberate on all major matters of government and party policy, and controlled the party's organisation and leadership. This simply formalised functions it had assumed as a *de facto* organ. It was also supposed to designate candidates to fill vacant ministerial posts and to succeed Mussolini as Head of Government, and discuss the succession to the throne. This was a significant challenge to the authority and powers of the king as head of state. What had started as a party organ was now being given constitutional powers to ensure the permanence and continuity of Fascism beyond the lifetime of Mussolini.

The Grand Council's powers, however, remained potential rather than actual from the moment they became law. As Head of Government Mussolini controlled the Council, its membership, when it met and what it discussed. In contrast with its often busy schedule between 1922 and 1929, Mussolini chose to call the Grand Council much less frequently during the 1930s. It was not even consulted on all major policy decisions, such as the Conciliation with the Catholic church and Italy's entry into the Second World War, which Mussolini took himself. The Council's designation of his successor, which conditioned the King's right to appoint the Head of Government, was never taken seriously. Mussolini refused to allow the consideration of alternatives to himself. By a 1929 amendment to the Grand Council law, Mussolini took from the Council and vested in himself as Head of Government the power to appoint the top PNF leaders and draft its statutes. The Grand Council's increasing marginalisation was a striking example of the way Fascism's own new constitutional order, the basis, after all, of Fascism lasting beyond Mussolini, could be subverted by the workings of a personal dictatorship.

The concentration of government powers in his own person was exemplified in the almost ludicrous accumulation of ministerial posts held by Mussolini from 1925 onwards, except for a temporary period of delegation between 1929 and 1932. In 1933 Mussolini was Head of Government and held seven of fourteen cabinet posts. Government came to resemble Mussolini in endless dialogue with himself. The outcome of personal government of this kind was hardly efficient administration of the country's affairs, since it divorced power from responsibility. The accumulation of offices fed the image of an omnipotent and omniscient *Duce*. But it left Mussolini with the nominal responsibility for running ministries over which he could hardly expect to exercise real control. Management passed to the Under-Secretaries. But they could not employ the full weight of ministerial authority nor feel they were able or required to act decisively while Mussolini was their titular head. The result of this circular passing of the buck was probably that things did not get done. Italy's deficiencies in military planning and preparation during the lifetime of a regime committed to territorial expansion and war could in part be attributed to the in-built inefficiency of dictatorial government: Mussolini was head of all three armed service ministries from 1924 until 1929, and again from 1933 to 1943.

These various reforms amounted to a violation if not an absolute elimination of the Constitution of liberal Italy. Meaningful parliamentary government had given way to a centralised and unaccountable system of executive rule, vested in Mussolini and the state bureaucracies. Significantly, the personal will and power of Mussolini as dictator undermined the operation of Fascism's most characteristic constitutional innovation, the Grand Council, designed to ensure the continuity of Fascism.

But even these institutional changes represented a kind of balance between Fascism and the monarchy, respecting the king's support through inaction for Mussolini's government which went back to October 1922, and continued during and after the Matteotti crisis. There can be little doubt that Mussolini ruled Italy and made the major policy decisions. Although the king was a political cipher, he retained, just, the latent but decisive power to appoint and dismiss the Head of Government. The monarchy had not been abolished as a national institution and head of state. Mussolini had quite evidently calculated that it was too risky to eliminate the monarchy at a stroke. He had attempted through the constitutional changes to find a diminished place and role for the king within the Fascist system of government. This sort of institutional compromise with a force which was still too strong to confront definitively was used to consolidate and stabilise the dictatorship. It dovetailed, for instance, with the party's subordination to the state. Retention of the monarchy and its neutralisation by incorporation into the Fascist system widened the acceptance of the Fascist regime among important groups such as the armed forces and the state administration. They still looked to the monarchy as at least a symbol of national unity, tradition and state authority.

5. THE CONCILIATION WITH THE CATHOLIC CHURCH

Much the same strategy was applied to the 'co-ordination' of the Catholic church in the evolving Fascist system of rule. Formal and bilateral negotiations between the Vatican and the Fascist government for a church–state agreement began in August 1926. The timing was significant, as Fascism was in the process of erecting the 'totalitarian' state. The Vatican needed to enter into a comprehensive and lasting relationship with the new state which would guarantee and preserve the church's position in society. This was exercised exclusively through Catholic Action's network of lay associations, now that the PPI and the CIL were on the point of extinction.

The specific cause for alarm was the government's establishment of the National Balilla Agency (ONB) in April 1926, a body initially dependent on the Interior Ministry and led by the *ras* of Carrara, Renato Ricci. Created to organise and indoctrinate children and adolescents in broadly the eight to seventeen age groups, it demonstrated how from a very early stage the Fascist government intended to monopolise the formation of young people and 'fascistise' them. This could only be achieved by squeezing out its rivals in the field. The Catholic Boy Scouts were dissolved by the prefects in early 1927 in small and medium-sized communes, forcing the Vatican to close them all. The formation of other youth groups was banned, as was the provision of sporting and athletics activities by groups not affiliated to the ONB. By *force majeure*, the members of Catholic sports clubs drifted over to the Balilla organisations. A proposed general ban on all non-ONB youth organisations stalled the church–state talks for a while in 1928, and they only resumed on Mussolini's decision to exempt Catholic Action's youth clubs. The Vatican's need to ensure Catholic Action's survival against the depredations of the 'totalitarian' state was both the reason for breaking off negotiations with the government, and for pushing them towards a definitive conclusion.

The Lateran agreements of February 1929 formally reconciled the church to the Italian state which it had condemned at the moment of national unification. A treaty involved the mutual recognition of the

Italian nation-state and the Vatican city-state, while a financial settlement compensated the church for the loss of the papal states during unification. But the part of the package to which the Pope attached the greatest importance was the Concordat regulating church–state relations in the country. Mussolini made significant concessions in the Concordat which both recognised and legalised the church's special position in Italian society. Church marriage now had civil force; religious education taught by priests, already part of the curriculum in elementary schools under the 1923 Gentile law, was introduced into state secondary schools; and Catholic Action was allowed to exist, becoming the only non-Fascist organisation legally operating within the 'totalitarian' state.

The Vatican and Mussolini approached the agreement from different perspectives. Pope Pius XI hoped that the church's privileged position, recognised and buttressed by the Fascist state in the Concordat, would allow it to extend its influence throughout Italian life, a platform for the clerical reconquest of state and society. Mussolini's view was equally instrumentalist. He had always acknowledged the importance and strength of Catholicism as the religion of most Italians, and as an orga-nisation with a national network of social, economic and cultural bodies inspired by religious ideals. The church was so rooted in Italian life in a civil as well as religious capacity that it could not be challenged directly and immediately without endangering the government's stability and survival. Mussolini rejected both before and after the Concordat any party anti-clerical campaign: 'A holy war in Italy, never; the priests will never bring out the peasants against the state.'[9] The reverse was, of course, true. An agreement ending the church's official alienation from the state would reconcile Catholics to the regime which brought it about. It could help to harness the support of the church and Catholics denied to the liberal state, in both internal and foreign policy.

In this light, the Conciliation was probably the most important con-tribution to the consolidation of the Fascist government in power on a wider basis of support and consent. It brought Mussolini and Fascism enormous internal and international prestige. It temporarily killed off active Catholic anti-Fascism at home and abroad, because the church, through the pacts, was seen to be endorsing and legitimating the Fascist regime. The ex-PPI and CIL men who had passed to Catholic Action, an organisation closely controlled by the Vatican and bishops, 'could not conspire against a regime constantly backed by the blessings of the Church'.[10]

Catholics could now rally unreservedly to Fascism, and Catholic priests and organisers could be expected to involve themselves and their flocks in support of Fascism. This was demonstrated immediately in the plebiscitary elections of 1929. Bishops and clergy publicly urged Catholics to vote for the single government list of candidates, in the knowledge, of course, that the new parliament would have to ratify the Lateran agreements. But the explicit endorsement was repeated in the 1934 elections, and reflected a more general alignment of the church with many of the regime's economic and social policies. It was difficult to see how else Mussolini could have reached an agreement with the church. But the Conciliation traded the short-term broadening of support for the regime, for the longer-term risk of the 'totalitarian' state recognising an alternative and rival for the control and organisation of the country.

The Fascist dictatorship had been built by 1929 around the position of a single leader, Mussolini, and a highly centralised system of government. It was founded on the primacy of state authority, to which were subordinated both a purged and reconstructed single party and the syndicates. At this stage of its development, the Fascist state did reflect and formalise a series of compromises and a kind of power-sharing with institutions which had helped or tolerated Fascism's coming to power in 1922 and its retention of power during the Matteotti crisis. The dictatorship recognised and rested on important centres of power and influence, the monarchy, the armed forces, the state apparatus, *Confindustria* and the Catholic church. Mussolini had estimated that they were too strong to challenge head-on and simultaneously. It was best to co-opt and incorporate them as far as possible within the Fascist state, if only because this contributed to the regime's stabilisation.

6. THE REVALUATION OF THE LIRA

The construction of the 'totalitarian' state coincided with economic difficulties, which led to the Fascist government's first serious intervention in economic policy. The government's actions and the laws and decrees setting up the new state did not run in parallel, but intersected. From 1925 Fascist policies were being aligned with the kind of governmental system which was evolving.

Mussolini proclaimed in the parliamentary debate on Rocco's syndical bill in December 1925 that 'I consider the Italian nation to be in a permanent state of war . . . To live for me means struggle, risk, tenacity . . . not submitting to fate, not even to . . . our so-called deficiency in raw materials.' He said that the nation's 'permanent state of war' necessitated, as in the First World War, the end to labour conflict and a state conciliation apparatus through which 'we will achieve the greatest possible productive efficiency of the nation'.[11] This speech contained all the characteristic elements of Fascist rhetoric and style, applying the language of struggle and conflict to the resolution of the country's economic problems. It clearly echoed the 'battle for grain' which had been launched that summer, and the 'battle for the lira' soon to be engaged. The ethos of squadrism was being applied to economic policy. Objective economic weaknesses could be overcome by acts of political will which defied caution and rationality. The wartime model and analogy signified Fascism's 'totalitarian' aspirations: permanent war meant permanent mobilisation of the nation, internally disciplined by and around the regime in defence of the national interest.

The speech addressed a bill which would become a fundamental law of the regime, putting organised economic groups under state control to maximise the nation's economic strength. But it also connected the establishment of these permanent structures of state control to the solution of a long-term weakness of the national economy, which was being exposed during the current economic difficulties confronting the government. How the government interpreted these economic problems and how it tried to tackle them were the first real exercise in 'totalitarian' control.

The economic problems of 1925–6 were rising inflation and growing deficits in the balances of trade and payments. Partly due to a poor 1924 harvest, grain imports rose rapidly, along with those of industrial raw materials which manufacturers were accumulating to offset the effects of a simultaneous devaluation of the Italian currency. This was caused by the revaluation of the dollar and sterling, and continuing uncertainty over the payment of Italian war debts to Britain and the United States. The lira's devaluation contributed to general price inflation in 1925–6, and to stock market speculation which in turn accelerated the lira's decline in value.

The dramatic rise in grain imports at high international prices prompted the government's launching of the 'battle for grain'. The aim was to increase Italy's production of wheat and cereals to the point of self-sufficiency. The successive wheat tariffs of 1925, 1928 and 1929 were the traditional recourse to government protection of home producers. But the programme was given a Fascist intonation by the enormous propaganda campaign. Farmers and the public were mobilised behind the regime's self-proclaimed efforts to emancipate the country from the 'slavery of foreign bread'[12] and achieve national economic independence in the event of war. Italy produced enough grain to feed itself by the late 1930s. But the 'battle' was won at the cost of reversing the diversification into export cash crops. It protected the unproductive southern *latifundia* as much as it benefited the entrepreneurial farmers of the north and centre.

The lira's eventual stabilisation was largely dictated by the deflationary demands of the US and British governments and financial markets, and Italian industry's concern to gain access to these sources of capital and investment. Some of the way was cleared by the Italian government's negotiation of war debt repayment settlements with the United States and Britain in late 1925 and early 1926. Linked to these settlements was the release of large US loans and investments, which went to Italian industry and to the Italian government to stabilise the currency. A stable lira was itself a stimulus and security to further profitable US investment in the Italian economy.

The Fascist government's monetary policies were being largely determined by Italy's subordinate place in the international economy dominated by Britain and above all the United States. But again, Mussolini transformed the Italian economy's adjustment to general deflationary trends into a Fascist 'battle' for the country's economic independence. Mussolini quite deliberately hitched the prestige of the regime to the fate of the lira. In a speech at Pesarò in August 1926, he launched the 'battle for the lira', which was to be revalued at the rate of 90 lire to the pound, the currency's level at the time of his coming to power in 1922.

Most industrialists were convinced of the need to revalue, but 'Quota 90' was probably higher than what they desired or expected. The dispute over the level of revaluation soon faded. The government compensated those large industries producing for the domestic market, introducing higher protective tariffs, placing orders and cutting wages. It also underwrote the bigger firms' takeover and merger of smaller businesses least able to sustain the lower profit margins of a deflationary policy.

Nevertheless 'Quota 90' was Mussolini's political decision, dictated in part by prestige rather than economic rationality. The 'battle' to realise the rate was achieved in late 1927. It was conceived as a national mobilisation for economic survival, in which the PNF, now being reorganised by Turati, and the newly legalised syndicates performed their first services as instruments of the Fascist state. The PNF took the lead in announcing as a matter of national necessity wage reductions in both agriculture and industry in 1927. These cuts were to align pay to the revalued lira, and should have been matched by an end to inflation and a lower cost of living. In fact, the fall in wages occurred more rapidly and steeply than the fall in prices, especially in agriculture and textiles, which meant that the costs of deflation were met by workers and consumers.

To ensure that the officially imposed wage cuts were implemented and that corresponding action was taken to lower prices and rents, Turati extended to all provinces the Party's Intersyndical Committees. An equivalent organisation at the national level was also established. These had already sprung up on the initiative of some local PNF federations to oversee the stipulation of labour contracts and conciliate labour disputes, which were really matters for the Ministry of Corporations, in the wake of the syndical law. Presided by the provincial PNF secretary, or *federale*, these committees were liaison bodies bringing together the representatives of the provincial employer, traders and worker syndicates. As the regime's 'corporative' presence at the local level, with a labour relations role and now assuming responsibility for wages and prices control, they were potentially an important lever of the PNF's influence and interference in economic and social life.

It was difficult to say how effectively the committees carried out the task of carrying the regime's economic 'battle' to employers, traders and workers. In some areas, it made a difference that as *de facto* bodies their decisions were not legally enforceable, a let-out for employers unwilling to recognise their authority in labour disputes. With no statutory control over prices, they certainly found it hardgoing setting accurately and fairly the retail prices of essential foodstuffs, which usually found their own market level. As with the whole campaign, the committees, whose pricing functions lapsed in 1928, were more effective in enforcing cuts in wages than in prices. The committees remained in existence, however, as instruments of PNF political control of the syndicates and their cadres. They assumed a near-permanent role in the arbitration of labour disputes, almost to the point of replacing the syndicates altogether.

The revaluation campaign was important both for its effects on the economy's general orientation under Fascism and for the way it was staged. A revalued currency made trading more difficult for Italy's agricultural and industrial exporters. Together with the government's protective measures against cheaper imports, it generally favoured those large concerns in the chemicals, engineering, iron and steel and agribusiness sectors producing mainly for the home market. It also encouraged import substitution, of which the 'battle for grain' was the clearest example. Only with the Great Depression from 1929 did the Italian economy, like others, become progressively isolated from international trade and finance. But there was an increasingly autarchic feel to the shape of the economy because of revaluation. This was consistent with the government's projection of its economic battles as the struggles of a nation unified around the regime and mobilised into action by the PNF, to revive the country's economic strength and independence against foreign 'domination'.

7. 'RURALISM'

The 'battle for grain' anticipated and became part of the Fascist government's more general campaign to 'ruralise' Italy. Self-sufficiency in cereals was meant to ensure that the country had enough food in the event of war. On the same lines, Fascist 'ruralism' was connected to population concerns, and from there to Fascism's longer-term aspirations to create an empire for Italy.

Both 'ruralism' and the demographic 'battle' were announced officially in Mussolini's keynote 'Ascension Day' address to the Chamber of Deputies in May 1927. Here, Mussolini asserted that what determined the political, economic and moral strength of the nation was the size and growth of its population. Numbers, quite literally, meant power. A growing population was both the reason for and means of achieving imperialist expansion. Settlement colonies were an outlet for surplus population, and a large army was needed to conquer them. This was a self-justifying, circular and anachronistic argument for empire, and a lopsided view of what constituted power to wage modern wars. But Mussolini took his own formulations seriously and made them the basis of policy. Industrial urbanisation was leading to a declining birthrate in Italy and elsewhere. To be populous and hence powerful, Italy had to protect and promote agriculture and its fecund peasantry, turning out the peasant soldiers who would win and colonise the empire. The hackneyed exaltation of the superior values and virtues of rural life clearly mirrored Fascism's own large social base among the small farmers of northern and central Italy and its suspicion of the industrial proletariat. Mussolini admitted in his speech that workers were 'still distant, and if not opposed as they once were, absent'.[13]

These concerns lay behind a whole swathe of co-ordinated, or at least connected, government policies in 1927–8, which continued in the years to come. Various pronatalist measures favoured early marriage and large families, including the notorious and lucrative tax on bachelors first levied in 1927, which funded provision for the improved healthcare of mothers and infant children. An 'empty the cities' campaign launched by Mussolini in Autumn 1928 was backed up by the prefects and police being given powers to prevent temporary and permanent migration to towns and cities. Such repressive measures were accompanied by concrete action to make rural life more attractive and agriculture more productive. It involved a shift in public spending to the agricultural sector to fund a vast programme of *bonifica integrale* or comprehensive land reclamation and improvement, established in the law of 1928. The scheme was designed to provide public works employment on infrastructural improvements, and extend the land area under cultivation to be settled and worked by new small farmers.

'Ruralism' was clearly tied to the conquest of empire, and to that future period of 1935–40 which Mussolini had identified in the Ascension Day speech as when 'we will make our voice heard and see our rights finally recognised'. The campaign was also a response to the impact of the lira's revaluation on the economy. The anti-urban police measures came just at the point when another rural exodus was threatened, as deflation affected the agricultural sector far more severely than the government expected or wished. Keeping people on the land or, rather, keeping the unemployed in the countryside and not in the cities, made the growing social problem of unemployment less visible and more easily policed.

Historians have often been rather puzzled by the 'ruralism' campaign. Some regard it as a gigantic bluff or sleight of hand. It has been described as the way Fascism disguised the onset of serious economic problems in agriculture, 'ideological compensation for crisis'.[14] It was supposedly how the regime deliberately masked the transition Italy made during Fascism to a mainly if not predominantly industrial and urban economy, and its subordination to the interests of industrial and financial capitalism. For once, it seems that the policy is best understood by separating the reasons behind it from its actual effects.

The measures to restrain urban growth, increase the population and stimulate an agricultural sector of small peasants were certainly largely unsuccessful. They proved unable to stem, let alone reverse, long-term trends of a declining birthrate and the shift to urban and industrial habitation and employment. The rural economy was increasingly penetrated by industry and finance, in the shape of the near-monopolistic chemical and machinery firms supplying fertilisers and tractors under the regime's own 'battle for grain' and *bonifica integrale* programmes.

'Quota 90' certainly improved the purchasing power of the relatively fixed incomes of large parts of Fascism's urban middle-class constituency among public officials, professional men and property owners. Revaluation ended a ten-year cycle of inflation starting during the war, which they associated with the erosion of their own living standards and the material and political advances of the working classes. But currency stabilisation also devastated many of Fascism's own rural supporters, especially those newly established peasant proprietors and tenants who found their debts being revalued upwards at a time of falling land and agricultural prices. The regime showed a clear propagandistic preference for agricultural sharecropping during the 'ruralisation' campaign. *Mezzadria* purported to embody a kind of social solidarity between peasant and owner, and necessitated large and stable family units to work the land under such contracts. But the spread of sharecropping was not only a result of upgrading landless labourers, and hence cutting the ground from under rural socialism. It was also the outcome of proprietors and tenants moving downwards to farm under far more onerous and exploitative forms of sharecropping.

Bonifica integrale, especially in the south and the islands, often went no further than the infrastructural improvements at public expense. The 'partners' in *bonifica*, the landowners, refused to make and pay for land improvements, and the government lacked the political will to expropriate them and disrupt the alliance that had eased the Fascist 'conquest' of the south. This situation not only reduced the amount of newly cultivable land available for prospective farmers. Those that did make it were also saddled with the financing and undertaking of such improvements themselves in burdensome tenancy contracts.

If the effects of these policies were inconsistent with their aims, one has to admit that the government's agricultural policies often also had contradictory goals. It was difficult to see how the countryside could be repopulated and agriculture made more productive – the intention of both the 'battle for grain' and *bonifica* projects – when wheat was best cultivated extensively and in a labour-intensive way. It was no surprise that the farmers who made the real killing in the 'battle for grain' were the large-scale commercial farmers of the Po Valley. They increasingly employed machines rather than men, in switching from cash crops whose prices were falling to the safety of the protected grain market. So it appears unlikely that 'ruralism' did or could have had the anticipated impact on Italian agriculture. Nevertheless it remained one of the abiding themes of fascist propaganda and policy, and had its logic in Fascism's wider concern to shape a nation which would be populous and independent enough economically to found and rule an empire.

Part II
The Fascist Regime, 1929–36

4 The Years of the Great Depression, 1929–34

1. THE PARTY AND THE *INQUADRAMENTO* OF THE NATION

It is tempting to say that Fascism did not evolve beyond the point in 1929 when the construction of a repressive dictatorship was largely completed, based on centralised and extended state power administered by the existing state apparatus. Certainly, one of its major rationales both as a middle-class mass movement and in power was the permanent destruction of working-class organisations and the postwar threat of a significant advance in the political and social position of workers. This was the lowest common denominator of the compromise or alliance of Fascism with the institutions and forces of the existing order. The advantages to that order of the Fascist state's disciplining and control of labour were apparent in the way the government had handled the revaluation crisis. But the development of the Fascist regime during the period of the Depression indicated that Fascism was something more than a repressive conservative dictatorship.

Coercion alone was insufficient as a means of control. It was inadequate to keep the lid on a society marked by deep social, economic and political divisions and where both industrial and agricultural workers were used to being represented by their own independent organisations. The regime needed a base of 'consent' broader than its middle-class constituency if it was to survive, be stable and, most importantly, perpetuate itself. Yet the Fascist state was founded on the denial and repression of the free articulation and satisfaction of social and political demands. No political parties were allowed other than the PNF; no unions other than the syndicates. In this context, 'consent' had to be 'manufactured', through the development and extension of the regime's own organisations and structures, particularly the party and its auxiliary agencies. Already under Turati the PNF was becoming a 'mass' party, with an organisational network beginning to reach into the localities and involve large numbers of people in a wide range of activities sponsored and controlled by the regime. This incipient process of 'fascistisation' was called *l'inquadramento*, meaning something between organisation and re-gimentation, with the sense of framing, enclosing, integrating.

Allied to the 'totalitarian' imperative of attempting to create 'consent' in an unfree situation, there was a more immediate and contingent in-centive behind Mussolini's injunction to the party to 'go resolutely to the people'.[1] *L'inquadramento* was a response to the actual and potential popular distress and discontent arising from the effects of the revaluation crisis, and then the Depression from 1929. The basic aims of *l'inqua-dramento* were combined to varying degrees of emphasis and intensity in all of the regime's organisations, which expanded greatly from the late 1920s. They were to erect a more efficient organisational apparatus for exercising control and surveillance over the population; to generate a wider basis of 'consent' for the regime; and to mobilise and identify the population with the regime's policies and goals. The organisations re-sponsible for the attempted 'fascistisation' of Italian society were at least potentially and in intention a way of giving independence and permanent life to Fascism. They were the models and agencies of a new social and moral order which might eventually supersede the compromises and bargains struck with non-Fascist institutions. They were the basis on which Fascism could reproduce itself, and arguably made the PNF the most important organ of the Fascist state in the 1930s.

The party had been geared up for its tasks in the Fascist state under Turati. But the outcome of his reorganisation might well have hampered its performance. It would be difficult to activate a party that was subject to centralised discipline and control, where internal debate and self-government had been stifled. The PNF had also lost some of its earliest and most combative members, and its leaders, appointed from above, could be treated as itinerant public officials. Giovanni Giuriati, like Turati, whom he succeeded as Party Secretary in 1930, retained the idea of an élite party, maintaining the official closure of party ranks which restricted entry to graduates of the Fascist youth organisations.

But Achille Starace's Secretaryship, from December 1931 until October 1939, inaugurated the mass party, removing the boundaries between the party and the nation. The reopening of the party to new members deliberately coincided with the public celebrations of the tenth anniversary of the 'March on Rome', and the sense of the regime's triumphant consolidation they were meant to convey. Enlargement of the PNF would formalise the identity of Fascism with the nation, and its general acceptance by the nation. Membership leapt from about one million in 1932 (2.4 per cent of the national population) to over 1 800 000 in 1934, and after another prewar influx of members in 1936, reached 2 600 000 (6 per cent) by 1939. Decrees of 1932–3 made PNF membership indispensable to gain employment in local and central government, eroding the voluntary character of membership.

It was perhaps hard to see how a party weighed down by such numbers could be active and dynamic, especially when many members were not committed volunteers but conscripted by the requirements of their job. But the party's bureaucratisation and consequent devitalisation can easily be assumed or overemphasized. Making the party bigger facilitated the 'totalitarian' control of more of the population. Greater demands could be made of someone who was inside rather than outside the party. This was recognised by the Pope in his famous encyclical, *Non Abbiamo Bisogno*, at the height of church–state conflict in 1931. He allowed a kind of mental fingers-crossing when it was difficult to reconcile being both a Catholic and a party member. Party leadership at all levels remained the preserve of 'first hour' Fascists or those who had entered the party through the youth organisations. Some of this inner core of activist leaders were clearly capable of maintaining and enhancing a vigorous and influential party presence which owed something to past squadrist traditions. They often did so, as in Florence and Bologna, by associating the party with the revival of the local economy and the development of a strong sense of municipal pride and public achievement in culture and sport. Under Starace particularly, who had a simplistic 'totalitarian' vision of the party covering every square yard and every person in the country, the PNF was constantly widening and deepening the scope of its activity and competence in society. Where the party went and who it organised in its empire of dependent and auxiliary bodies were more important than the affairs of the party proper.

2. THE ORGANISATION OF THE YOUNG, WELFARE AND FREE TIME

The regime's efforts to control the formation of the nation's children and young people became more intensive and focused from 1929, in part to mitigate or minimize the effects of the Concordat's concessions to the church. Indeed, in his speech to parliament on the ratification of the Lateran agreements, Mussolini quite brutally emphasised the Fascist and 'totalitarian' nature of the state, and its exclusive right to mould the mind and character of the young through an 'education for war'.[2] This crudely formative view of the educational process under Fascism was carried over into the Ministry of Public Instruction's change of title to Ministry of National Education in September 1929. The ONB became a branch of this Ministry, with Ricci the Under-Secretary for youth and physical education.

The ONB provided premilitary physical training in the form of drilling, gym and callisthenic exercises, and crucially, sports activities. It intended its work to be integrated into the school curriculum and timetable. School teachers, especially physical education staff, were expected to become local ONB organisers and instructors. The fusion of school and ONB was actual and complete in the thousands of small rural schools run directly by the agency between 1928 and 1935. The ONB's direct connection to the school system facilitated recruitment and access to equipment and premises, membership always being heaviest among children up to the age of twelve, the statutory school leaving age until it was theoretically extended to fourteen under the 1923 educational law. It also accelerated the 'fascistisation' of the personnel and pedagogy of the elementary schools in particular. An oath of loyalty was required of elementary and secondary school teachers from February 1929. As public employees they were subject to the later decrees on obligatory PNF membership to join the profession. The first Fascist textbooks for obligatory use in all schools, public and private, were ready for introduction in the 1930 scholastic year. They and their successors were designed to impart an education which was nationalistic and militaristic in tone and content.

The PNF itself only retained direct control of the university students associations (GUF) on the formation of the ONB in 1926. It always resented the ONB's special status, and argued in a long series of jurisdictional disputes with the ONB that only a party organ as opposed to a state body was suitable to inculcate the Fascist spirit and mentality in the young. Were Fascist youth to be left to a 'lazy bourgeois bureaucracy, which after thirteen years of the regime, remained more or less what it was?' complained Starace to Mussolini in 1935.[3] Under the irascible *ras* of Lucca and party Vice-Secretary, Carlo Scorza, the PNF founded the Young Fascists' organisation in October 1930. It was deliberately aimed at plugging a real gap in the joint ONB and PNF regimentation of young men. These were the eighteen to twenty-one year olds already at work or attending trade or vocational schools but who had not gone on to higher education, the same age range but a different social class to most university students. These young peasants and workers were to be a new source of PNF members and lower level cadres. Their premilitary training came from the Militia and their political education in special courses of political preparation. Their often unruly behaviour and aggressive demeanour, vented to the full in the attacks on Catholic youth clubs in 1931, were the nearest the party got to recreating the bravado of the squads.

But it was clearly among university students that the regime expected the next generation of Fascist leaders to emerge. Here, it was grudgingly recognised that the formation and selection of the new Fascist élite required some attempt to engage them intellectually and politically. A certain latitude to debate and criticise without it was hoped, breaking the bounds of Fascist orthodoxy, was allowed in student circles if denied elsewhere in society. Held annually between 1934 and 1940, the *Littoriali* or student games, were a good example of the atmosphere of repressive tolerance in which the regime raised its prospective ruling class. Attending something between a student conference and academic talent show, students competed for the title of 'lictor' in a wide range of examinations for the creative arts and discourses on various themes of Fascist doctrine and practice. Prize-winners and participants could expect to be earmarked for jobs in the burgeoning bureaucracies of the party, syndicates and corporations.

The Young Fascists' motto, 'Believe, Obey, Fight', gave a sense of the kind of 'new Fascist man' the regime hoped to forge in the controlled environment of the educational system and the youth organisations. Essentially, the Fascists wanted to create an Italy made in their own image, a nation of ready-made warriors, physically fit, mentally agile, disciplined, courageous and obedient, committed believers and fighters in the cause of the nation. To achieve this, Fascist propaganda and indoctrination projected a series of images and models of the kind of conduct and behaviour for the 'new' Italian to emulate. To diffuse a culture of warlike and patriotic endeavour, the regime could draw on and propagate the virtues of some of Fascism's own heroic figures, the First World War combatant, the squadrist, and of course, Mussolini himself. The slogan, 'Mussolini is always right', was first coined and employed by the party under Turati. He used the idealisation of a single, undisputed and infallible leader to cover the imposition of a centralised order and discipline on the party itself in the late 1920s. Under Starace, the cult of the *Duce*, the charismatic, omnipotent figure shaping the nation's destiny, assumed ludicrous proportions in the 1930s.

But increasingly the prevailing myth on which Fascist propaganda focused was that of ancient Rome, which identified Fascism as the re-creation of a glorious and exalted past, and also justified imperialist expansion. The setting of Fascist Italy to the image of imperial Rome allowed the regime to convey and legitimise its desire to make Italy great and powerful, through the foundation of a new empire and as the carrier of a new 'civilisation'. It combined the will to empire with the 'making of Italians': the aim was to mould a nation of citizen-soldiers which would be fit to conquer and rule an empire. It was easy to get carried away with all this, and Fascist pretensions now appear hollow and unrealisable. But it is important to recognise that when Fascists talked of 'revolution', they usually meant a 'spiritual' revolution, not so much a transformation of socio-economic reality as its sublimation in a changed national consciousness. The idea was to reshape attitudes, mentality and perceptions, to change the way people thought and behaved. Even what would become during the Depression Fascism's claim to universality, a new social and economic order in corporativism, was given an ethical as much as a 'productivist' dimension. The corporations supposedly brought all kinds of producers together in a collaborative system of production. They were the practical training ground where through the experience of organised co-operation, employers and workers would exchange a class and sectional outlook for a national awareness. This was why the PNF, as the guardian and apostle of national values and the national interest, was always represented on each corporative council. Changing Italy then, involved changing the character of Italians in a controlled educative process; hence the priority which the regime gave in the 1930s to propaganda and organisation.

One of the most important aspects of the 'going . . . to the people' campaign during the Depression was the party's organisation of welfare. By late 1931 the party's welfare agencies (EOAs) had added to their operation of summer health camps for young children, the running of a winter relief programme coinciding with the worst months of seasonal unemployment. This lasted until the dissolution of the EOAs in 1937, when responsibility for winter welfare passed back to the local authorities and the summer camps went to the PNF's new unified youth organisation. There was, of course, nothing exceptional about a government providing emergency aid to alleviate the distress of those suffering most from the effects of a deep and prolonged economic crisis. For one thing, welfare was a way of trying to head off the likely repercussions for public order of widespread economic distress. But the party's involvement gave a

Fascist imprint to the provision of welfare, and a further impetus to 'totalitarian' organisation which lasted beyond the actual period of the Depression. Party-run welfare was regarded as an act of 'civil mobilization' and 'a most effective means of propaganda and penetration of the people'.[4] In the rhetoric if perhaps not the reality of Fascist welfare, it was a demonstration of class collaboration and national solidarity, because the party was collecting contributions from all who were able to give and distributing aid to all who were in need. Such was the Fascist moral community in the making, the outcome of the growing connection between people and regime through the medium of the party. This certainly strained the moral significance of the way the party actually collected the funds for winter relief. Much EOA funding came from a kind of party levy on the syndical bodies of employers and workers and the Fascist associations of schoolteachers, railwaymen and other public employees, and similar subscriptions extracted by party pressure on local banks and credit institutions. So workers would find that their syndicates had agreed to them donating a certain proportion of their wage to the EOA. In the spirit of class emulation, employers in the same economic or professional category contributed at least the same amount.

Perhaps more important was the way welfare provision could be used to 'penetrate' areas of the country and parts of the population which might otherwise be untouched by the regime or anyway unresponsive to more overtly political contact. The provincial EOAs were umbrella organisations for various private and public bodies working in the welfare field, through which the party monopolised the collection and distribution of relief funds for the unemployed and their families. The centralised collection of funds and pooling of resources was matched by the decentralisation of welfare distribution to the area groups into which the *fasci* of towns and cities were territorially subdivided. Welfare was synchronised with the spread of the party's 'capillary' structure. From the early 1930s, the area groups were encouraged to establish 'sectors', in turn subdivided into 'nuclei', corresponding to groups of streets or individual streets. Each sector or nucleus was to have a party social-worker, who made home visits to assess and report on need in her patch.

Winter welfare became one of the regime's largest organisations. The Padua Party, for instance, was providing regular welfare for about 19 000 families, affecting 80 000 people in city and province, the equivalent of about 1 in 20 of the total provincial population, in March 1935. Starace's official global figures were that nearly 1 750 000 families or almost three million individuals received daily welfare in the 1934–5 winter.

The party organisation of welfare stimulated the development of the Women's *fasci*. Significantly again, the party's drive to create a female section alongside each male *fascio* started with the onset of the 'going . . . to the people' campaign launched in 1931. The regime's demographic concerns and policies relegated women to the role of child bearing and raising and home management. The involvement of women's *fasci* in various forms of voluntary and welfare work was the natural organisational extension of this child-caring slot. From them came the neighbourhood social workers, the mainly middle-class women who prepared and distributed the clothing and cooked meals for winter relief, who helped out at the summer camps, the 'fascist Epiphany' and other 'fascistised' popular festivals. Welfare organisation during the Depression quite literally gave the party access to the backwaters of town and countryside. By providing the moral and material benefits of welfare, the party was extending the regime's network of control and surveillance of the population.

Along with welfare, the regime's efforts to provide for people's free time through its national afterwork agency, the OND or *Dopolavoro*, was characteristic of the 'mass' organising of the Depression years. The OND matched welfare in the large numbers of people it reached and involved, including groups hostile and indifferent to, or simply ignorant of Fascism, and in what followed from this, the apolitical nature and appeal of its activities. The OND was originally set up in May 1925 as a state agency responsible to the Ministry of National Economy, with the job of unifying and running the workers recreational clubs established by the Fascist syndicates and taken over from the Socialists. The OND became a party auxiliary in 1927. Thereafter its national president was the PNF Secretary, the provincial counterparts were the *federali* and its local administration was staffed by party cadres. Turati's takeover of the OND was part of the PNF's mobilisation for the 'battle for the lira', offering social welfare and rest and recreation facilities for blue- and white-collar workers in a difficult economic situation. Already the largest adult organisation by 1931, with 1.75 million members, it moved beyond the initial phase of affiliating and 'fascistising' existing socialist and democratic working-men's clubs, to build up a new network of sections during the Depression. By 1939 the OND had about 3.8 million members. It retained the character and function of its PNF relaunching during the revaluation crisis, providing some compensation in the form of facilities and services for the low pay and living standards which prevented many workers from becoming serious consumers. The OND's cumulative impact was probably to alleviate and divert some of the social distress and discontent arising during the Depression years.

The regime's organising drive crossed with and reinforced employer paternalism and 'scientific' management practice which saw a healthy and rested worker as a more productive one. Industrial employers also encouraged the OND in order to isolate and marginalise the Fascist syndicates among their workforce, since however toothless, they remained class-based organisations defending workers' interests. Most of the OND's industrial workers' membership and a good part of its white-collar members, belonged to occupational sections organised around the factory, firm and branch of the state administration. The territorial sections at the level of the communes were meant to catch the families and the whole population of the area. The typical OND section had a library, a radio, a sports and recreation ground and a clubhouse in which tosocialise. It organised sporting activities and local festivals of a folklorist character, and arranged showings of films and performances of the OND-sponsored travelling theatres. It offered to its members rail and other consumer discounts, welfare and social insurance benefits, and probably the most patronised activity, subsidised trips and excursions, a kind of low-level, low-cost tourism. The OND was introducing and spreading forms of popular mass leisure and recreation, which in other countries was occurring more spontaneously as part of the stirrings of a 'consumer society', rather than under the auspices of a 'totalitarian' state.

The OND clearly also played a part in persuading the regime of the utility of modern means of mass communication: the cinema and, especially, radio. These were increasingly incorporated into a more refined propaganda apparatus as the 1930s went on. Organisationally, this was reflected in the constant upgrading of the government bodies made responsible for the control and manipulation of opinion. The Press Office of the Council of Ministers, primarily concerned with the meticulous daily control of journalists and newspapers, was enlarged in 1934 into a sub-ministry for Press and Propaganda. This assumed overall control also of radio, cinema, theatre and tourism. On its elevation in 1935 into a full Ministry, there began a concerted attempt to shape popular culture through the controlled use of mass communication media.

Cinema-going certainly increased, partly because it was facilitated by the regime's own organisations like the OND. There were a few historical and contemporary film dramas conveying something of the Fascist message and style. But the fare was mainly diversionary entertainment

provided by both American and Italian-made films. What official propaganda there was, came in the obligatory showing in all cinemas of the
weekly documentary or newsreel produced by the government-controlled
film agency, LUCE. Their output obviously dramatised the regime's
major achievements and policies, placing some emphasis on rural and
imperial campaigns and themes.

Rural life was also the focus for radio transmission, which from the
start was controlled by a government-run public agency. Radio was
clearly a more flexible way than a relatively low circulation press to
convey the regime's presence and message to rural populations traditionally indifferent to government and its agencies and isolated by illit-
eracy and distance. Radio quite literally spanned these social and
geographical distances, and was capable of delivering a single, uniform
message to many different places simultaneously. The poverty of the
Italian domestic market for consumer goods, accentuated by the regime's
own economic policies compressing wages and purchasing power, constantly inhibited the diffusion of radio. This was to an extent offset by the
government providing what the individual often could not. A special rural
radio agency (ERR) was set up in 1933, and significantly was presided by
the PNF Secretary, Starace, from late 1934, reflecting the Party's drive to
control all the channels of contact between regime and people. Besides
operating as a programme network for specifically rural audiences, the
ERR distributed sets to elementary schools and other outposts of the
regime in the countryside, like the communal OND. These sets had to
service the whole community: collective listening in public places and
premises was another improvised response to the problems of access.

3. THE IMPACT AND LIMITATIONS OF 'TOTALITARIAN' CONTROL

Assessing the actual impacts of the great expansion of the regime's 'capillary' organisations and initiatives during and after the Depression is a
far harder task than defining Fascism's 'totalitarian' goals and the mechanisms it used to achieve them. One is always struck by both the
unique scale and extent of the regime's organisational achievement in the
1930s, and how far it nevertheless fell short of what the regime claimed.
The runt in the litter of Fascist organisations, the workers' syndicates,
legally represented all workers after the 1926 syndical law, but organised
barely half of the country's waged labour force in 1930, as little as 15 per

cent in the highly industrialised Milan province. The situation did improve, partly because syndicate membership was useful if not compulsory for gaining and keeping a job. But industrial workers especially never warmed to the syndicates when they were generally if not uniformly ineffective in, for example, upholding the terms of labour contracts against the constant spoliation of employers. Perhaps it was an achievement to survive at all as a class organisation in a regime wedded, at least rhetorically, to the overcoming of class conflict and class loyalties in the national interest.

It was scarcely accidental that the syndicates were increasingly bypassed in favour of the OND, the regime's main point of contact with an industrial working class which Mussolini continued to recognise as hostile to or distant from Fascism. Here again, the figures were impressive without being 'totalitarian'. By 1936 the OND has as members about 9 per cent of the national population, including an estimated 20 per cent of all industrial workers, who represented at this point about 70 per cent of total OND membership. In 1939 40 per cent of industrial workers were in the OND. But the OND was the 'mass' organisation of the lower middle and middle classes, both in terms of relative membership levels, the people who ran it and the atmosphere pervading it. In 1936 80 per cent of all state and private-sector salaried employees were enrolled in the OND.

Then again, the OND's profile was culturally lowbrow, folksy and geared to providing popular entertainment, leisure and recreation rather than explicit propaganda and indoctrination. When a zealous *federale* complained that the OND was not being used to proselytise actively among workers, Mussolini replied that 'the important thing is that people are able to meet in places where we can control them'.[5] The OND's neutral approach was both its greatest advantage and its greatest limitation. Workers and their families could join in order to enjoy what it offered, without having to make any uncomfortable political choices about their general view of Fascism. Involvement in the OND contributed to what the analysis of oral testimony seems to indicate as a 'mix' of attitudes in workers' families: a pragmatic acceptance of benefits coexisting with other critical or indifferent postures. But it was unlikely that the OND, precisely because of its popularity, could instil or reflect in its activities the militaristic ethic of Fascism. Despite its cross-class membership the OND did not even necessarily foster a sense of national community. If not class specific, its activities were often class separate: the manual workers did things together, but apart from the group activities of the white-collar workers.

The Fascist organisation of women certainly expanded, though never at the pace and to the extent of the male and catch-all organisations. Specialised and neglected groups of women were enrolled in the euphemistically named Rural Housewives' organisation, set up in 1935, and in that for female domestic and industrial workers founded two years later. This still left urban working-class housewives and mothers outside the organisational net. But it was always difficult for the regime to give the same attention and resources to female as to male organisations. Its warlike values were so evidently masculine, and organising women at all might remove them from their officially located place in the home, giving birth and bringing up the family.

There were also regional, social and gender nuances to the overall picture of youth organisation. A sizeable minority of children and adolescents in the eight to eighteen age range, perhaps between 30 and 40 per cent, did not join the ONB at all. The ONB was so intertwined with and dependent on the school system that membership was inevitably concentrated among children of statutory school age, and membership did sometimes lapse once children left school. This was both cause and effect of the greater degree of overt 'fascistisation' of the teaching staff and curriculum in elementary schools. But the ONB always regarded the considerable presence of women teachers as a hindrance to its work of forming the young. Since those children who continued their schooling were usually of middle-class parentage and boys rather than girls, the absentees from the ONB were mainly working-class teenagers and particularly young females. The membership of GUF simply reflected the overwhelmingly middle-class background of university students.

Whatever the less than 'totalitarian' coverage of youth organisations, there was little doubt that the young were the most susceptible to Fascist propaganda and indoctrination. For many of the young people growing up after 1925, there were no alternatives to Fascism, no pre-Fascist precedents or memories unless they could be transmitted by their family. Fascist regimentation was accepted as the norm. The Fascist regime was the only permissible outlet for and source of youthful idealism, political ambition and activity, career opportunities and more mundanely, services and facilities from sport to welfare.

For the PNF itself as well as its dependent and auxiliary organs, membership and activity generally declined from north and centre to south and the islands. Part of the explanation was that Fascism started from a lower organisational base. In many areas of the south Fascism was unknown before 1922 and scarcely established by 1925. Starting from scratch, the PNF lacked the already high membership and proven organisational network of its strongholds in some northern and central provinces. In other cases, the party found that backwardness had built in obstacles to organising southern populations which were difficult to overcome. Getting the PNF off the ground meant confronting problems of physical remoteness, inadequate communications, the general lack of resources and facilities, low school attendance because of agricultural child labour, a lack of tradition or experience of organisation and public activity among peasants, especially for women.

But basically Fascist organisations in the 1930s were paying the price for Fascism's renewal of the 'transformistic' deal by which Mussolini's government extended its political control to the south. Fascism's putative organising effort among peasants and their families cut across the support it had won in the south from the local notables, now in Fascism, who controlled the levers of patronage and clientelism. In some rural communities, for whom the state had always been no more than the policeman and the taxman, organisations like the OND at least presented a more benign face to state authority. But in much of the south the Fascist government was too associated with the large landowners, who were the ones favoured by its agricultural and 'ruralistic' policies. Fascism would not have appeared to peasants as anything other than the continuation of a socio-economic order which had always been buttressed by the state's policing and judicial apparatus.

The most important limitation or obstacle to the regime's 'totalitarian' pretensions was self-imposed. The 1929 agreement with the Catholic church gave a fresh impetus to Catholic Action, whose membership reached one million in late 1930. Under the terms of the Concordat this appeared to the church as a legitimate extension of clerical organisation and influence in Italian society. Mussolini recognised the undoubted contradiction of an autonomous non-Fascist body operating within a self-declared 'totalitarian' Fascist state. He expected it to be overcome by the PNF's superior competitive organisational powers, and by the annexation of the church's moral and social authority and presence to serve the state's ends. In a way, this approach simply restated the contradiction. Making, for instance, parish priests the chaplains of local ONB sections was a kind of co-option by association with Fascism. But using the church's prestige and status among the population as a form of guarantee that Catholics would support the regime and its organisations, naturally allowed the clergy to continue and extend their contact with the people.

Fascist organisations registered with alarm the post-Concordat Catholic activity and the presence of ex-PPI organisers within Catholic Action, and tried to retaliate in the way Mussolini anticipated. The PNF's foundation of the Young Fascists was a response to the low incidence of membership in Fascist youth organisations among Catholic young men. But the open conflict between church and Fascist state was precipitated by the Fascist syndicates' press attacks in March 1931 on Catholic Action's formation of occupational groups among Catholics. These 'professional sections' were with some justification seen by the syndicates as embryonic rival unions, infringing their legal monopoly. The issue was particularly sensitive because of the deepening economic crisis and attempts to exploit it by clandestine anti-Fascist groups. The church was also staging an international public celebration of the fortieth anniversary of Pope Leo XIII's famous encyclical on Catholic social policy. This, and the present Pope's restatement of the Catholic position in his May 1931 encyclical, *Quadragesimo Anno*, more than implied that the Church had a superior version of a new economic and social order.

In late May Mussolini brought the simmering conflict to a head by ordering the prefects to dissolve Catholic youth organisations, after a wave of PNF and Young Fascist attacks on Catholic premises and members. The Pope's response, the encyclical *Non Abbiamo Bisogno*, formally drew back from a condemnation of Fascism 'as such'.[6] Nevertheless it exposed the real basis of ideological dispute, rejecting the state's 'totalitarian' claim to abrogate the rights of individual, family and church in the education of the young.

Neither side was prepared to push the conflict to the point of 'holy war'. The September 1931 agreement banned former PPI leaders from holding positions in Catholic Action, whose centralised national structure was dismantled for a diocesan basis of organisation. Catholic bodies were to have a strictly moral and religious character. This stipulation confirmed the earlier prohibition on youth organisations engaging in sports and athletic activities, and apparently pre-empted the transformation of 'professional sections' into unions. The sections were to ensure that the Fascist syndicates 'conform more and more to the principles of class collaboration, and to the social and national objectives which in a catholic country, the state seeks to achieve through the corporative system'.[7] Did this mean a Catholic endorsement of Fascist corporativism, or an opportunity to influence it in a Catholic direction? It could be read all ways, as could the settlement as a whole. Mussolini obviously felt that the restrictions on the content and scope of Catholic activity would allow the regime to press home the organisational advantage and squeeze out the rival Catholic bodies, while continuing to make use of the church in support of the state. But the church regarded all its activity as 'moral and religious' and all its lay organisations, whatever their function, as having 'moral and religious' ends. So in the general revival of Catholic Action activity from 1934, 'professional sections' re-emerged under this rubric. Catholic youth groups were not abolished, as Giuriati and Scorza demanded. The return of their confiscated premises allowed their reconstitution, and they remained as an alternative to the ONB for Catholic young people. Article 43 of the Concordat was still intact.

These Janus-like agreements pointed to the overall complexity of the working relationship between the Fascist regime and the church in the mid-1930s. The church never really shook off its role as both an ally and rival of the Fascist state. The Pope's theoretical reservations about Fascist statolatry, revealed in the 1931 incidents, made little practical difference to relations between church and state, and Catholics and government. The 1931 events might well have forced the Vatican to revise its hopes of a clerical reconquest of state and society. But there had been and would be plenty of occasions for the church to express its support for the regime and its policies. Anti-communism remained the constant and central element of the common ground between church and state. It assumed an international importance for the Vatican, with the apparent spread of atheistic communism and its persecution of the church to the Popular Front governments of France and Spain. Italian intervention to support the military rebellion against the anti-clerical republic in Spain from 1936 was portrayed as the struggle of Catholic Europe against Bolshevism. The church wholeheartedly backed and participated in the regime's demographic and 'ruralist' campaigns from the 'battle for grain' onwards. In doing so, it stereotypically evoked the disappearing world of a sober, prolific and god-fearing peasantry, set against a sterile, materialistic urban-industrial society, the corrupter of religion and morals. This was the complementary spiritual equivalent of the regime's own more secular assumptions and expectations behind its promotion of rural life. The church also willingly associated itself with the myth of a civilising imperial and Catholic Rome, made actual in the conquest of Ethiopia. Even Fascist corporativism could be generally welcomed and accepted as an imperfect stab at realising Catholic social teaching, though these affinities were not usually recognised or acknowledged by Fascists themselves.

A Catholic slant was always given to these expressions of support for Fascist policies, which could be backed because they approximated to

Catholic ideals and models. At times, particularly with the philofascist intellectuals and teachers of the Catholic University of Milan, there was the sense that Catholics were inventing a Fascism which would match their hopes of realising a Catholic society through the regime. All this indicated an apartness and a concern to avoid total identification with Fascism, embodied concretely in the jealous preservation of a separate body for Catholic laity in Catholic Action. But the evident symmetry between the policies and outlook of the regime and the church must have satisfied Mussolini's instrumentalist view that it was more advantageous to get the church on the regime's side, than push their differences to the point of rupture.

For De Felice, the Italian historian writing an encyclopaedic and sometimes opaque 'life and times' biography of Mussolini, 1929 – 1934 were the years when the Fascist regime was most stable and enjoyed the greatest 'consent'. At first sight this is a questionable proposition, because no government could expect to have the people's support during a period of economic depression. Certainly in Italy, clandestine anti-Fascist activity undertaken by communists, socialists and a new liberal-socialist group called 'Justice and Liberty', was more intense in 1930-1 than at any other point before the war. These groups were very efficiently broken up by the police. Only sometimes could they be connected to the incidence of popular disturbances, including illegal strikes, of which there were 101 according to official records in 1933, the highest figure for the Depression years. The Vatican, along with others, was expressing doubts in 1931 on the regime's ability to survive the impact of the economic crisis. They did so hardly from the view point that they wanted the government to fall. It is at least arguable that 1930-1 were years of 'dissent'.

What De Felice appears to mean by 'consent' in relation to workers' attitudes to the Fascist government was an absence of political opposition to it. This, he explains with reference to the police's undoubted efficiency, and to the regime's largely successful efforts to mitigate the effects of the crisis in its 'going . . . to the people' campaign conducted through the PNF's organisations. The whole debate cries out for greater rigour in the use of the concept of 'consent'. Who exactly was 'consenting' to what, and how and when? 'Consent' can best be understood as a continuum of attitudes, ranging from, yes, the lack of dissent to enthusiastic commitment. It is ephemeral, varying in quality, intensity and location through time; 'consent' over one issue often evaporates over another.

This kind of analysis is a quagmire for the historian and sometimes of doubtful utility. Exactly how do you measure 'consent' in a repressive

Fascist dictatorship, which prevented any free expression of popular opinion? About 17 000 people were sent to *confino*, or internal exile, under Fascism, and police files contained the names of about 160 000 Italians who were under surveillance or police restraint. Does this convey a climate of 'consent' or conformity? But the figures were deceptively large precisely because Fascist Italy was a 'totalitarian' and police state, and demanded and prohibited more than in other systems. Under Fascism the police had very wide powers, hence almost infinitely enlarging the compass of actually and potentially unacceptable behaviour.

The difficulty if not the futility of assessing 'consent' and 'dissent' under Fascism should now be apparent. But the question raises some important points about the distinctive nature of the Fascist 'totalitarian' system. The context of life in Fascist Italy was repressive, and necessarily so. No alternative or contradictory viewpoints to those put out by the regime were allowed, and where they appeared they were repressed. The police state created a kind of blank space of opinion, clearing the ground for the attempted indoctrination of the population. This indoctrination could only be the outcome of an organising process. The Fascists expected to change people by putting them through the experience of being organised in the regime's own bodies. There was an inescapable element of compulsion and dictation in this process, which permeated all the regime's initiatives. In the case of the PNF's provision of welfare through the EOAs, what was portrayed as the spontaneous display of national solidarity bringing together the haves and the have-nots, was in fact the result of organisation. By leaning on its own members and other bodies it controlled to subscribe on a regular and systematic basis to winter relief, the party was organising 'spontaneity'. There was an obligation to contribute, though clearly not one marked by violence.

The contradiction of 'orchestrated spontaneity' was clear also in the attempt to indoctrinate. There was a real debate or dispute within the regime, never entirely resolved, over the kind of formation the young should undergo in the youth organisations. Bottai and his journal *Critica Fascista* constantly argued that Fascism's future leaders should be allowed the relative freedom to discuss, and even criticise, within the Party's framework. This was the only sure way of producing an élite with a sincere and enthusiastic, rather than conformist and opportunistic commitment to Fascism. Scorza, the head of the Young Fascists, emphasised instead the regimental and blind faith approach. The *Duce* and Fascism 'do not need political brains which lose their way in the esoteric', but 'an army organised in closed ranks: huge and imposing, firm and disciplined, masculine, unshakeable in faith, irresistible in its advance: in short, an armed religious order'.[8] The combination of the two sets of attributes was the ideal, according to the official aphorism, 'Book and Rifle Make the Perfect Fascist'. But all the regime's mass organisations havered between functions of control, surveillance and regimentation, and mobilisation to gain support, consent and participation, a unique and paradoxical combination of force and consent.

Historians of any political system will continue to speculate on the extent and degree of harmony between government and governed. But the accepted polarities of 'consent' and 'dissent' are generally extrapolated from the experience of democratic and pluralist systems. They are not easily applied to the analysis of the methods and goals of a regime which aspired to be 'totalitarian', mobilising 'consent' in a context of repression and dictatorship. The Fascist 'totalitarian' state was novel in its attempt to keep control of and win active support from the population. To secure the identification of people with the regime, society was aligned to the state through the state's organisations. The party did organise among social, age and gender groups, many of them previously untouched by Fascism. But there was a considerable gap between 'totalitarian' claim and performance in the 1930s, not only in terms of the numbers organised. In its organisation of the population the party could never overcome the contradiction, inherent to the 'totalitarian' system, of exercising both a repressive and educative role. A consciously willed acceptance of Fascism was unrealisable within the system erected to create it.

4. CORPORATIVISM AND THE GREAT DEPRESSION

Mussolini's personal dictatorship was strengthened by his ministerial shake-up of July 1932. This undid the apparent delegation in 1929 of important government office to prominent figures of the regime other than himself. Rocco went from the Justice ministry, Grandi from Foreign Affairs and Bottai from Corporations. Mussolini personally reassumed headship of the latter two, and in further reshuffles in 1933 once again became the nominal minister for all of the armed forces. The changes probably ran deeper than Mussolini's congenital suspicion of collaborators who knew their own mind. They clearly reinforced the reality and the impression that Mussolini was, effectively, the government, and that the regime's future was ultimately dependent on himself and what he achieved. The depersonalised figure of the cult of the *Duce*, a leader of more than normal talents and qualities, above and beyond the fray, did correspond in some way to Mussolini's self-imposed solitude in government, and reinforced his sense of being a man with a mission.

The self-elevation of the *Duce* coincided with the first serious official attempts to launch Fascism as an international phenomenon, which were clearly related to the deepening of the worldwide economic Depression. Its severity, duration and extent gave ample scope and justification to Fascist claims that it marked the crisis *of* liberal capitalism and parliamentary democracy, and the start of the fascist era. The formal statement of Fascist doctrine was published under Mussolini's name in 1932. Fascist movements were emerging in other European countries and the Nazis were on the verge of power in Germany, lending credence to Mussolini's prediction that Europe would shortly be fascist or 'fascistised' on the model of Fascist Italy. The officially sponsored international Volta conference in late 1932 discussed the 'universal' aspects of fascism. It anticipated the regime's effort to create a fascist 'International' of European movements recognising the primacy of the Italian version. The launch and, as it turned out, culmination was a multinational conference in Montreux in December 1934. This gathering attracted some obscure fascist adventurers keen to get Italian patronage and funding, as well as fascist movements of some significance, such as the Romanian Iron Guard. It agreed, albeit in the loosest terms, that a defining element of international fascism was corporativism. The Fascist 'corporate state' was projected as a new social and political order, a 'Third Way' alternative to both the socially unjust and self-evidently dysfunctional liberal capitalism, and the state collectivism of communist Russia. As such, Italian Fascism exercised during the Depression years an appeal and fascination in European politics that was not confined simply to fascist movements.

Corporativism occupied a major place in Fascist ideology and propaganda in the Depression years, and significantly remained largely a matter for international consumption. In Italy itself the corporative structures reflected only too well the balance of forces and compromises underpinning the foundation of the regime. In 1929 Bottai had urged on the Grand Council the actual enactment of a provision in the 1926 law setting up his Ministry, for a National Council of Corporations. Established in March 1930, it was made up of seven large sections, corporations in embryo, bringing together the employer and worker organisations covering the main branches of the economy, which also met in a general assembly and were represented on a Central Corporative

Committee. The National Council appeared to have normative as well as consultative functions, which suggested a role in the co-ordination and planning of production itself. This was carried over into the 1934 law which finally created twenty-two corporations for the productive cycles of the major sectors of industry, agriculture and services. The corporations could fix the prices of goods or rates for services in their own areas, and issue norms 'to regulate economic relations and the unitary discipline of production'.[9]

Such provisions were for self-governing, inter-class organs of producers which could manage production in the various branches of the economy and also co-ordinate production between sectors. In practice, they were inoperative. Deciphering what the corporations actually did was, to re-apply Gaetano Salvemini's phrase, like 'looking in a dark room for a black cat which is not there'.[10] But there was a basic unreality to the idea of producers' self-management of the economy in the conditions of Fascist dictatorship.

The corporations were basically councils where workers' and employers' representatives met in the presence of PNF or Ministry of Corporations officials embodying the 'national' interest. Only one side, however, was genuinely representative. Members of the employers' organisations were usually technically equipped managers actually chosen by the employers. Despite confirmation in 1934 of the barely observed principle of election to major syndical posts, the representatives of workers' syndicates in the corporations were generally not workers or men close to workers and the environment of work. The ex-revolutionary and interventionist syndicalists had given way since the *sbloccamento* of Rossoni's national workers' confederation in 1928 to a new breed of middle-class and careerist syndical officials drawn from the PNF and the Ministry of Corporations. There was little possibility of the corporations becoming a real forum for the harmonisation of all producers when representation was so unbalanced. Those who were most strongly represented, won out. Without some equivalence of interest representation, the corporations were easily dominated by employers, and by the pro-employer 'productivist' rationale which informed every government measure in the field from the 1926 syndical law onwards.

Again, the corporations' formal powers of economic co-ordination were deliberately circumscribed by the government. All deliberations of the corporations had to be approved in the National Council of Corporations assembly or, after 1935, by the Central Corporative Committee, whose convenor and president was the Head of Government.

Corporative regulations only had effect when issued as a decree of the Head of Government. It was the executive's ultimate control which reassured *Confindustria* that economic decisions would be a matter for Mussolini and the government, and that the corporative system would not become an economic planning mechanism interfering in production. This really revealed that the corporative ideal of delegated economic decision-making by self-run producer organisations was incompatible with the centralised state authority at the centre of Fascist 'totalitarianism'. As party leaders liked to point out, Mussolini led a Fascist not a 'corporate state', and political control was not to be passed down to even the regime's own permanent economic organisations.

Practically all the government's economic measures during the Depression years were proclaimed as advances of the corporative economy. But in reality, as Bottai and other Fascist corporatists realised, these were mainly emergency and 'acorporative' actions, a response to the depth of the economic crisis. Industrial production in Italy and worldwide was at its lowest point in 1932. It was at this juncture that the government intervened, in a way that continued the policies of the revaluation crisis of the late 1920s. In June 1932 a law made the formation of consortia or cartels obligatory where a large majority of firms in any sector favoured it. By dividing up a shrinking market among existing producers, cartels deliberately limited competition and held up prices in a depressed economy.

The January 1933 law setting up a licensing scheme for new and expanded industrial plant could have become a lever for state direction of industrial investment and development. But it worked in the same way and served the same interests as government-endorsed cartelisation. Competition was restrained to protect the current market share of existing firms. Industrialists applied for authorisation to set up new factories and then did nothing, simply to pre-empt the entry of any potential rival firms onto their patch.

The government connived at this use of its economic rescue package, even when these emergency measures were eventually integrated with the corporative structures. From 1935 the corporations supposedly supervised consortia established in their areas. In 1937 they were responsible for the running of the licensing system, having always been expected to give an opinion on new plant applications. The Ministry of Corporations anyway in practice relied on *Confindustria*'s technical expertise in the evaluation of applications, while the employers' dominant position within the corporations ensured that 'productivist' criteria prevailed. There was a real sense here of the private use of public power, of business or its biggest exponents carving up the domestic market with official endorsement.

The intrinsically Fascist character of the regime's economic crisis management was in the continued coercion of labour through the PNF and syndicates. As in 1926–7 there were more officially imposed wage cuts between 1930 and 1934, heavier in agriculture than in industry, which prevented employed workers from enjoying the full benefits of falling prices during the Depression. A forty-hour week was similarly enforced in industry in October 1934 in order to create more employment. Industrial workers with large families were in part compensated for loss of income through shorter working hours, by the introduction of family allowances, a measure soon subsumed in the regime's continuing demographic 'battle'.

The government's resistance to lira devaluation throughout the Depression meant a constant revaluation of the currency, as, crucially, sterling and the dollar devalued in 1931 and 1933. An overvalued lira contributed to a growing balance of payments deficit and the outflow of Italy's foreign currency and gold reserves during 1933–4. It was this situation which led the government in early 1934 to set up yet another special agency, the Institute of Foreign Exchange, through which it could both monopolise and regulate foreign exchange and currency trading. From February 1935 quotas were imposed on imports, related to the availability of foreign currency to pay for them. This gave a further impetus to import substitutionism and autarky.

The most important government salvage operation during the Depression occurred completely outside the corporative framework and was never even formally accommodated to it. A special feature of Italian capitalist development from the late nineteenth century had been the interlocking of the major banks and industries. Banks lent to and invested in industry, and held industrial shares as collateral. The crisis in industrial production was so severe during the Depression that the stability of the country's banking system was also threatened. The banks had lent money to now ailing industries, whose shares in the hands of the banks were declining in value.

A series of attempted rescues of banks and industries using public money was made in 1931. Mussolini in late 1932 delegated the working out of a definitive salvage operation not to the Ministry of Corporations, but to the Finance Minister, Guido Jung, and Alberto Beneduce, a technocrat with feet in both private industry and state-run credit institutions. The outcome was the establishment of the Institute of Industrial Reconstruction (IRI) in 1933, a kind of giant state holding company. IRI took over the industrial share assets of the three banks, in return for paying off the banks' enormous debts to the Bank of Italy, incurred during the unsuccessful operations of 1931. This colossal public payment of private industrial and banking losses finally ended the connection between the banks and industry. It was the start of a reorganisation of the entire banking and credit sector culminating in the 1936 banking law. The banks were restricted to supplying normal short-term commercial credit, while for medium- and long-term capital investment, industries went to the stock market and mainly state-owned financial institutions.

These were very significant and lasting changes in the organisation of the capitalist economy in Italy. But it was probably not the original intention to make IRI anything other than a temporary dispensary for sick industries in extraordinary economic conditions. IRI was meant to reorganise, rationalise and reprivatise the industries whose shares it now held, and this happened in the case, for example, of the profitable electricity companies. But not all of IRI's holdings were as attractive to private enterprise. IRI's existence during and beyond Fascism rested on its continued responsibility for administering the loss-making industries which the private sector would not touch, especially the iron and steel, shipbuilding and navigation companies. With IRI, state intervention in the economy took on a new institutional form. Through the entrepreneurial public body, the state had a sometimes majority shareholding in many firms which retained the structure and management of private companies. The boards of IRI's companies were filled by the same men who were on the boards of businesses in the increasingly monopolistic private sector.

All this ran parallel to the corporations, and resembled a 'consortial' rather than a 'corporate' state. It was clear that the government was not prepared to entrust its economic rescue measures during the Depression, which had to be rapid and functional in effect, to the complicated mechanisms of the corporations. The problem was how to reconcile the corporative apparatus with increasing state direction of the economy. The government resolved it by ignoring the former and developing an alternative network of public bodies with economic functions.

State economic intervention was initially made necessary by the severity and duration of the Depression, and then by the imperatives of Fascist foreign policy. By late 1934 planning and spending for the conquest of Ethiopia was under way. The various public agencies which had originated as emergency measures of the Depression were now used to regulate an economy being geared up for war. Italy's growing isolation from the international economy was reflected in the collapse in value of its foreign trade. As for other countries which sought some kind of refuge in protected domestic and imperial markets, this was a consequence of the Depression and also in Italy's case, of the government's refusal to devalue. But in the end it was the Fascist government's military and imperialist foreign policy, and the knock-on effect of directing the economy towards autarky, which finally scuppered the corporative system as a way of organising society and the economy.

5 The Creation of the Fascist Empire, 1935–6

1. IMPERIALISM, REVISIONISM AND THE LIMITS TO FASCIST FOREIGN POLICY IN THE 1920S

From its inception, Fascism was imperialist. Mussolini had cynically abandoned D'Annunzio in Fiume in 1920, calculating correctly that Fascism's opportunity lay in combatting 'the enemy within'. But the movement consistently had as its declared aim a general commitment to realising the grandeur of Italy, specifically through the foundation of an empire. Self-consciously drawing on the legacy of interventionism and the war experience, Fascism claimed that under its rule Italy would at last be recognised as a major power and achieve hegemony in the 'Italian' sea, the Mediterranean.

Recognition as a Great Power and Mediterranean expansion should, of course, have been the natural outcome of Italy's participation on the winning side of the war. But in the Fascist view Italy's 'mutilated victory' was plain to see in the peace treaties of 1919, which had not delivered the anticipated gains in the Adriatic, the Near East and Africa. Responsibility rested with the pusillanimous liberal governments, both cause and victims of the country's deep postwar internal divisions, which were unable to defend the country's national interests. Blame was shared with the un-grateful ex-Allies and already well-established imperialist powers, France and Britain.

This reading of the war and its outcome was hardly original. It re-gurgitated wholesale the Nationalist position, whose war aims Mussolini had practically adopted as his own during 1918. From the Nationalists too, Mussolini and Fascism took the notion of the struggle between rival imperialisms as an inescapable fact of international relations, and of war as the inevitable and even desirable test of a nation's will to power and expansion. There existed a ready-made Nationalist rhetoric about inter-national 'class war' between up and coming 'proletarian' nations and satiated 'plutocratic' ones, for a redistribution of territory and resources. It was employed regularly by Mussolini in the late 1920s, even if the realisation was delayed until the 1930s. From the very start then, Fascism was tendentially bound to be 'revisionist' of the Versailles settlement, anti-pacifist and anti-internationalist. It had little time for the principles of parity and respect between countries which purportedly inspired the new international order enshrined in the League of Nations, even though Italy was a member.

Revisionism seemed to put Italy at odds with France in particular, since France regarded the retention of the postwar territorial settlements as a guarantee of security against Germany. France had built up in the early 1920s a network of alliances and agreements with Czechoslovakia, Poland, Romania and Yugoslavia, the beneficiaries of the treaties and of the collapse of the Austro-Hungarian empire in Central, Eastern and South-eastern Europe. The lands bordering the Adriatic were not only the focus of Italian irredentism, but a bridgehead for the spread of Italian influence in the Balkan and Danubian regions now that the Habsburg empire was gone. Control of the Adriatic was also seen geopolitically as crucial to the wider goal of Mediterranean hegemony, the realisation of which was again hindered by French and British colonial possessions and mandates in North and East Africa and the Middle East.

It is obviously dangerous to divine the actual diplomatic and military alignments of 1940 in the grandiose pretensions of early Fascism, as if the one was the logical and inevitable outcome of the other. There was much ground to cover before the outbreak of a general war of the fascist powers against the 'plutocracies', and some historians, notably De Felice, try to argue that Italy's choice of allies and enemies was still open as late as spring 1940. But whether it was expressed in political and economic influence or military conquest and direct control, Fascist foreign policy always went in two directions, towards the Balkans and Danubia, and to Africa. Both prongs potentially cut across France's European and im-perial interests. This was not so much Fascist as Italian foreign policy, or at least that of conservative liberals and Nationalists both before, during and after the 1915–18 war. Fascist foreign policy could be seen as con-ventional or the extension of a certain tradition. The continuity with much of what had gone before helps to explain why the Fascist gov-ernment's policy was for a long while broadly supported by Italy's establishment, including the monarchy and the top career diplomats in the Ministry of Foreign Affairs.

Italy was a small power in European and world terms, lacking the kind of economic and military muscle which would allow the country to be an independent player in international power politics. Italy's attempted economic penetration of the Balkan and Danubian countries, one of the arms of its diplomacy in the area, always met superior competition on the same ground from richer nations. This came from France in the 1920s and early 1930s, and then later from Germany during the late 1930s and into the period of war and occupation. Such inescapable and objective weakness meant that it was difficult for Italy to contemplate going it alone. She always needed the help of other major powers, or the opportunity to exploit to her own advantage the balance, tensions and rivalries among these more powerful countries. Italy's entry into the First World War was a classic demonstration of this kind of makeweight diplomacy. Although formally allied to Germany and Austro-Hungary in the Triple Alliance, the Italian declaration of neutrality in 1914 indicated that she was open to offers from both sides at war. Even continuing neutrality would have a price. Italian irredentism might well have been pushing the country towards intervention against Austro-Hungary. But the decision to fight alongside France and Britain in 1915 was clinched by the secret Treaty of London, where the Western Allies were able to offer the better territorial deal.

Mussolini's first dramatic foreign policy coup in government was his provocative escalation of a dispute with Greece over the delimitation of the Greek–Albanian border. The bombardment and occupation of the Greek Adriatic island of Corfu in late Summer 1923, the prelude to its expected annexation, was not only an example of Mussolini's exhibitionist, bullying and bellicose style. It showed the extent of the Fascist government's aspirations to dominate the Adriatic and its Balkan coast, and the then insuperable barrier to their achievement. Although Mussolini managed to avoid mediation by the League of Nations, to which Greece had referred the dispute, the island was evacuated on the implied threat of British naval action in the Mediterranean.

This was a demonstration of where real power lay, and an increasingly forward policy in the Balkan and Danubian regions in the late 1920s could not really shift the reality of Anglo-French domination of European affairs. The resort to largely secret and 'dirty tricks' political activity in the area was both a recognition of the situation, and the sign that Mussolini was prepared to use undiplomatic and unconventional methods in foreign policy. As Secretary-General of the Foreign Ministry, the top position in the career service, Salvatore Contarini has been credited with both restraining Mussolini's natural mischief-making in foreign affairs during his first years of government, and in rallying the career diplomats to Fascism. His resignation in March 1926 was basically in protest at Mussolini's conduct of foreign policy, which barely respected the norms of diplomatic activity.

Mussolini sought to extend Italian influence in South-eastern Europe by meddling in the internal politics of countries. He attempted particularly to exploit their ethnic and national antagonisms. These had been fuelled rather than dampened by the corrupted form of national self-determination inspiring the 1919 peace treaties, where strategic and economic as well as ethnic criteria had been used to determine national territorial boundaries. Involvement in the dynastic rivalries of the Albanian royal family had reduced Albania to an informal Italian protectorate in 1925–6. A footing in Albania was also a wedge into Yugoslavia, with its own Albanian minority. Destabilisation of the new Yugoslav state was again actively pursued through aid to the separatist and fascistic Croatian Ustasha movement from early 1929, and similar support from 1927 to Macedonian nationalists. In defiance of the treaties Italy also secretly armed and supplied Hungary, which had revisionist territorial claims against all its neighbours, including Yugoslavia.

Subverting states from within might not have been new, but both fascist regimes made it a regular instrument of policy. Mussolini applied it in North Africa and the Middle East against the British and French empires, as well as in the Balkans. As early as an official visit to the Italian colony of Libya in 1926, Mussolini declared himself the defender of Islam as an incitement to native anti-colonial nationalism in French and British territories bordering on the Mediterranean. At the time the Italians were engaged in their own nasty internal pacification of Libya's Arab population. Mussolini's intermittent interest in Zionism was again related to the concern to shake the British hold on its Middle Eastern mandates and its place in the Mediterranean. The abortive destabilisation of Yugoslavia anticipated the highly manipulative Nazi dismemberment in 1938–9 on the phoney grounds of national self-determination, of Czechoslovakia, which as Mussolini liked to say, was not simply 'Czecho-Slovakia' but also, 'Czecho-Germano-Polono-Magyaro-Rutheno-Romano-Slovakia'.

As a revisionist country herself, Fascist Italy was in league with the other revisionist countries, specifically Hungary. The regime's contacts with some sections of the revanchist German right in the 1920s pointed in the same direction, even though such a revisionist axis created other contradictory tensions, notably over Austrian independence and the German-speaking population of the Italian alpine border region. Revisionism also indicated a growing ideological convergence and division in Europe. Antipathy to France, the barrier to Italian influence in the

Danube and Balkans, was heightened by Fascist anger at democratic France 'harbouring' Italian anti-Fascist emigration. The Fascist government had dealings with the right-wing opposition in Weimar Germany, and sponsored imitative, violently nationalistic groups to undermine the Yugoslav state. It co-operated with a succession of rightist if not fascist governments under Admiral Nicholas Horthy's regency in Hungary, again to attack the democratic beneficiaries of the peace treaties. With the rise of the Nazis in Germany, Mussolini could see in a 'fascistising' Europe the extension of Italian power and influence on the continent.

It seems difficult to describe Fascist foreign policy in the 1920s as basically one of peace and reconciliation. Some historians do see incidents like that of Corfu in 1923 as aberrant interruptions of a decade of calm in Fascist foreign policy, a period of good conduct largely determined by the need to consolidate power in Italy itself, which required a low profile internationally to reassure both foreign and domestic opinion. Italy, after all, was with Britain the co-guarantor of the 1925 Locarno agreement bringing Germany into the League of Nations and securing the French and Belgian borders with Germany, which contemporaries regarded as cementing peace between former enemies. But we know also that Mussolini was hardly an initiator of Locarno, and tried and failed to link it to a European guarantee of the Italo-Austrian frontier. He eventually participated in bad grace, seeing it at most as a recognition of Italy as a Great Power arbitrating the fate of Europe in a way which anticipated the abortive four-power scheme of the early 1930s. He certainly shed no tears over the dispelling of the illusions of peace nourished by Locarno, and indeed contributed to this through his revisionist actions in Eastern Europe from 1926.

No Eastern Locarno here; imperialism and revisionism were consistently held and publicly declared goals, and both meant changes to the postwar territorial settlement. Such changes could occur peacefully, of course. A 1926 Italo-British agreement slightly modified the border between Somalia and Egypt in Italy's favour. But Mussolini's predilection was to make trouble wherever he could and disparage the forms of conventional diplomacy, using methods of internal political subversion as covert, undeclared warfare on countries he regarded as Italy's enemies. The point is not that Mussolini could be credited with a decade of good behaviour in foreign policy, but rather that the damage he could do in the 1920s was limited, because of Italy's intrinsic economic and military weakness, and the lack of any counterbalance to effective Anglo-French dominance in Europe which Italy could exploit.

In the late 1920s this external and objective obstacle to the realisation of Great Power aspirations was reinforced by international political economy. The Fascist government's revaluation of the lira in 1926–7 was achieved as part of a wider currency and economic stabilisation involving other European countries, and was arranged and funded by the American and British governments and financial markets. Although Fascism had just embarked on the construction of its own system of government in the form of 'totalitarianism', Italy was still integrated into and dependent on an international economy dominated by Anglo-Saxon finance and capital. It was difficult to run a foreign policy which ignored these realities of economic and financial dependence, which were only transformed by the impact of the great Depression.

2.   THE 'TOTALITARIAN STATE': INTERNAL POLICY AS FOREIGN POLICY AND VICE VERSA

In another very important sense, too, Fascist foreign policy could not be regarded as essentially peaceful or demonstrating 'realistic' restraint. It is usual for historians to separate their treatment of a country's foreign affairs from the analysis of domestic policy. This chapter, dedicated to international relations, shows how difficult it is to kick the habit of considering foreign policy as an autonomous, even superior, field of governmental activity. We conventionally see foreign policy as being relatively stable and consistent through time in both line and approach. This is because the 'national interest' of any country can apparently be defined in relation to certain constants, such as its economic and military resources and potential, and its geographical and strategic position. So far this chapter has handled Fascist foreign policy in a similar way, and argued that broadly comparable constraints shaped the diplomacy of both liberal and Fascist Italy, hence establishing a basic continuity between the two. As 'the least of the Great Powers', an Italy governed by liberals or Fascists had generally the same aims, oscillating between the Balkans and Africa, and employed some of the same means, oscillating between the Great Powers, the perpetual makeweight. To an extent the traditional approach holds up, as we shall see in the later discussion of the invasion of Ethiopia. But the customary separation of foreign and domestic matters is artificial and distorting, in both fact and interpretation, for Fascism. Internal and external policies were explicitly linked and interacted in a synchronised way.

It was not just simply a matter of Mussolini using dramatic foreign policy coups to enhance his own and the regime's internal popularity and prestige. This was one of the earliest views of Mussolini's diplomacy, argued out with some verve by the exiled anti-Fascist historian, Salvemini. He described a gadfly foreign policy, inconsistent, volatile and surprising, because its only rationale was the constant pursuit of momentary advantage and success for primarily home consumption. The patriotic tub-thumping over Corfu in 1923 was certainly designed to demonstrate to the Italian public that at last Italy had a government which stood up for and defended the nation's interests. But this was not all that the Corfu incident represented. Focusing exclusively on the internal clamour gives the whole affair a sense of improvisation, which disguises the longer-term drive to realise control of the Adriatic and Mediterranean. Also, the use or abuse of foreign adventures to build up prestige internally or to save the skin of governments floundering on the domestic front, was and is hardly the preserve of fascist regimes. It is the last resort of all kinds of government, as the recent experience of the Falklands War would indicate.

The interdependence of domestic and foreign affairs lay also in the connection between the Fascist 'totalitarian' state and an imperialist foreign policy. Mussolini made this linkage explicit in the speech of October 1925 where he first used the term 'totalitarian' publicly. He spoke of the party imposing the 'discipline of a state of war' on the nation, unavoidably caught up in the continuous 'competition between peoples in the arena of world civilisation'. 'The present century must be the century of our power', and the 'magic key' to national spiritual and material power was 'the disciplined will'.[1] Once again, this was a reworking of the Nationalist perspective that internal policy was the premise and preparation for an expansionist foreign policy, which provided the incentive and reason for internal discipline and order. The deliberate association with the 'totalitarian' state showed that the intention was not to preserve and reinforce the existing order. Only a new internal political and socio-economic order, unifying and concentrating the nation's resources through 'totalitarian' controls, could enable the country to fight and win its battles in the international arena.

The Fascist 'totalitarian' state thus gave concrete and practical form to the fusion of domestic and foreign policy. Put simply, the purpose of the 'totalitarian' state was to equip Italy and Italians for war. This was evident in the government's policies and actions from 1926 onwards, described in the previous chapters, however partial and contradictory they were in effect. The single-party state put an end to the divisive and competitive political parties which placed factional and sectional interests before those of the nation. From its monopolistic position the PNF could organise and mobilise the nation in support of the regime and its goals, re-educating and forming the 'new Italian', a breed capable of founding and civilising an empire. Demographic and 'ruralist' policies were intended to move the country in the same direction. A 'productivist' corporative system would organise and discipline all 'producers' in the overriding interest of national production, so as to make Italy economically independent of other countries and materially strong enough to expand.

This is admittedly a tidied-up and perhaps over-rationalised reading of Fascism's conduct of the country's affairs, which deals with intentions rather than effects. The interplay of events at home and abroad which lay behind the invasion and conquest of Ethiopia was more complicated than that suggested by the schematic relationship between internal and external affairs represented above. The full interaction of domestic and foreign policy distinctive of the Fascist way became more evident from 1936.

3.   THE DEPRESSION AND FASCISM'S OPPORTUNITY

If not the aim, then the opportunity for and timing of Italy's imperialist war was undoubtedly consequent on changes in the international situation during the years of the Great Depression. For one thing, the international economic context in which all countries worked out their economic and foreign policies was rapidly changing under the impact of the Great Depression. By 1934 the interdependence of international finance and trade had largely broken down, as had the various attempts to manage the Depression through multilateral co-operation. The United States had abandoned its pivotal position in the world economy, looking to protectionism, devaluation of the dollar and internal pump-priming to revive its economy. US tariff protection provoked similar counter-measures elsewhere, as countries developed their own variants of autarky and economic self-help, Britain and France in tightening and exclusive links with their empires.

By defending the value of the lira at the cost of reducing its gold and foreign currency reserves, Italy could at least pay off its dollar debts on advantageous terms and more rapidly. Even before 1934 Italy was trading less with the United States and more bilaterally with Central and

Eastern European nations, including Germany. Italy was increasingly no longer a part of or dependent on a framework of international trade and finance dominated by the United States, and such a dependence could no longer inhibit the pursuit of a more forward foreign policy. Italy's weaker economy meant that it would be difficult to avoid another form of dependence on a stronger economic power. But her trading and economic links were less and less determined by her place in the international economy, and more by the drift towards autarky and the realisation of nationalistic goals. The collapse of international trading and financial connections during the Depression encouraged or facilitated in Italy's case the matching of economic policy and trade patterns to the direction of her foreign policy.

Also, the growing strength of the Nazis in Germany, the largest single party in the German parliament by mid-1932, raised the imminent prospect of a revanchist Germany challenging the 1919 settlement and the Anglo-French domination of European affairs. Make-weight diplomacy had some prospect of success in a situation of equilibrium rather than hegemony, and the emergence of Hitler's Germany provided the balance which Mussolini thought to exploit.

The hope was to prey on Franco-German conflict, avoiding binding alliances and blackmailing both sides for Italy's gain. Grandi, Foreign Minister between 1929 and 1932, gave a characteristically Fascist intonation of bellicosity and opportunism to his summary in 1930 of Italy's position as the so-called 'determining weight': 'With everybody and against everybody. Arming ourselves and isolating ourselves even more, in order to sell ourselves at a high price at the time of future great crisis.'[2] For a while Grandi tried to work through the League of Nations and for disarmament, as a way of bringing about a parity of France and Germany which would allow Italy to oscillate between the two. He seemed to appreciate the potential risk as well as the opportunity of German revisionism, not least for its likely impact on Italy's position in the Balkans. A Franco-Italian agreement on colonial questions, and a tacit restraint on Germany in Central and Eastern Europe, almost exactly what eventually emerged in 1935, was a possibility in 1931–2. The prospect temporarily disappeared once Mussolini replaced Grandi at the Foreign Ministry in July 1932. Mussolini disliked giving any credibility to the League, and wanted to push the German lever even harder.

His idea of a four-power pact in 1933, which came to little in the end, envisaged a kind of Great Power directorate to rearrange European affairs. Part of its purpose was to get Italy recognised as a major power alongside Britain, France and Germany, bypassing the League. Its talk of Great Power collaboration to revise Versailles, German equality in armaments, and co-operation on colonial issues was a scarcely coded attempt to use Germany against France, while intimating to all sides that Fascist Italy was Nazi Germany's minder and patron. The idea of reintroducing a revisionist Germany to European affairs under the auspices of an Italian-sponsored arrangement among the Great Powers did not survive Hitler's unilateral and simultaneous decisions in late 1933 to withdraw from the League of Nations and resume rearmament.

Hitler's actions were a clear warning that German revisionism would be a difficult horse to ride. Relations with Germany deteriorated also as a result of the activities of the Austrian Nazis, perceived as the long arm of the German Nazi government. To defend Italy's own frontiers against the weight of German revisionism, Mussolini became the protector of Austrian independence. The murder of the Austrian dictator, Engelbert Dollfuss, in an abortive coup by Austrian Nazis in July 1934 intended to precipitate union with Germany, might well have tipped Mussolini towards the kind of understanding with France which he had earlier resisted. There was nothing explicit in the written record and agreement of Mussolini's talks with the French Foreign Minister, Laval, in January 1935. But the nature of the tacit bargain was understood on both sides. Italy could have a free hand in Ethiopia, and in Europe would join France in resisting *Anschluss*.

4. THE INVASION AND CONQUEST OF ETHIOPIA

What we know of the planning and preparation of the Ethiopian conquest is at least consistent with the view that changing international circumstances gave Mussolini the opportunity to achieve Italy's and Fascism's empire in East Africa. Actual invasion plans were commissioned by Mussolini from the Colonial Ministry and presented to him by the Minister, De Bono, in late 1932. This coincided with the awareness of the unsettling effects on international relations of the prospect of a revanchist Germany under a nationalistic government. The Italian military became involved later in planning discussions, but the definite decision to invade was taken by Mussolini and communicated to civilian and military leaders in December 1934. One of Mussolini's stated premises for war was a period of European stability or balance from 1935. It could scarcely be coincidental that the tacit arrangement linking the containment of

German revisionism and action in Ethiopia was made in the Franco-Italian talks of early 1935.

But the internal dimensions of the decision to attack Ethiopia can scarcely be ignored. It is too simplistic to argue that rearmament and war were the only way that the regime could find to stimulate a depressed economy. The worst point of the Depression was 1932, when planning for an invasion started. But the economy was beginning to recover during 1934. That recovery was certainly aided by the government's war-related commissions and contracts, which began to flow in late 1934 and early 1935, coinciding with and consequent on Mussolini's decision to invade and the Italian-French understanding. Preparation for war undoubtedly had an impact on employment, which by spring 1935 was down 250 000 on 1934 levels. Some sectors benefited hugely from mobilisation, the war itself and colonial administration, obviously enough those supplying arms, clothing, equipment, transportation and other logistical services for the war effort and the running of the empire. Few industrialists do badly out of a war, but those that profited did so as a result of the government's initiative to go to war, not as that war's prime movers.

The Fascist government had an economic rationale or perception of the war. It was projected endlessly and unoriginally before and during the invasion as that of a 'proletarian' nation fighting for its share of territory and resources at the expense of the richer 'plutocratic' imperialist powers. An empire would guarantee raw materials and markets for Italian industry and agriculture, and its colonisation would satisfy the land hunger of the overpopulated south and islands. This familiar rehash of imperialist rationalisations was not directly concerned with a way out of the Great Depression. Such a poor man's imperialism was couched in more general terms of rectifying an historical political and economic inferiority which had consigned Italy to the second rank of nations.

In economic matters, then, what happened was dictated by the pursuit of the government's foreign policy aims for overseas expansion. But other domestic pressures did arguably help to shape foreign policy decisions. It is again too glib to say that the Ethiopian war was simply a diversionary foreign policy adventure to distract attention from internal political difficulties and recoup support and prestige for the regime. There was certainly no political crisis, arising from the effects of the Depression or not, which seriously threatened the regime's stability. At least internationally, the corporatist 'Third Way' could be taken as a demonstration that it was the liberal democracies rather than Fascism which were struggling to ride the Depression.

But objectively, as we have seen, the regime's corporative reforms had swollen the state's bureaucracy, without changing or affecting much in the way the economy and society were managed. *Confindustria*'s largely successful evasion or use of the corporative apparatus indicated the strength and persistence of the compromises with conservative interest groups and institutions, on which the regime had consolidated itself in the late 1920s. The prospects of an internal Fascist transformation of society seemed to be on hold, as long as the regime did not challenge the established interests which it had itself incorporated into its system of rule. In foreign affairs, however, Mussolini could act with more freedom than seemed possible domestically, and a dramatic and successful foreign policy coup could unblock the road to the further 'fascistisation' of Italian society.

So far this might appear to be a subliminal or over-rationalised argument, but some indication of its plausibility comes from the way Mussolini communicated his decision to invade Ethiopia in December 1934. He stated that the aim was the total conquest of Ethiopia, by war: 'the empire cannot be made in any other way'.[3] This explicitly rejected a diplomatic rather than military solution to Italian claims on Ethiopia. It sat uneasily with Mussolini's apparent willingness to consider a negotiated settlement short of complete annexation in November and December 1935, after the invasion had been launched in October. In the event Mussolini avoided having to decide whether to accept or reject the compromise terms of the Hoare–Laval agreement of December, which gave Italy part of Ethiopia and informal control of the rest. The British government was forced to disown the deal arranged by its own Foreign Minister. The arrangement rewarded Italy for an act of war, and contradicted Britain's public support for and application of limited economic and financial sanctions imposed on Italy as aggressor by the League of Nations.

The Hoare–Laval plan was motivated by the British and French governments' fears that the possible extension of League sanctions to measures which would really bite, including an oil embargo, might precipitate a real war with Italy. Mussolini had every reason to be anxious about League action of this kind, which, if implemented, could seriously handicap military operations in Africa and cause hardship in Italy. It seems likely that Mussolini's openness to the possibility of settlement was his attempt to head off the consideration of more severe sanctions, which would, of course, be made superfluous by victory in the field.

Certainly, the sheer scale of Italy's military preparation and commitment, which ran to an army of 400 000 men to wage a small colonial war, indicated that the intention was to achieve a rapid, decisive and comprehensive conquest of Ethiopia by the overwhelming force of arms. The massive mobilisation leading to war was an end in itself for the regime. The winning of an empire was the opportunity to demonstrate and enhance 'totalitarian' mobilisation and control, to rally and unify the nation around the regime and a Fascist war. The barrage of preparatory propaganda working on the anti-British theme of the justifiable imperialism of the 'proletarian' nation was building up from the summer of 1935, matching the actual concentration of arms, equipment and men on Ethiopia's borders. Significantly, the Under-Secretariat for Press and Propaganda, which under Mussolini's son-in-law, Galeazzo Ciano, was expanding its jurisdiction to radio, films, music, theatre and literature, was made a full ministry in June 1935. The ministry's creeping monopolisation of the making and dissemination of information and control of cultural activity was both boosted and tested during the period of the Ethiopian war, when the regime embarked on a systematic propaganda campaign to rouse opinion in support of the war.

However ephemeral the effects, the regime, milking the sense of outrage at the sanctions imposed by the League from November 1935, did seem to manage to arouse a reactive nationalism and xenophobia among Italians of all classes and backgrounds. As far as this was measurable, the Ethiopian war marked the high point of support and consent for the Fascist regime. One of the peaks of the propaganda campaign was the organisation of the 'day of faith' on 18 December, when the royal family, along with thousands of Italians and with the blessing of the church, publicly and emotionally symbolised their marriage to the nation by ceremonially handing over their wedding rings. An estimated 20 million Italians listened to Mussolini's public radio broadcast announcing the invasion in October, and again to his proclamation in May 1936 that 'Italy has an empire at last, . . . a Fascist Empire'.[4] If nothing else, the Ethiopian war finally convinced the regime of the utility of radio as a means of controlled mass communication.

The conquest of Ethiopia then, was a Fascist war, even though it clearly drew on Italy's pre-Fascist legacy of colonial aspirations and achievement, and won the endorsement of the country's establishment. It was Fascist in the commitment to victory by force, and in the deliberate exposure of the nation to the test of war, both a measure and justification of 'totalitarian' mobilisation and control. Fascism's new order was the nation in a perpetual state of mobilisation for war, and in this sense

Fascist foreign policy was also an act of domestic policy. Mussolini's sneering conclusion to his December 1934 directive to prepare for the invasion of Ethiopia was that 'the remnants of the old world fear the "adventure" because they believe that the war will be conducted with their systems, but they deceive themselves, and besides, politically and socially they count for nothing'.[5] The way in which the regime handled the war as an exercise in organisation and control of the nation's resources and energies indicated that this was not just gratuitous anti-establishment rhetoric. Victory in a war planned for by the regime and using its own 'totalitarian' apparatus to organise and generate support, undoubtedly strengthened the position of Mussolini and the regime in the country. The Fascist system had apparently been validated by the achievement of empire. From the sense of the regime's enhanced popularity and control came the confidence and will to push harder on the pedal of 'fascistising' the country, both the premise for and result of fighting and winning wars. The period after 1936 was perhaps the real 'totalitarian' phase of Fascism, marked by the almost total complementarity of foreign and domestic policy.

Part III
Fascist Expansionism at Home and Abroad, 1936-43

6 The Axis Connection and the 'Fascistisation' of Italian Society, 1936-40

1. THE AXIS WITH GERMANY

Foreign policy decisions were the most important and revealing of the regime's nature and intentions, and must be harmonised with any view of domestic and economic policy between 1936 and 1940. The Ethiopian invasion could be regarded as a successful exercise in 'determining weight' diplomacy. Exploiting the threat of Germany to Anglo-French hegemony in Europe, Mussolini had won what he thought was a free run in East Africa in return for restraint on Germany in Europe, specifically resistance to *Anschluss*. The question is, what options were still open to Mussolini during and after Ethiopia? Could he maintain a position of 'equidistance' in international relations, and did he actually want to?

Except for De Felice and his 'school', most historians see the working out of a kind of 'logic' in the sequence of events leading from League of Nations sanctions against Italy over Ethiopia, through the Axis and then alliance between Fascist Italy and Nazi Germany, to the decision to enter the war on Germany's side in 1940. The 'logic' lay in the force of changing international circumstances apparent even during the Ethiopian campaign, and in the nature of the Fascist regime as an imperialistic totalitarian dictatorship. To support his view of a Mussolini still pursuing makeweight diplomacy, manoeuvring between Germany and Britain and France, De Felice focuses on Italo-British relations. Mussolini's intention and priority, he argues, was to achieve a general Mediterranean settlement involving British recognition of Italy as a Mediterranean power, which more or less revived Mussolini's idea of a four-power directorate of European affairs. The more conventional view sees Italo-German relations as central to Mussolini's foreign policy in the late 1930s.

There is something in the force of circumstances argument, since the so-called Axis of the two fascist powers had its immediate origins in the Ethiopian crisis. In early 1936, League of Nations sanctions confronted

Italy with a degree of international isolation, and in bad need of friends. Germany obliged. Hitler refused to apply sanctions against Italy and became a major supplier of materials and energy crucial to the Italian seige economy. He simultaneously armed the Ethiopians in secret, presumably to keep the war on the boil and increase Italy's alienation from France and Britain. In return, Mussolini wavered on the Austrian question, the very issue which allowed Italy to straddle Germany and the Western democracies. In 1934–5, Mussolini had propped up the Dollfuss–Schuschnigg regime as the guarantee of an independent nationalist Austria. Now, he indicated to Germany that Austria and Germany should reach agreement on the status of Austria, and later leaned on Kurt Von Schuschnigg to make concessions to Germany and the Austrian Nazis.

The mutual benefits of synchronised action by Italy and Germany were demonstrated by the German reoccupation of the remainder of the Rhineland in March 1935, deliberately timed by Hitler to catch France and Britain with their attention diverted to the Ethiopian affair. Hitler's action broke the terms of Versailles and of the 1925 Locarno treaty, which made Italy and Britain the guarantors of France's frontiers with Germany. But Mussolini, who knew of Hitler's intended coup, declared he would not support any possible League of Nations retribution against Germany. Hitler's move increased the attractiveness of hitching Italy to German revisionism. A German Rhineland pinned France down in the west, made her more worried about her own security and her ability to stand by her treaties with the East European 'successor' states. Co-operation with a dynamic Germany was clearly the best way of hammering concessions for Italy out of a more vulnerable France.

These connections and perceptions of mutual advantage persisted after the Ethiopian invasion. The autumn 1936 talks between the newly appointed Foreign Minister, Ciano, his German counterpart, Konstantin Von Neurath, and Hitler, discussed a range of issues where collaboration was possible and forthcoming. These included Italy's endorsement of the July 1936 Austro-German agreement, set in train by Mussolini himself, which effectively made Austria a 'German' state and eased the way to actual *Anschluss* in early 1938. This surrender of Austrian independence was traded off against German recognition of Italy's new African empire. The two sides agreed on military aid to Franco's rebellion against the Spanish republic, and more broadly, on a common front against communism. These meetings also apparently affirmed respective and parallel spheres of interest, Germany in Northern and Eastern-Central Europe and Italy in the Mediterranean and Balkans, as the basis for collaboration in foreign policy. Italy tried ritually to extract German recognition of this division of labour in subsequent meetings, though it was never formally written into the agreements between the two countries.

These productive meetings enabled Mussolini to declare in November 1936 the emergence of the Rome–Berlin alignment, which was not only a relation between two states but 'an axis around which all the European states animated by the will to collaboration and peace can also collaborate'.[1] The 'peace' aspired to was clearly not meant to be that prevailing at the moment. Mussolini's appeal for collaboration was at face value multilateral and inclusive, but would turn on the two linked and dominant poles of Italy and Germany.

It is just possible to argue that couching Italo-German co-operation in the form of an Axis rather than an alliance, still bound Mussolini to no one and did not mark any definitive break with France and Britain. Mussolini did not take up German approaches in 1937–8 to transform the Axis into a full military alliance, which in the nature of a treaty of alliance would be exclusive in its obligations and commitments. It was also the case that despite Italian anger and hostility over the part played by Britain in sanctions, diplomatic contact was resumed, in the context of Italy's intervention in the Spanish Civil War. The nebulous 'Gentleman's Agreement' of January 1937 acknowledged the status quo in the Mediterranean. It was followed by the rather more concrete 'Easter Accords' in April 1938, which won British recognition of the empire in return for an Italian promise to disengage from Spain. But these agreements did not lead to a comprehensive settlement of Mediterranean issues between Italy and Britain, let alone France. If this was Mussolini's intention, as De Felice says, then why was it not achieved? A study of Mussolini's *actions* indicates that it was neither intended nor possible, and that the declaration of the Axis marked a new point of departure in Fascist foreign policy.

The Axis could be seen as the blackmailer's card and the continuation of a kind of balancing act, which is how De Felice interprets both the Axis and, incredibly, the alliance between Italy and Germany in May 1939. Closeness to Germany might well be the lever to extract concessions from France and Britain. Yet allowing a *de facto Anschluss* can hardly be construed as using the threat of Germany to win something from the West. It is difficult to see how Mussolini's public declaration of a new international alignment in the Axis could ever, in fact, lead to or make possible, Italy's independence of both sides, as the 'determining weight'. The Axis, after all, became an alliance of the fascist countries, and was not dissolved in the wake of some peaceable and conciliatory accommodation among the European powers. In both timing and content, the Axis indicated that Mussolini had made a choice. It was a statement of a perceived division in Europe between the dictatorships and the democracies, which was accentuated by Mussolini's actions in both foreign and internal policy thereafter.

The Ethiopian conquest was, then, a watershed in interwar international relations. It was the occasion which brought out a basic convergence of interest between Fascist Italy and Nazi Germany. They were both expansionist, and revisionist of the 1919 settlement, and united in their hostility to the beneficiaries and defenders of that settlement which stood in the way of achieving their expansionist goals, France and Britain. Certainly from *Mein Kampf* onwards, Hitler had always regarded an alliance with Italy as central to German revision of Versailles and the attainment of a German racial empire in Europe. The Italian ally would tie down the French on the Alps and in North Africa, and the British in the Eastern Mediterranean, which was exactly the role allotted to Italy in the period of Italian so-called 'non-belligerency' between September 1939 and June 1940.

For his part, Mussolini recognised that only a revanchist Germany would back the Italian challenge to Anglo-French hegemony in the Mediterranean and help Italy become a Great Power. For Mussolini was not really interested in security in the Mediterranean, which could have been achieved by some accommodation and balance between Italy, France and Britain. It was clear from Mussolini's summary of the international situation and Fascist Italy's aims to a secret meeting of the Grand Council in February 1939 that he aspired to control and dominance of the Mediterranean. Mussolini spoke of war with the Western democracies as inevitable, if Italy was to break out of the 'prison' of the Mediterranean and remove the 'bars' and 'guards' of French and British possessions and colonies in its 'march to the oceans'.[2] Mussolini's pacing of this Italian Mediterranean stage-by-stage plan did not anticipate war in 1939, and such a qualification was important. But his keynote address, consistent with earlier and later public and private pronouncements, ruled out any compromise with France and Britain.

This was unlikely, anyway, after the Gallophobic war scare propaganda campaign deliberately mounted in November 1938, which had Fascist deputies in the Chamber screaming for Corsica, Tunisia, Nice and Savoy, students rampaging outside the French embassy, and vicious anti-French articles in the press. The campaign was staged shortly after Mussolini's 'mediation' of German claims on Czechoslovakia at the Munich conference in September 1938. Here, Mussolini had appeared to be the peacemaker, as broker of a deal between Germany and the Western democracies to dismember the country. Was the public airing of Italian grievances and claims against France, Mussolini's reminder to the democracies of the price Italy would exact for 'restraining' Germany in the interests of general peace? If so, it was a clumsy piece of blackmail and led nowhere, except to a hardening of the Axis relationship. Vigorous French remonstrations at the campaign, and Britain's support of the French position, showed Mussolini that threats would not extract concessions out of the French and that more pressure needed to be applied, in the shape of an actual alliance with Germany. The events of November 1938 were probably the immediate backdrop, even the immediate incentive, for Mussolini's decision in January 1939, communicated to the German Foreign Minister, Joachim Von Ribbentrop, through Ciano, to proceed to an alliance. Even if we apply here the logic of De Felice's line about Mussolini trying to extract advantage for Italy by straddling the two camps, we are still left with a non-existent 'equidistance'. Mussolini's Mediterranean dreams only actually required France and Britain to give something up, and the 'logic' of this situation impelled Mussolini to an ever greater reliance on Germany, a choosing of sides, in other words.

It is important to realise that the Axis, in Mussolini's view, met the *interests* of both countries in the ways outlined above, since historians have been keen to emphasise their differing and conflictual interests, as well as their apparent ideological divergence. The differences were real enough, and persisted into the war years in the uneasy and unequal condominium of the Balkans area. But the conflicts of national interest were never insuperable or a cause of rupture in the relationship. They were, to some extent, resolved by the tacit understanding on the Italian side, at least, of separate and parallel German and Italian 'living space'. Austrian independence, apparently so crucial to the security of Italy's land frontier in 1933-5, ceased to be an issue between the two countries once Mussolini had effectively withdrawn his support for it during the Ethiopian campaign. The attempted 'Italianisation' of Italy's German-speaking alpine border provinces rankled with both Weimar statesmen like Gustav Streseman and Nazi pan-Germans, as much as German complaints offended Mussolini, whose concern was to secure the nation on a contested frontier. But again, Hitler had decided very early on, in the 1920s, that making the South Tyrol German was not going to endanger an Italian alliance, a commitment he maintained until the later stages of the war.

If the Axis was sustained by a sense of common interests being served by action against common enemies, then it was also sustained by ideology. This was another factor eroding Italy's 'equidistance' between the two sides. There has always been some debate over the impact of ideology on foreign policy. If foreign policy is that function of government which defends national independence and the national interest, however defined, then ideological differences in the political systems of countries should be irrelevant to the conduct of foreign policy. Parliamentary and republican France allied itself to tsarist Russia in the 1890s and to communist Russia in the 1930s, because both countries saw their national interest in taking precautions against a common German threat. From this perspective, the fact that Britain was a democracy and Italy a Fascist dictatorship was no barrier to diplomatic relations between them. So, for all his talk about Mussolini being inspired by the Ethiopian success with a sense of historical mission to realise the grandeur of the Italian nation, De Felice schizophrenically portrays the dictator as a normal player on the international stage in the late 1930s. This approach is comparable to A.J.P. Taylor's view of Hitler as a normal German statesman in his *Origins of the Second World War*, which misses the peculiar and essential dynamic of the foreign policy of a totalitarian state.

Such a simple separation of ideology and interest is difficult to maintain in interwar Europe, even for the example of the Franco-Russian alliance. That of 1935 was the cause of serious political division in France, enough to render it inoperative. Sections of the French right were not convinced that the real danger to the nation came from Nazi Germany. They rather feared that the Soviet alliance would strengthen the position of the French Communist Party internally, fears apparently borne out by the formation of the centre-left Popular Front government which rested on the PCF's parliamentary backing.

The separation is even less justifiable in the case of the fascist powers. The hostility to France and Britain was compounded by the dictators' constantly expressed conviction, confirmed as they saw it by events, that the democracies were on the slope of irreversible decline. Ultimately, they were victims of their own social Darwinist assumptions and propaganda, that these enfeebled countries would inevitably give way to the rising, aggressive fascist powers. That the Axis was not open to all, despite its apparent multilateralism, was evident from the sense of ideological affinity which the dictators gave to the relationship from the start. As

Mussolini put it in March 1939, the Axis was the 'meeting of two Revolutions which declare themselves in direct antithesis to all other conceptions of contemporary civilization. Here is the strength of the Axis, and here are conditions for it lasting.'[3] This meaning was carried over into the formal alliance, 'the Pact of Steel', which was signed shortly after in May 1939. The text spoke of the basis of the alliance being 'the close relations of friendship and solidarity which exist between National Socialist Germany and Fascist Italy . . . closely bound together through the complete affinity of ideologies and through comprehensive solidarity of interests'.[4]

The meshing of interest and ideology can be seen in Italian involvement in the Spanish Civil War between 1936 and 1939. Franco's military rising against the Popular Front government in Spain would not have survived at all without the early logistical and transport support from Italy. Intervention extended to the commitment of about 60 000 Italian troops alongside Franco's forces, some of them camouflaged as Militia 'volunteers'. The deception itself was significant. Mussolini could disclaim any 'official' involvement, and at the same time the sending of the armed guard of the Fascist revolution would show that the struggle against antifascism was now indivisible and Europe-wide. There is no evidence that Mussolini deliberately used the lever of Italian aid to install a Falangist regime in Spain, when the Soviet Union was certainly manipulating its aid to the Republic in order to increase Spanish Communist Party influence in the Popular Front government. But Mussolini clearly backed the rebellion because he wanted the Popular Front government and the parliamentary Republic to fall. He feared an agreement between Popular Front governments in France and Spain, which would allow France to use Spain as the land bridge to its North African empire, and might even introduce communism to Spain and, by extension, the Soviet Union to the Mediterranean.

The Mediterranean was to be the Italian sea, and any strengthening of the French position there had to be resisted. Franco's victory, achieved with Italian support, would increase Italian influence in the Western Mediterranean and give access to Spanish ports and naval bases, from which to threaten French North Africa. Many of these hopes were disappointed by Franco's neutrality during the Second World War, and Mussolini certainly did not anticipate the Civil War dragging on for so long. But Italian intervention connected Mussolini's strategic and geopolitical concerns for primacy in the Mediterranean to the particular form of the Spanish government. Who governed Spain and how Spain was governed, made a difference to the promotion of Italian interests in the Mediterranean. This, after all, was the rationale of the Axis. A similarity in political systems was some measure of the mutual support which each could expect from the other in the international arena.

The Axis brought together war-mongering dictatorships, whose 'totalitarian' structures were designed to mobilise the populations behind the regimes and prepare them for war. Any agreement with the Western democracies not only meant Italy abandoning Great Power ambitions and dreams of Mediterranean supremacy. Peace also made it difficult to continue the Fascist 'totalitarian' state, whose premise and justification was organising the nation for conflict.

The interdependence of domestic and international politics for the Fascist regime was directly and immediately felt on at least two emblematic occasions. At the time of the Czech crisis in late summer 1938, Mussolini was clearly not ready for war, and this partly explains his willingness to 'arbitrate' the dispute at the Munich conference. But his contempt for the democracies was reinforced by his perception that they were capitulating to German demands, without war. Yet Mussolini was equally disgusted at the popular enthusiasm in Italy for his role in avoiding a European war. The response was one of his periodic tirades to Ciano about the unwarlike demeanour of the Italian people, and especially of the country's establishment and bourgeoisie, whose values and conduct were still modelled on those of the pacifist and cowardly democracies. The popularity of peace in Italy was to be a further stimulus to the 'fascistisation' of society, in the shape of the 'anti-bourgeois' campaign confirmed in Mussolini's speech to the PNF National Council in October 1938.

The second, more painful occasion was whether to intervene or not in the war which Germany had started in September 1939. As the ex-Nationalist journalist and senator, Maurizio Maraviglia, confided to Bottai, war was always preferable to peace, since even if with peace the country might be saved, 'the regime goes to the bottom, because it rests on the prestige of military, warlike indoctrination'.[5] 'Non-belligerency' in 1939–40 will be broached later. But there are no starker illustrations of the line drawing together foreign and internal policy in Fascist Italy, and simultaneously driving apart Fascist Italy and the democracies. It was literally the case that Mussolini could not and did not contemplate reversing the evident drift of the Axis: estrangement from France and Britain, and proximity to Germany.

2. FORCING THE PACE OF 'FASCISTISATION'

Between 1936 and 1940 the regime consciously stepped up and intensified its attempts to 'fascistise' Italian society. The structures and organisations of the 'totalitarian' state were already in place, of course. It is possible, then, to see what happened in the late 1930s as the continuation, extension and refinement of the system of 'totalitarian' controls, though the successful conquest of Ethiopia undoubtedly provided an extra impetus to the process.

The invasion had been the first great test of and opportunity for the controlled manipulation of opinion, using all available sources of information and means of communication. The institution co-ordinating this propaganda effort, the Ministry of Press and Propaganda, was renamed the Ministry of Popular Culture in May 1937. The new title denoted more ambitious tasks, never fully realised before the collapse of the regime. These were to achieve full control of all cultural activity and of the means to transmit an official and uniform culture on a mass scale. Such ends were more readily achievable, at least at the level of bureaucratic control or co-ordination, than that of actually defining and forming what was to be projected as the standard culture. Still, 'Minculpop', in name and function, was a further step towards the 'totalitarian' submersion of the private sphere in the public or political domain. Culture was no longer seen as a free-standing, self-generating activity, but as propaganda, produced or directed by the state to serve the ends of the state.

The main prop of the Fascist state was, of course, the party, which more than any other body was meant to ensure the permanence of Fascism beyond Mussolini by creating the 'new' Italian. After years of bickering competition with the Ministry of Education and the ONB, the party at last achieved the complete and integral control of youth organisations that Starace had long regarded as necessary for effective 'fascistisation' of the young. In 1937, the ONB was merged with the Young Fascists to form a unified, party-run youth organisation, *Gioventù Italiana del Littorio* (GIL, or Italian Youth of the Lictors), which organised young people of both sexes from the age of six to twenty-one.

The formation of GIL marked a more 'Fascist' education of the young, both in and after school. GIL's instructors, now increasingly the young Fascist men graduating from the Fascist Academies of Physical Training, ran all the sports activities and physical education in state elementary and secondary schools, as well as that provided in the youth organisations themselves. From early 1938, GIL also organised the premilitary training of the eight to eighteen age group. Racial themes were introduced into the training manuals of GIL, as they were in school curricula and text-books, coinciding with and marking the regime's incorporation of racism into its 'anti-bourgeois' campaign.

The reforms announced by the Minister of Education, Bottai, in the School Charter of February 1939, were meant to equip schools to provide training in and for life. Bottai's balance between academic study, hands-on experience of manual work and physical fitness might well have stood up outside its Fascist context and provenance. But that was inescapable in Bottai's own stated belief in the merging of GIL and the school system as 'a single instrument of Fascist education'.[6] Whether Bottai felt that the PNF, rather than his own Ministry, should take charge of the process, was another matter, but the momentum of party control was difficult to resist. One of the recommendations of a joint ministry–party working group in July 1940 was for a uniform school timetable which would make over every afternoon in the school day to GIL activities. Enactment in wartime conditions was impossible, but it recognised the PNF's more than equal role in what was glibly perceived as a total educational experience. As such, it indicated the scale of the party's growing intrusiveness in school life from GIL's formation, and the increasing emphasis on militaristic and physical preparation of the young to match 'the climate of Empire'.

The party and the corporations, together the most evidently Fascist of the regime's institutions, were also given formal and official standing in the constitutional framework of the Fascist state. In January 1937, the PNF Secretary was given ministerial status, and could, for instance, by right of office, sit in the Council of Ministers. After consideration of the issue by a Grand Council commission between 1936 and 1938, the law of January 1939 replaced the Chamber of Deputies with the Chamber of Fasces and Corporations, a change in more than name. In its even greater strengthening of the executive arm of government, the law carried on the work of the constitutional legislation of 1925–8. The nominal elective and representative character of the old Chamber disappeared completely. The new Chamber was composed of members of the PNF National Council, the National Council of Corporations and the Grand Council, who were there by virtue of their offices, all of which were nominated by the government. The executive appointed the legislative body, in other words, which was now an assembly of officials, leaving the Senate as the only unreconstructed element.

The timing and purpose of the reform were significant. It was a further attack on the constitutional position of the monarchy, which apparently disappeared from the legislative process altogether. The bill stated that Senate and Chamber collaborate with the government in the formation of the law and made no mention of the king at all. There were other straws in the wind. In a stage-managed wave of enthusiasm which deceived no one, the old Chamber of Deputies had rushed through a bill in April 1938 which created a new honorific title, First Marshal of the Empire, and bestowed it on both the king and Mussolini. This appeared to put the Head of Government on a par with the Head of State. A relatively trivial matter in itself, the incident came shortly after Mussolini's far more serious suggestion to the Senate that he should be the country's military commander in war, and not the king and the generals. On the eve of intervention in the war, he broached the question again with the king, whose fudging compromise was to give Mussolini command of operational, but not all, armed forces. The fact that the king had delegated control just about preserved his formal constitutional position as Commander-in-Chief of the armed forces.

These frictions at least give some credence to Mussolini's intention, often expressed in his private conversations with Ciano, to eliminate the monarchy. The Italo-German Axis never allowed the question of the monarchy to go away in the late 1930s. This meant that the attempts to clip the crown's prerogatives could not only be regarded as the resumption of a long-standing campaign of attrition. It was known that the king was critical, or at least sceptical, of Mussolini's pro-Axis foreign policy, even if his reservations did not lead to any overt resistance to that policy, nor appear to make a real difference to Mussolini's conduct. Almost inevitably, this made the king a potential rallying point for others' unease about where the Axis alignment was leading, including by 1940, Fascist leaders like Balbo, Grandi, Cesare Maria De Vecchi and De Bono. None of these men broke with Mussolini and the regime over the Axis, at least not until 1943. But Mussolini was only too aware that the king's residual prerogatives lay precisely in military command of the armed forces and in foreign affairs, including that of the declaration of war. So, insisting that he, like Hitler, should be military commander was a way of ensuring that the country would enter a Fascist war under Fascist command, and that the hoped-for victories of war would redound entirely to the regime's credit. Mussolini expected the conclusion of a successful war to provide the opportunity for a final settling of accounts with the monarchy. This fitted the king's own gloomy assessment of his position in 1940 – that win or lose the war, the monarchy was doomed. If the Allies won, it would be compromised by the 'dyarchy' with Fascism; if the Axis powers won, Mussolini would abolish it. These were prognostications of an unpredictable future. But Mussolini's growing intolerance of the monarchy's existence as a drag on Fascist policy and power were evident in the late 1930s, yet another indication of the nexus between internal 'fascistisation' and the German connection in foreign policy.

The most extraordinary aspect of accelerating 'fascistisation' after 1936 was the grotesque efforts to reform the conduct, habits and attitudes of Italians. The party set the example and spearheaded the campaign, which began in early 1938 but was at its peak in the period between summer 1938 and late 1939. The PNF banned the use in its own organisations of the impersonal form of second-person address, 'lei', described as a foreign import to the language denoting servility, and insisted on the more comradely 'voi'. The fraternal 'you' was also formally required of all in state employment from June 1939. Other obligatory lessons in Fascist style handed out in 1938–9 included the abolition of the unhygienic handshake of greeting for the raised arm of the Fascist salute; putting state officials in uniform as a mark of their readiness to serve the nation from their desks; and the introduction of the goose-step (*passo romano*) as the marching step of the Militia and the army.

Some of Starace's initiatives were laughable, and deliberately parodied by Mussolini to show how plainly daft they were. When the PNF Secretary ordered that all official correspondence had to be signed off with a ringing 'Viva il Duce', Mussolini concocted in his presence some imaginary letters: 'Dear Sir, . . . you have been dismissed. Viva il Duce!'[7] Not that Mussolini distanced himself from the campaign. He initiated and extended it, and seemed to share Starace's view that the way in which things were done actually indicated some inner spiritual transformation. It was as if forcing the nation to adopt in its daily life the rituals and symbols of the military barracks would put the country on a war footing and make the people warlike: the style was the substance.

The campaign broadened into a concerted attack on the so-called 'bourgeois' outlook and lifestyle, to the extent that the term 'anti-bourgeois' was applied to the campaign as a whole. Many of the slogans used and attitudes conveyed were evocative of the adventurous, dare-devil and violent days of squadrism, and the associations were apparently deliberate. As Mussolini put it to Ciano in July 1938, 'henceforth, the revolution must impinge upon the habits of Italians. They must learn to be less sympathetic in order to become hard, relentless and hateful – in other words, masters.'[8]

The dynamic of Fascist 'totalitarianism' connecting internal regimentation and control to expansion externally, was evidently at work
here. Fascism needed to accelerate the formation of a nation of
'squadrists', bold enough to rule and extend the empire. In Mussolini's
view time was pressing, especially now that international politics were
changing so quickly, and the opportunities for increasing Italian power
correspondingly greater because of Fascist Italy's association with the
dynamic 'revisionism' of Nazi Germany. This rapidly evolving international situation justified the intensifying efforts of the regime to create real
Fascists out of Italians, so that the nation could successfully confront the
inevitable conflict to come.

It could be argued that the anti-bourgeois campaign shared the same
basic mystification of the actual squadrism of 1920–2, as well as reviving
its myths. The squadrists, after all, glorified and acted out a life of risk and
violence, inimical to the outlook of the property owners who payrolled
their 'punitive expeditions'. Squadrism gave a revolutionary and heroic
veneer to the sordid defence of threatened middle-class social and economic interests. Did the same sublimation lie behind the anti-bourgeois
rhetoric, in the sense that it did not really target social and economic
inequality, and gave the regime a sense of dynamism while disguising its
inability and unwillingness to bring about real social change? Some
young Fascists, who took seriously Fascism's pretensions to embody a new
social order, tried in their GUF journals to extend the attack to the social
and economic privileges of the bourgeoisie. Syndicalists and labour organisers did the same. It may be possible to relate to the anti-bourgeois
campaign the government's decision to make official in October 1939 the
extension of the appointment of factory agents (fiduciari di fabbrica) to most
large-scale industrial plants. The Fascist syndicates had long argued
before and since the ban on such agents in 1929, that only a live representative of the syndicates on the shop floor could ensure that employers stopped violating labour agreements, and sceptical workers saw
some point in the syndicates.

But the brunt of the campaign was certainly directed at the 'bourgeois
mentality', not at middle-class wealth. This was consistent with Fascism's
own view of itself as a 'spiritual revolution', concerned with the recasting
of consciousness and perception, of how Italians saw themselves and
others. In this light, the term 'bourgeois' was not applied to a specific
class, a socio-economic category, but rather to an outlook and a demeanour which the regime condemned as un-Fascist.

Particularly after the Munich Conference, the internal stereotype of the 'bourgeois' was given a foreign incarnation, in order to emphasise that 'bourgeois' behaviour was imported, unpatriotic, and that Fascism's martial values were in fact authentic Italian national values. So the 'bourgeois' was cosmopolitan, defeatist, pacifist not by conviction but for the easy life, complacent, passive and materialistic. Infertility was the consequence of these moral failings, typical of 'bourgeois' egoism and a sure sign of national decline. The 'bourgeois' supported the Western democracies and peace with them rather than war alongside Nazi Germany, and modelled his conduct on the unheroic stance of the French and British people. These images revealed the self-fulfilling nature of propaganda. The Italians would both avoid and prey on the inevitable decline of decadent peoples, because they were being toughened up for national aggrandisement in the hard school of the Fascist totalitarian state. The campaign's focus on mentality was not simply sublimation, then. Because 'bourgeois' was not class specific but an attitude of mind in need of correction and redirection, it could take root everywhere and in anybody. In an obviously circular and self-justifying way, the anti-bourgeois campaign was the vehicle of the Fascist totalitarian regime and its claim to exercise total control over everybody and every facet of their conduct and personality.

Important strands of the anti-bourgeois campaign were race and anti-Semitism, still a puzzling and contentious episode in the history of Fascism. Many historians see the race issue as a qualitative mark of distinction between Fascism and Nazism. If they accept an ideological dimension to the Axis, then this ideological convergence is regarded as instrumental, adopted for political reasons of state. So in 1933–4 Mussolini's opposition to *Anschluss* was to keep a revanchist Germany from Italy's frontiers, and also a bridge to an agreement with France in Europe and Ethiopia. Being publicly contemptuous and critical of Nazism's racial policies was Mussolini's way of reinforcing the diplomatic alignments and divisions of the time. Equally his decision to introduce anti-Semitic measures in 1938–9, thereby removing the one major ideological difference between the two regimes, was almost a pledge to Germany that he was serious about the Axis. From this perspective, ideological affinity was the product not the cause of the closer relations between Fascist Italy and Nazi Germany.

This was exactly how Germans and Italians saw the introduction of the anti-Jewish laws at the time. German state and party officials were caught on the hop by the publication of the Race Manifesto in July 1938. This list of purportedly 'scientific propositions' about race had been concocted on Mussolini's instructions in the Ministry of Popular Culture, using the names and work of fellow-travelling academics and intellectuals. If the Germans were surprised, they were pleasantly surprised, because the Manifesto apparently endorsed a biological view of race. It asserted that the Italians were a pure Aryan race, not something accepted by all Nazi race ideologues, and that the Jews were not of the Italian race and therefore unassimilable. There appears to be no evidence of pressure from Hitler or anywhere in the Nazi system for the regime in Italy to come into line on the race question. However, Nazi German observers were unanimous in their assessment of the international repercussions of such moves: Fascist anti-Semitism would bind Italy to Germany and make it very difficult for Italy to reach an understanding with the democracies.

Reaction in Italy exactly mirrored the Nazi response. The Pope quickly and roundly condemned the move, to an audience of Catholic students, as an un-Italian imitation of German Nazism which was a further step in the regime's descent to pagan totalitarianism. The Manifesto was popularly stigmatised as 'the Axis Ten Commandments', and from what the police and other sources tell us about the public's view, official anti-Semitism was regarded as Italy's capitulation and subordination to Germany in the Axis. If Mussolini's intention was putting on a show of ideological solidarity in order to make the Axis stick, then it clearly had that effect.

These contemporary perceptions were important, not least because they shaped the Italian people's response to the Fascist regime in the late 1930s. But it is still difficult to be absolutely sure that Mussolini, the undoubted instigator of the race measures, saw and intended them as the necessary cement of the Axis alignment. Or at least, this aspect did not exhaust the reasons for their introduction.

Mussolini seemed to hold rather conventional political prejudices about Jews, sharpened considerably by League of Nations sanctions against Italy and then by the Spanish Civil War. Jews were associated nationally and internationally with anti-Fascism in the shape of Masonry, democracy and communism, and 'controlled' international finance and business. These prejudices came together in the anti-Jewish propaganda of the sanctions period, which portrayed sanctions as the work of the Jewish international conspiracy of plutocracy and Bolshevism. Such simple-minded connections hardened with the emergence of what were portrayed as communist, Jewish-inspired Popular Front governments in France and Spain. Mussolini also appeared to be concerned about the assumed dual identity of Italian Jews as both Italians and Zionists, especially when the totalitarian state made such heavy and inescapable demands on people's loyalty to the nation. The Axis certainly did not help resolve the question hanging over the Jews' divided loyalties. Nazi racism was hardly likely to endear those Jews in military and civilian government service to the idea of an Italo-German alliance.

As a result of sanctions and the Axis then, the Jews in Italy, though small in number, had become a political problem for the regime. The conquest of Ethiopia also brought race issues in general to the political foreground. It gave an added dimension and point to the regime's long standing demographic policies, which had always been related to the stocking of an empire with healthy and well-bred Italians. The first miscegenation laws were applied in the Italian East African colony of Eritrea in 1933. Similar measures to enforce the separation of races were introduced in Ethiopia in 1937, since over-familiarity with the natives apparently undermined the principle of European racial superiority and the civilising mission. The race problem could logically be exported from the empire to Italy itself, which explains how the Grand Council could justify its racial measures of October 1938 as the domestic aspect of a general racial problem, rendered acute by the conquest of an empire. If it was wrong on racial grounds for Italians to mix with Africans, then it was wrong for Italians to mix with Jews, as members of a different race.

The jump still had to be made, however. The impetus came from the regime's quickening of the tempo and intensity of internal 'fascistisation' from 1936, in Mussolini's view made necessary by the conquest of empire itself. Italians needed to acquire an 'imperialistic' mentality, a racial consciousness, a sense of their own superiority and fitness to dominate and rule. A general resolution of racial issues emerging in both Africa and Italy after 1936 was therefore made possible and pressing by the regime's commitment to forcing the pace of the campaign to remake Italians. Speaking to Ciano in June 1938 of the imminent unleashing of the Fascist revolution's 'third wave', Mussolini incorporated racism into the anti-bourgeois campaign, as an integral part of the regime's attempt to tone up the population. The connection was even more strikingly made later. In an implicit recognition of the unpopularity of the measures against the Jews, the anti-bourgeois propaganda of late 1938–early 1939 condemned the 'pietism' of especially Catholics' attitudes to the Jewish community. Any trace of compassion, pity or sympathy for the Jews was a mark of the 'bourgeois' mentality, and unworthy of Italians being raised in the climate of empire and war.

Perhaps one would expect the regime to insist that anti-Semitism was internal to Fascism, a natural and unavoidable extension of the race issue from Africa to Italy, and deny that it imitated Nazism. The Race Manifesto's biological racism made the charge of imitation difficult to counter. But the package of discriminatory measures announced by the Council of Ministers in September and the Grand Council in October 1938 were an odd hybrid of non-racial nationalism and biological racism. Besides action against foreign-born Jews resident in or citizens of Italy and the colonies, there was a ban on intermarriage and sexual relations between Italians and Jews, and the exclusion of Jews from the PNF and all public employment, including education, the armed forces and the civil service. Jews were also to be prevented from entering or exercising the professions, and from owning and inheriting property.

But religious and other criteria were used to dilute the racial definition of the Jews subject to these measures. The children of mixed Jewish–'Aryan' marriages who were not practising Jews were categorised as 'Aryan'. No Nazi would have religious beliefs override the evidence of blood. The exemptions violated biological determinism too. Patriotic and Fascist Jews and their families, meaning, for instance, war veterans and those joining the PNF early on, were not affected by the anti-Semitic laws. About a fifth of all Italian Jewish families were exempted as a result, probably more after the partial and corrupt way in which the laws were actually applied.

This discretionary rather than deterministic view of 'race' marked the survival of the original Fascist conception of the nation as a 'spiritual' community, unified by and through the consciousness of all its members that they belonged to and identified with the nation. So not all Jews were strangers to the nation. Fighting in its wars and participating in the movement which embodied the best of the nation, showed a real sense of being and feeling Italian and validated their membership of the nation. This idea of nation underpinned the whole process of 'fascistisation' within the framework of the 'totalitarian' state. No one was *a priori* excluded from the nation; anyone and everyone could be reformed and 'made' into Italians in the regimented and controlled atmosphere of the regime's organisations. A kind of racism might well have been adopted and adapted by Mussolini for political reasons of state. But these were as much to do with the 'fascistisation' of Italian society as with making the Axis credible as an international alignment.

The race laws were the occasion and one of the causes of the confrontation between the regime and the church in 1938–9. The underlying problem was the Catholic lay organisation, Catholic Action, which the government thought it had contained in the 1931 deal ending an earlier conflict. Catholic Action activity was picking up from the mid-1930s, at the very time that the regime was pushing harder at the 'fascistisation' of the country. In successive administrative changes it had managed to resurrect itself as a unitary, national organisation, when the whole point of the 1931 agreement had been to fragment Catholic Action into separate diocesan pieces.

It was clear that particularly in the areas of youth organisation and quasi-union activity, Catholic Action was the umbrella for networks which duplicated and thus offered alternatives to the regime's own organisations. The church appeared to have cordoned off a section of the country's educated young men in the Catholic university students' federation, its graduates' organisation and various professional associations. The parallel and competitive nature of Catholic Action was evident from the relatively small numbers of its members and leaders who were simultaneously participating in the equivalent PNF bodies. The church, building on its uniquely privileged position in the Concordat, was hoping to continue and extend its influence in society through laymen organised in the church's own orbit. The party and police reported on and urged action against a rival organisation which to their eyes and not without reason, was assuming the dimensions of an embryonic Catholic movement capable of outlasting Fascism.

Mussolini's preferred response, as always, was to combine low key PNF and police harassment of Catholic activity in order to make life difficult with a belief in the natural wastage of Catholic Action as a result of superior party organisation. A kind of *modus vivendi* was restored in the August 1938 agreement between the party and Catholic Action, which probably took both sides back to the terms of the 1931 arrangement. This was scarcely reassuring from the party's viewpoint, since the commitment to purely religious activity had hardly inhibited Catholic Action. But there was an inbuilt caution to the Pope's jealous defence of Catholic Action, because he never wanted to risk offending the Fascist state to the point of calling the Concordat into question. This became clear from the relatively muted reaction to the race laws, which never lived up to the Pope's vigorous attack on the Race Manifesto.

Racial legislation violated the Concordat in a specific and general sense. The ban on intermarriage made invalid those church marriages involving Jews converted to Catholicism, but the Vatican's protests got nowhere and this 'wound' to the Concordat remained open. On a broader front the laws challenged the church's claims to minister to the needs of all Catholics, and to a special and protected position in society based on the Concordat. The laws were to apply to everybody, including Catholics. The abuse heaped on Catholic 'pietism' in that accentuation of the regime's anti-bourgeois propaganda showed they could expect the same treatment as anybody else from a 'fascistising' regime. The Vatican limited its defence of the Concordat to the specific point of marriage, and did not broaden its resistance to defend the Jews against legalised discrimination. This was a measure of the Pope's concern not to allow the confrontation to rupture church–state relations and endanger the very survival of the Concordat, which he continued to see as the guarantee of the church's presence in society.

3. AUTARKY AND ECONOMIC PREPARATION FOR WAR

There was a demonstrably high degree of alignment between Mussolini's foreign policy, increasingly centred on the Axis with Nazi Germany, and the drive to 'fascistise' Italian society. The government's continuing commitment to autarky indicated a similar alignment of economic to foreign policy. Mussolini's speech in March 1936 making autarky official explicitly linked a strong foreign policy to economic independence, and spoke of the need for a state-run 'regulatory plan'[9] for the exploitation of the country's economic resources to meet the inevitability of war. Mussolini's reference to a planned war economy cannot be taken at face value. It is quite difficult to show that economic and foreign policy were exactly matched, because Italy was not ready for war when she joined it in 1940. This apparent puzzle needs explaining.

Autarky was at the start as much impelled by circumstances as by choice. The circumstances were first, those of the Depression and the universally protectionist responses to it, which destroyed Italian and international trade between 1929 and 1935. Italy's trading position was worsened by Mussolini's political decision to stick to an overvalued lira, but overall Italy's trade declined in the same proportions as world trade. Second, there were the economic sanctions of the Ethiopian war, and the goal of self-sufficiency made a virtue out of the necessity of finding a way around them. Sanctions were lifted in July 1936 and the Depression was easing too, even though this did not automatically involve any return to the world trade of the 1920s. As for foreign policy, the question was whether there was a choice, between continuing autarky or returning to the international economy.

For the Fascist regime any such choice was political and ideological, or would have such repercussions. International trade could only revive in conditions of international peace, and if Italy wanted to trade with the United States and Western Europe, relations with them had to improve and continue to improve. It was no wonder that anti-Germans like Fulvio Suvich, Under-Secretary at the Foreign Ministry until he was removed in July 1936, were urging a restoration of trading relations with those countries as a way of slipping out of Germany's embrace. But Mussolini was not interested in international stability and peace, nor in a non-ideological and accommodating foreign policy towards the Western democracies. The Axis exacted a kind of economic price.

After 1936 trade certainly resumed with Italy's usual trading partners, including countries which had applied sanctions. But two things were different. First, trade was increasingly conducted through bilateral clearing agreements, where the value of imports exactly matched the value of exports. For Italy this was a way of curbing and controlling imports, a vital aim of autarky, without paying for them by scarce gold and foreign currency reserves. Connected to this, the government's import licensing system and its control of foreign currency were strengthened and made permanent *after* the lifting of sanctions. The agency it had set up for this purpose to control foreign trade in preparation for and during the invasion, became the Ministry of Exchange and Currency in November 1937. The lira's belated hefty devaluation in October 1936 to improve exports – another autarkic aim – suggested a return to international trade, except that exports were often part of bilateral deals rather than multilateral exchange.

Second, the clearing arrangements with the countries that had not applied sanctions, such as Germany and Hungary, were more advantageous than the others, which marked a more general shift in the pattern of Italian trade during and after the Ethiopian war. Italy traded more with the empire and the countries of Central and Eastern Europe, and traded less with Western Europe and the United States. German imports were 18 per cent of the total in 1936 and 29 per cent in 1940. Imports from East Africa were small, but Italian exports to the empire were about 25 per cent of the total by 1939, and to Germany another 25 per cent. Germany supplied coal and industrial goods; Italy sent agricultural produce and labour to Germany. Here were the worrying signs to Italian businessmen of Italy becoming the agrarian client of its powerful industrial neighbour, and clear confirmation that the two economies were drawing together as the Axis hardened into the alliance.

There were other telling indications of an autarkic and war economy. State intervention in the economy continued and increased. IRI, initially the device for banking and industrial salvage operations in the Depression, became a permanent body in 1937. It ran a huge complex of largely publicly-owned heavy industries through subsidiary holding companies, like Finsider in the iron and steel sector, and had powers to take over private firms where this was justified by reference to national defence, autarky and empire. State-controlled and monopolistic agencies mushroomed, run like private companies on public money, and often indeed capitalised jointly by government sources and the near-monopolies dominating the private sector, like Montecatini and Fiat. They were responsible for developing import surrogates, whether through finding and exploiting indigenous sources of energy, metals and raw materials or producing synthetic substitutes. Obligatory requisitioning was introduced in 1936–7 for cereals, beet, hemp, wool and other agricultural foodstuffs and raw materials, in the hope that stockpiling would end market volatility and guarantee a regular supply at stable prices.

Government spending increased wildly, about 30 billion lire in 1934–5, rising to double that in 1938–9. Middle class incomes and savings were squeezed to pay for it, through government loans, the renegotiation of Treasury bonds, and four extraordinary direct taxes on property, capital and shareholdings. But even these increased tax revenues did not cover the state deficit, which rose from about 2 billion lire to 28 billion between 1934–5 and 1938–9. The money was going to autarkic and heavy industry servicing the armed forces. By 1939 probably between a quarter and a third of all government spending was on the military, including Spain and the empire. Nearly 80 per cent of the ballooning state deficit between 1935 and 1939 was accounted for by mainly military 'exceptional' expenditure.

Autarky bred abnormal and distorted economic growth, in itself a measure of the priority being given to war preparation. High-cost domestic industries were producing a range of products which could be bought cheaper on the international market. Since the contractor and consumer was the state, it did not matter that this made little economic sense. The goal was not productivity and market efficiency, but producing enough of what the country required for war.

Whether the autarkic economy was a planned economy in the way announced by Mussolini in 1936 is debatable. There was no central planning agency to co-ordinate the six economics ministries and innumerable economic bodies working in specific sectors, unless that job was done by the Commission for Autarky, set up in 1937 and later replaced by an inter-ministerial committee. The main organs of state control or regulation worked effectively enough in their own areas. IRI's Finsider, for instance, had reached the planning stage in 1938 for the coordination of production and investment in the iron and steel sector. Foreign trade was covered by the Ministry of Exchange, which by controlling raw materials imports and the currency to pay for them could discriminate among industries dependent on those imports. The requisitioning and stockpiling of cereals was an attempt to plan outside the market, for adequate food supplies in the eventuality of war. A prices policy of sorts was applied to contain the inflationary spiral set off by devaluation and increased public spending. A two-year block on rents and the prices of utilities and basic items was imposed in 1936. But as in the revaluation crisis of 1926–7, the Party's pricing committees were unable to stem price inflation. The corresponding award of quite significant across the board pay rises in 1936, 1937 and 1939 was hardly a sign of the control of labour in line with war mobilisation.

Italy's evident economic and military unreadiness to sustain a big war in 1939 might suggest the absence of economic planning for war, or at least a lack of synchronisation between economic and foreign policy. The second position has more validity than the first. It is difficult to deny the connection of autarky to war preparation, and not just because Mussolini insisted on the linkage. There was the evidence of the misshapen economy of the late 1930s, as the government poured public money into military and military-related spending. Much of these economic and military resources were consumed in the local wars and actions undertaken by the regime between 1935 and 1939, from the conquest, pacification and administration of Ethiopia, through the Spanish Civil War, to the annexation of Albania. This was another important reason for the situation on the outbreak of a more general European war in 1939.

Again, autarky was certainly an unattainable goal for a relatively poor and ill-resourced country like Italy, which would always need to import coal, oil and raw materials. But the fact that it was unrealisable in present conditions was the very reason pushing Fascist Italy towards war alongside Germany. Within the Axis bloc of fascist powers, German resources were already making up for some of Italy's economic shortfalls. Whatever the illusions about Ethiopia's economic potential, the empire was an attempt to make Italy economically independent and powerful by war.

Future expansion and conquest would achieve that redistribution of territory and resources which had always been behind Fascist 're-visionism'. Talk of 'living space' (*spazio vitale*) was as common in Fascist Italy before and during the war as it was in Nazi Germany.

4. 'NON-BELLIGERENCY' AND WAR, 1939–40

The problem was that the Axis partners were moving at a different pace and according to a different timetable, and Italy was being dragged along by its stronger ally. Partly as a result of this, Italian economic, military, political and diplomatic preparation were put out of joint, and led to Mussolini's humiliating decision not to join Hitler's war in 1939.

This was clear from the extraordinary and irresponsible alliance, the 'Pact of Steel', signed in May 1939. It envisaged permanent political consultation between Fascist Italy and Nazi Germany with a view to agreement and joint action on all matters. It bound each side to auto-matic military intervention when the other went to war, and planned for military and economic co-operation enabling such automatic military aid to occur. It was an agreement for war, in other words. Mussolini and Ciano had Ribbentrop's verbal assurances about the separate and par-allel spheres of interest of Italy and Germany, and that war, though inevitable, would not occur in the immediate future. A breathing space of two to three, perhaps even four to five years, was presumably why Mussolini felt he could enter such an alliance, though none of the German nods and winks about the timing of war were actually written into the Pact.

It was self-deluding not to be aware of the dynamism of the German partner. Already in March 1939 the Czech agreement nominally bro-kered by Mussolini at Munich had been destroyed by Hitler's seizure of Bohemia and Moravia – without consultation. As a reassertion of Italy's Balkan sphere of influence, the bad-tempered and anxious Italian re-sponse was to annex Albania in April, a country already so tied to Italy that it was 'like raping your own wife'.[10] Not that the Germans seemed to mind. The annexation gave the impression of the Axis powers acting in unison and with irresistible force, and kept Italy apart from the Western democracies. Again, immediately after the alliance was signed, which in Hitler's view made it even more unlikely that France and Britain would resist further Axis coups, he ordered the invasion of Poland. Ciano was dismayed to learn in his meetings with Hitler and Ribbentrop in August that a Polish war was not only inevitable but imminent.

The news of German plans for immediate war put Mussolini in a corner. He was bound by the alliance to join Hitler in a war he had not anticipated would happen so soon, and which he knew Italy could not really fight. It was not only a matter of Italy's military and economic unreadiness to sustain a long war. Mussolini and Ciano paraded this in front of the Germans, in order to get them to delay things or at least accept that the alliance could not be activated then. The other reason or pretext for prevarication was the need for more time to make the Axis popular in Italy and prepare the nation politically and psychologically for war.

This was some admission for a regime and a system predicated on war, but it pointed to what some historians have seen as Fascism's 'crisis of consent' in 1939–40. Fascist foreign policy and its complementary internal policy had the effect by 1940 of beginning to break through the crust of compromise under which the regime had stabilised itself in the late 1920s. More evidently Fascist foreign and domestic policies, marked by the Axis, internal 'fascistisation' and autarky, did not now necessarily serve the interests of those semi-autonomous centres of power which had come to terms with the dictatorship. Important sections of the establishment, the church, the monarchy and *Confindustria*, along with some major Fascist leaders, were against the German alliance and appalled at the prospect of war at Germany's side. Their concern, whether communicated privately or occasionally in public, made little apparent difference to Mussolini's commitment to the German connection, except to play its part in heightening Mussolini's sense of national unreadiness in 1939.

Mussolini's own police sources were telling him that anti-Axis feeling was not confined to these areas, and that warlike indoctrination was not taking hold in the country. Indeed, it was probably counter-productive, as 'fascistisation' imposing on people's outward behaviour and conduct invited resistance, annoyance, even ridicule. The anti-bourgeois campaign attacking their values, together with a spendthrift government taxing their income, were a strain on the largely uncoerced sympathies of the middle classes for Mussolini and Fascism. The more Fascist the regime became, the more it put at risk its broad base of 'consent'. Although it did not result in much opposition to the regime, the idea and approach of war made many apprehensive, and the Axis was unpopular precisely because it seemed to be leading to war.

Going to war was a gamble for all sides. The king realised that Mussolini by his actions in 1938–9 was gunning for the monarchy, and acknowledged that war, whether resulting in victory or defeat, could mean the end of the monarchy. The Vatican faced the same basic dilemma. The understanding between the church and regime had produced the Concordat. But again, this would be threatened by either a triumphant Fascism completing its 'fascistisation' of society on the back of a successful war, or in the event of defeat by anti-Fascism taking revenge on those institutions compromised with the regime. Neutrality in the war and Mussolini still in power preserved the benefits of Fascism without incurring the risks.

As for Mussolini and the regime, war was both the test and gauge of 'fascistisation' and the means of completing it, as was clear from his dark threats to finish with pope and king once the war was won. The dilemma was inescapable. Taking to war 'a race of sheep'[11] who had so far resisted their transformation into wolves, courted disaster for the regime if things went badly. But if the Italians were reluctant fighters and Fascists, then the Fascist solution could not be peace, only exposure to the test of war.

There was an immediate way out of the problem of wanting but feeling unable to go to war. This was Hitler's agreement in September 1939 to Italy remaining in the alliance without actually fighting, providing instead political and diplomatic support and acting as Germany's economic and military 'reserve'. It is important to realise that Mussolini's face-saving declaration of 'non-belligerency' was nothing like neutrality. As in 1914–15, neutrality was 'equidistance', listening to and taking offers from both sides. But Mussolini quickly killed off the tentative idea of a Balkan bloc of neutral countries led by Italy, which the Vatican supported, once France and Britain seized on it as a wedge between the Axis powers. 'Non-belligerency' quite deliberately meant that Mussolini was keeping Italy in the alliance, but there would be no fighting war as yet. In the meantime Mussolini kept alive, at least in his own mind, the hopes of a parallel war, alongside but not subordinated to Germany. This was probably the intention behind Mussolini's letter to Hitler in January 1940, urging him to end the Nazi–Soviet Pact and seek his *Lebensraum* in Russia. Knowing that Hitler was contemplating a campaign in the West, Mussolini wanted to delay matters, so that Italy would have the chance to intervene in *its* war against France and Britain.

By the end of March 1940 Mussolini was informing the king that the only issue was the when and how, not the whether of Italy's intervention. Staying out of the war would put Italy at the mercy of whoever won, and reduce the country to the status of a 'Switzerland, times ten'.[12] Even the king could see the logic of that in May–June 1940, when the Germans achieved rapid and crushing victories against France and seemed set to decide the fate of Europe, with or without Italy. For the few weeks up to Mussolini's decision to declare war on France on 10 June 1940, there was temporary unity of Mussolini and the country in the perception that Italy could gain much and risk little by joining a war that was practically over. Since only a short and victorious war was in prospect, with easy pickings, Italy's unreadiness to wage a long campaign was irrelevant. What Mussolini's political journal, *Gerarchia*, called in July 1940 a 'revolutionary' fascist war, could begin.

7   Fascist Italy at War, 1940-3

1.   THE COLLAPSE OF ITALY'S PARALLEL WAR

War should have been the apotheosis of Fascism. In fact it was its
nemesis. Fascism failed the test that it had set itself, indeed the only
standard by which it wanted to be measured, as a mass-mobilising dictatorship forming the nation for victorious war and conquest. War was
what Fascism was about, whatever the opportunism of Mussolini's June
1940 decision to exploit the apparently overwhelming Nazi military gains
in Northern and Western Europe. The gamble for Mussolini and the
regime was huge, if calculated. The only justification for war was to win
it, and rapidly. The losing of a prolonged war exposed the regime's
growing unpopularity, already passively evident before 1940 as a result of
that combination of accelerated 'fascistisation' and the Nazi German
alliance. The wartime experience revealed the inevitable superficiality of
Fascist attempts at totalitarian mobilisation and the fatal flaws in the
institutional structures of the Fascist state, and completed the dissolution
of the broad conservative coalition of interests that had sustained Fascism
since the 1920s.

Fascist Italy claimed to be fighting a parallel war within the Axis
framework, alongside Germany and against the same enemies but in
different areas and for Italian aims. The idea of a separate if connected
war effort can be related back to the implicit Axis understandings of the
late 1930s for contiguous 'living spaces', the Italians in the Mediterranean
basin and hinterland, the Germans in Northern, Central and Eastern
Europe. It could also, just, be linked to 'non-belligerency', in the sense
that Mussolini had not committed the country in 1939-40 to a war
started by Germany and at a time not of Italy's choosing.

The war was also to be parallel in political terms, as the regime attempted to articulate a vision of a Fascist 'New Order' which was in part
emulation of and in part a rival to that of the Nazis. In the wake of
conquest, itself validating Fascism's superior value system and its claim to
universality, European politics and society would be 'fascistised' by im-

planting the totalitarian state governed by Fascist élites and the corporative social and economic structure. This remodelling of a conquered Europe on the Italian Fascist prototype would be the essential first step in the continent's economic reorganisation, both serving the immediate needs of the Axis war effort in a global conflict and marking out the shape of the postwar order. Opinion differed as to whether a subjugated Europe and its African and Asian hinterlands should be treated as one unified economic bloc managed by collectively agreed Axis policies, or whether Italy should carve out its own separate and autarchic Mediterranean regional economic zone. Both projections were clearly meant to prevent or dilute German hegemony in Europe, especially the more commonly aired second option. A bipolar system, with each of the Axis powers dominating, organising and exploiting its own *spazio vitale*, would be some guarantee of Italian political and economic independence in the new Europe. The regime's propaganda gave Fascist war aims a patina of Europeanism, but the rhetoric of an imperial 'community', to be conquered and then civilised by Fascist Italy, only thinly disguised the intention to dominate.

The Fascist New Order was and remained fanciful stuff, because the military parallel war was over by spring 1941. There were demonstrable signs of who dominated the Axis in June 1940, on the defeat of France. Italian territorial claims on metropolitan, insular and colonial France, essential to achieve a redistribution of power in the Mediterranean, were turned aside by Hitler's political argument that the war against Britain would be hindered by the permanent alienation of France at that juncture. Then Mussolini ordered the invasion of Greece from Albania in October 1940. This was entirely consistent with the goal of Mediterranean hegemony, but was improvised in timing, planning and execution. It was precipitated by Germany's unilateral action to secure exclusive control of Romania's oil fields, seen as yet another move to monopolise the Balkan and Danubian economies in disregard of Italy's regional sphere of influence. It was hastily carried out, to pre-empt German objections to a Balkan war which Hitler felt would invite Allied intervention and thus compromise his own plans for the invasion of the Soviet Union. Deliberate aggravation of the Albanian minority issue in Greece and the attempted corruption of Greek politicians raised hopes of an easy victory on the cheap. But the Greek army resisted and counter-attacked into Albania before the front stabilised. The botched invasion was a military and political disaster for the regime. It undermined the regime's credibility internally, and brought about the subordination of Italy's to Germany's war which it was designed to prevent. Hitler's successful invasion of Yugoslavia and Greece in April 1941 alone allowed Mussolini a part in the dismemberment and occupation of countries in the Italian orbit.

Similar bailing-out operations were necessary in Africa, the other theatre of Italy's parallel war. As early as May 1941, the Italian East African empire of Eritrea, Somalia and Ethiopia was lost to British armies and Ethiopian insurgents, and Erwin Rommel's German force was required to stem and then reverse losses in Libya.

The self-evident failure of the separate war inevitably nullified the parallel Fascist political New Order. As a result of being incapable of winning its own battles in its own recognised spheres of action, Italy simply lacked any political weight in asserting her version of a European order or influencing the course and conduct of the war. This subordination was revealed concretely in both military and political matters. Mussolini insisted in diverting troops and equipment better deployed in North Africa to support the German invasion of the Soviet Union in June 1941. This was for the sake of 'being there', of confirming Italy's presence in the Axis. But the impression was of Italians fighting Hitler's war, in a place where no national interests were served. Italian involvement made little difference to how Hitler conducted the war, there or anywhere else. He was deaf to Mussolini's suggestions from late 1942 for a separate compromise peace with Russia.

Initially the Italians had made pointed comparisons between what they saw as Germany's brutal incorporation of northern Slovenia and their own alleged attempt to 'associate' the Yugoslav territory they controlled. But German pressure and German priorities led inexorably to the extension of German methods of control in occupied and annexed Yugoslavia by early 1943. Italian political and military control of Dalmatia and southern Slovenia and of the supposedly satellite statelets of Croatia and Montenegro was tenuous and short-lived anyway, as Slav resistance was active from the summer and autumn of 1941. Increasingly concerned that Balkan unrest would encourage Allied landings and endanger the war on the Eastern front, the Germans insisted on co-ordinated repressive action against all Slav partisans and their host local populations, including the nationalist bands which the Italian military had tried to use as a check on the communist formations. This eventual assimilation of Nazi occupation policy stopped short at the racial question. Despite German diplomatic pressure and Mussolini's official assurances, the persecution and deportation of Jews were only implemented once the Germans themselves took over the Italian-occupied zones of France and the Balkans in 1943.

2. THE IMPACT OF WAR AND THE INTERNAL CRISIS OF THE REGIME

Italy's military performance might be taken as an object lesson in the weakness of dictatorial rule. In 1940 Mussolini was Head of Government, minister for all three armed services and commander of the armed forces in the field. He clearly wanted to emulate Hitler's personal control of military matters, but unlike Hitler deprived himself of the support enabling him to manage such a role. Mussolini apparently had all the power, or at least the positions, and took the basic military decisions, but had no staff, office or command organisation to ensure proper briefing and translation of the leader's decisions into operational action by the armed forces. This should have been one of the roles of a General Staff. But its nominal head, Pietro Badoglio, had a nominal staff, and never expected or attempted to co-ordinate and direct the three services according to an agreed military strategy. Things improved when he was replaced as Head of the General Staff in May 1941 by Ugo Cavallero, whose office at least operated as an intermediary between Mussolini as supreme commander and the services.

This serious lack of effective strategic and operational co-ordination between the army, navy and air force had blighted Italy's preparation for war, reflected in inadequate anti-aircraft defences and the failure to construct aircraft carriers. In wartime even communication between the services was laborious, and the lack of an overall view in individual actions as much as general strategy led to some disastrous military own goals. It appeared as if the three services were fighting three separate wars, with no one, not even Mussolini, capable of co-ordinating them. The point was that the problem was not new, but endemic to the regime's relationship with the armed forces. Mussolini's accommodation with a still largely monarchical officer corps was in part sustained by his tacit respect of the traditional autonomy of the individual services. When it came to that most Fascist of endeavours, war, Mussolini paid dearly for the customary inter-service rivalry which marked the regime's compromise with the armed forces.

In order to explain Italy's military failures, there is also something to the argument that in comparison with the major powers at war with Italy, the country simply lacked the economic resources and potential to fight a long war. The evidence suggests that the country was performing during the war to its productive, financial and physical limits. Industrial production, at least in the war industries, rose, only falling away from high levels during 1942, partly as a result of Allied bombing of the northern industrial cities. Agricultural production too, at least in the north, generally held to its prewar levels until declining significantly in 1942–3, as the call-up of labour and shortage of fertilisers began to bite. The problem was that agriculture was still not producing enough foodstuffs to meet consumer needs, and wartime blockade and the regime's own autarchic policies cut off imports. Industry, though increasing production, could not supply sufficient arms and equipment for a prolonged conflict, and suffered from an inadequate supply of the raw materials and fuel which Italy had usually imported, even under autarky.

This was what allies were for, and Italy became almost entirely dependent on German coal supplies to fuel its industries, though again such provision progressively declined to a point below sufficiency, forcing breaks in production in 1942. Significantly, Germany began to extract more economically from Italy than she gave, and this changing balance of trade was another facet of Italy's subordination in the Axis alliance. Forced to export labour and agricultural produce to Germany in return for essential but shrinking supplies of coal and iron, the country was penalising its own war effort by 1942. Agricultural exports reduced the availability of food in Italy, depressing consumption levels even further. In February 1942, an estimated 350 000 Italian workers were in Germany, at least half of them skilled industrial workers needed in Italy's own factories. It was bad enough that the war was not leading to that grand redistribution of territory and resources which was its justification and which would raise Italy to the position of a major power. During 1942 the war and the German alliance were actually draining away the country's current and inadequate economic strength.

Moreover, this was perceived and more importantly experienced by almost every Italian during the war, which made all the difference to the regime's will, solidity and credibility. If the economy within its limits met the test of war, society did not. Popular dislike of the war and of the German alliance which had brought it about, temporarily suspended in summer 1940, found constant and concrete reference points in the worsening daily conditions of wartime life. As in the late 1930s, the government tried to meet the spiralling costs of the war economy by printing money, inflation and the diversion of private surplus into public hands by loans and taxes on property and capital. But the country's capacity to pay was not limitless. State taxation was taking perhaps a quarter of national income in the war, but whereas tax revenue met about 60 per cent of government spending on the eve of the war, in 1940–2 it barely covered a third, its value constantly eroded by general inflation. The middle-class taxpayer and saver had had enough. By late 1942 there were declining returns on successive issues of Treasury bonds, the method by which the government borrowed money from its citizens. This was a precise indicator of the lack of confidence that middle-class savers had in the state, undermined by military reverses and a deteriorating economic situation where inflation and shortages made people spend rather than lend or invest whatever money they had.

The rising costs and shortfalls of basic food and consumer goods eating into the real incomes of white- as well as blue-collar workers could be and were directly attributed to the autarky, enemy blockades and priority to military production and consumption associated with being at war. Food shortages were worsened by the inefficient operation of the government's own measures to ensure consistency of supply or at least some equality of sacrifice for consumers. A rationing scheme of sorts existed, but was never intended to cover all food needs. The official normal daily bread ration was nearly halved from 150 to 80 grams in the course of 1942, but the actual rations distributed were always below the official rate. Such a system, which could not guarantee a supply of basic products, was practically an open invitation to the emergence of a black market during 1941, at prices way beyond the reach of most people. The obligatory stockpilings of agricultural products, a feature of the autarchic economy from the late 1930s, were meant to make unnecessary any recourse to a black market in wartime. But these were administered poorly, sometimes corruptly and speculatively, and became part of the problem they were set up to pre-empt. Farmers basically lost confidence in the operation of these *ammassi*, disaffected by the disproportionate difference between consignment and sale prices, and attracted by the money to be made in supplying the unofficial market. Evasion of their legal obligation to consign goods to the *ammassi*, widespread in 1942–3, set off a counter-productive cycle of forcible requisitioning and more hiding of produce, alienating farmers and further reducing supply to the consumer.

Finally, Allied bombings of industrial cities intensified in the second half of 1942, disrupting production, causing homelessness and mass evacuations to rural areas, a dislocation which strained urban and country populations alike. The cumulative effects of rationing, high prices, bombings and evacuation, and the longer working hours and tighter factory discipline of wartime production, together with a by-now noticeable revival of organised anti-Fascist activity, sparked in March 1943 the first great strikes by industrial workers for nearly twenty years.

Perhaps unavoidably in these wartime circumstances, the regime's 'capillary' organisation, the party, could not hold the disintegrating home front. By late 1942 Mussolini was privately and publicly acknowledging that the nation had failed its ultimate test, reflecting what he rationalised as the endemic mental laziness of the Italian people only superficially touched by the process of 'fascistisation'. This was unwitting self-criticism as much as contempt for his inadequate human raw material, and to a party audience he condemned the inactivity of a PNF of his own making: 'There are 4 million members of the *fasci*, 8 million in GIL. . . . The regime controls something like 25 million individuals. . . . Well what are all these people doing? I ask myself what are they doing?'[1]

The sheer weight of numbers was part of the problem, and Mussolini rather futilely pined for a streamlined élite party where membership denoted faith in Fascism. This from a leader who had endorsed Party Secretary Ettore Muti's decisions in 1939–40 to open PNF membership to the ex-combatants of all Italy's recent wars and to the 25–35 age group. Membership of male and female *fasci* swelled from 3.5 million in late 1939 to 4.25 million in March 1940 and 4.75 million in June 1943. This showy attempt to match the party to the young and not quite so young soldier-patriots posed an enormous administrative burden to the provincial PNF federations, forcing them to digest an army of new members.

This came just at a time when war placed the party in the same contradictory position as during the 'going to the people' campaign of the Great Depression. Mobilised to face the national emergency and involve itself even more in society, the party's capacity to cope with such an enhanced role was stretched by the extraordinary wartime conditions. Being at war put a premium on the PNF's functions of control, exhortation and surveillance. Together with responsibilities for organising civil defence, the welfare of combatants and evacuees and their families, and the direction and policing of price controls and the *ammassi*, these required extra human and material resources. Yet conscription and absence on military service of members, staff and leaders at all levels destabilised party organisation and reduced the regular income from subscriptions. The shortfall was not easily made up when other normal contributors to the funding of party activities, such as banks, companies and syndical organisations, were feeling the financial squeeze themselves because of the impact of war.

The PNF's involvement in the official price setting of basic consumer goods and the requisitioning of foodstuffs, unhappily not matched by its ability to do much about spiralling living costs and worsening shortages, took the party into areas of concrete disaffection with the war and made it and its activities unpopular. Fatally the party's capacity to carry the nation through the war and defend the regime was corroded by the perceptibly worsening course of the war on both the home and fighting fronts. It was difficult and ultimately pointless to counter 'defeatism' in all its forms and seek to maintain popular morale, when the regime's pretensions and propaganda were made incredible in contact with the awful reality of the war's impact. Hitler's scathing indictment in September 1943 of a Fascism melting away like snow under the sun at the time of Mussolini's fall from power in July, underestimated the demoralisation and isolation which party men and organisation experienced as a result of that unbridgeable gap between aspiration and reality opened up by the war. The appointment in April 1943 of the old squadrist lag, Scorza, as the PNF's fourth Secretary in four years, promised 'a relaunching of the Party with a strong hand, intervening in all branches of public life'.[2] It was too late to mean much by then. But this desperate last-ditch evocation of squadrist methods, the imposition by force of the will of an armed minority, captured the seige mentality of the PNF's successor in the even more untenable situation of Mussolini's Social Republic in 1943–5.

3. THE FALL OF MUSSOLINI

Italy's war had gone badly almost from the start. But the military situation had been retrieved by German intervention and there was some hope that Fascist Italy could achieve a Mediterranean empire under the cover of German victories. But the war finally turned against the Axis in Autumn 1942, with successful Allied landings in North Africa resulting in the loss of Libya in May 1943 and the start of huge Russian offensives. There was a real prospect of an Allied invasion of Italy itself, which occurred in July 1943, and this made the Anglo-Americans an influence on Italian political developments. The Allies talked of unconditional surrender, and it was evident that they would not negotiate a separate peace with Mussolini. He was more clear-headed than his ministers about the significance of this. In his view there was no possibility of disengagement from the Axis. A separate peace with the Allies, a renunciation of the German alliance, would mean the removal of Mussolini and the end of Fascism, while the

Germans would occupy Italy if it tried to leave the Axis.

Mussolini's stance closed down the options of those who realised the war was lost, invasion imminent and wanted to find a way out of the war. Since Mussolini would not leave the German alliance, the only possible way out of the Axis and the war was his removal as Head of Government and commander of the armed forces, and the king's resumption of his power over these positions. Here, the incompleteness of the Fascist constitutional arrangements of the late 1920s proved fatal for the regime. Although the king had been reduced to a political cipher, the monarchy was still an alternative focus of legitimate political authority. Even under Fascism's own 1928 law on the attributes of Head of Government the king could dismiss Mussolini, and he certainly could do so under the still-unrepealed constitutional statute. It was this Fascist–monarchist dyarchy which made Mussolini's fall in July 1943 as constitutionally ambiguous as his coming to power in 1922.

The loss of confidence in the regime and Mussolini's leadership was almost general as a result of the impact of the war and the near-certainty of Axis defeat. It extended to Fascists like Grandi, Bottai and Ciano, who were the main movers behind the calling of the Grand Council meeting in July, the first that Mussolini had allowed since December 1939.

Other conservative interests stood back from a now-discredited system. Industrialists had enjoyed high wartime profits, even the initial prospect of taking advantage of territorial gains, but by late 1942 the war was destroying their factories and interrupting production. The strikes of March 1943, involving over 100 000 workers in Piedmont and Lombardy, re-created the situation of organised labour agitation and left-wing political activity, the suppression of which had been one of the major reasons for their support-cum-connivance of Fascism over the past twenty years. Industrialists, whether individually or through *Confindustria*, probably took no direct part in the royal conspiracy to overthrow Mussolini. But the regime had clearly outlived its usefulness for them, and the eventual outcome of a military-bureaucratic government appointed by the king excluding both Fascists and anti-Fascists certainly best suited their concern to preserve their businesses under private management. Again, the Vatican could hardly go further officially than keeping to its traditional neutrality and pacificism in wartime. But its contacts with the American government were one of the channels through which it was made known to the king that a royal-nominated anti-Axis and anti-communist government was an acceptable premise for a separate peace, again a solution suiting the church.

If it was clear that only the monarchy, backed by the army, could and would take Italy out of the war, the king himself was hesitant in taking the initiative. Soundings between the king's advisors, army generals including Badoglio and police chiefs began in early 1943 on the practicalities of a royal coup. But the final decision to act was probably only taken a week before the Grand Council meeting arranged for 25 July. As much as the church and the industrialists, he realised that as in 1924 during the Matteotti crisis, removing Mussolini raised the prospect of a civil war if the Fascists resisted and an anti-Fascist and left-wing succession, which would hardly forget or forgive his involvement with Fascism. Dismissing Mussolini was a judgement of the fellow-travellers as well as of the regime. The Grand Council meeting at least gave the king some kind of constitutional setting to which he could respond. Time was really pressing now that the country was being invaded, Rome being bombed, and German troops entering the country in force after the July Hitler–Mussolini meeting confirming the Axis alliance.

Grandi's resolution to the Grand Council, winning a 19–7 majority, urged the restoration of military command to the king and the proper functioning of the constitutional organs, the monarchy, Grand Council, government, corporations and parliament. This certainly amounted to the end of Mussolini's dictatorship and his running of the war. But there was no explicit reference to replacing Mussolini, and it seemed to suggest that there was life for some kind of more collegial Fascist government or at least one containing moderate Fascists. The genuine confusion over the meaning of the passing of Grandi's motion might go a little way to explaining why there was no immediate action to defend Mussolini by the Militia and Fascists. Both Mussolini and the Fascist Grand Council members were surprised by the suddenness with which the moderate Fascist conspiracy was overtaken by the plan of the king and the military. Mussolini was arrested, and Badoglio appointed head of a military government ruling by royal decree, which ordered the dissolution of all the organs of the Fascist regime, the PNF, Grand Council, Chamber of Fasces and Corporations, the Special Tribunal and the MVSN. The war would go on, but the Germans were not deceived by this formal re-affirmation of the Axis alliance, and their move into Italy and Italian-occupied Europe both before and after the September 1943 armistice was the basis of the temporary resurrection of Mussolini's political career.

Epilogue: The Italian Social Republic, 1943–5

As Mussolini had realised, the first price to pay for leaving the Axis was his own fall from power. The second – German occupation of Italy and her territory – was completed speedily in September 1943 on the news of the Italian armistice with the Allies and her official changing of sides. The leisurely maladroit way in which Badoglio's royal government had opened its contacts with the Allies after July, and the king's irresponsible flight to the Allied-occupied south effectively delivered the whole of Italy's armed forces, men and equipment, to the invading Germans.

Mussolini was sprung from his prison in September and taken to Germany to join other Fascist leaders who had survived the July coup. The Germans obviously intended to fight in Italy to defend their own country from invasion, and exploit Italy's labour and resources for the German war effort. Against the advice of many in the Nazi and military leadership, Hitler decided to set up a Mussolini government in northern Italy, which was some confirmation of the personal and ideological basis to the Axis. This would indicate that fascism was not in decline, that it could be revived under German patronage as an expression of confidence in the ultimate victory of the Axis.

The anti-Fascist and anti-Nazi Resistance movement effectively began here, with the German occupation of Italy and the installation of a new Fascist government in September 1943. It was marked by the appearance of armed bands of escaping officers and soldiers reacting to the German invasion and the disbanding of Italy's army. They were basically loyal to the monarchical government of Badoglio, which from early 1944 was given jurisdiction over those parts of the south coming under Allied military administration and control. More generally, the Resistance was also the outcome of action by the anti-Fascist parties which had been driven underground or into exile after 1926, and painfully formed or reconstituted themselves in the late 1930s and especially during the later stages of Italy's Axis war in 1942–3.

The Communists, Socialists and a new liberal-socialist group, the

Action Party, were the first to translate opposition to Fascism into armed struggle. Behind their participation in an increasingly nasty civil war within the war was the desire to determine the shape of Italy on the collapse of Fascism. A broad alliance of anti-Fascist parties constituted the Committee of National Liberation for Upper Italy (CLNAI), founded in January 1944 to co-ordinate the activities of the armed Resistance and to act as a *de facto* clandestine government in German-occupied Italy. These same parties were also represented in the Bonomi-led government which succeeded that of Badoglio in June 1944, after the Allied liberation of Rome and on the subsequent military advance by the winter to a line running across Italy from the Ligurian Riviera to Rimini on the Adriatic. The important point was that what united the Resisters, irrespective of their political complexion, was the determination to defeat Fascism and its occupying Nazi patron. The Resistance could credibly stand as an anti-Fascist and patriotic force, and contest the Fascist claim to be the true nation.

The reality of German control of Mussolini's government was inescapable and killed the *Repubblica Sociale Italiana* (Italian Social Republic or RSI) on the ground. As in the rest of occupied Europe, the Nazis exported their own competitive jungle of administration to Italy, overlaying and countermanding the Republic's ministries and offices at central and local level. All the Republic's actions and measures had to be filtered through and approved by Rudolf Rahn, German ambassador to Salò and as Reich Plenipotentiary Hitler's direct representative in Italy, and SS General Karl Wolff, responsible for police and internal security. It was no joke that Mussolini had remarked to Hitler in their first meetings after his release, 'I have come to receive my orders.'[1] German control was so palpable that the Fascists, although claiming to restore national honour by sticking to the Axis alliance reneged on by Badoglio and the king, could no longer with any real authority portray themselves as the only national and patriotic force.

Worse still, and undermining the RSI's claim to embody the nation even more than the Allied occupation of the south, was the German reversal of Italy's territorial gains of the First and Second World Wars. Without consulting Mussolini, two Italian-held provinces, Zara and Ljubljana, were handed over to Croatia and eight in the South Tyrol, Venetia and on the Adriatic were 'provisionally' annexed to Germany and placed under Gauleiter administration.

The Republic's programme was agreed at the unruly congress of the *Partito Fascista Repubblicano* (Republican Fascist Party or PFR), the reconstituted successor to the PNF, held in Verona in November 1943. It was an attempt to give a meaning and content to the Republic other than doing the Germans' business, and to win the support of the population nominally under its jurisdiction, whose loyalties were contested by the anti-Fascist and anti-German Resistance movements. It called for a constituent assembly to replace the monarchy with a social Republic, an elected head of state on the US model, a scarcely credible charter of citizens' rights, a single party for the political education of the people, socialisation of the economy, treating the Jews as enemy aliens, and a foreign policy whose talk of 'living space' and European federation was a rehash of the former regime's New Order wartime propaganda.

The abolition of the monarchy and socialisation were both a rejection of and an alibi for Fascism's past. The desire for revenge and scapegoating was brutally evident in the extraordinary Special Tribunal's trial and execution of those of the July 1943 Grand Council 'traitors' who could be found, including Ciano. It was they, in league with the king and conservative bourgeois and capitalist interests, who were charged with not only bringing about Mussolini's fall and the Allied invasion but also subverting and sidetracking the Fascist Revolution during the twenty years of the regime. Now shorn of its conservative fellow-travelling elements and liberated from the 'pluto-monarchical compromises of 1922',[2] Fascism could 'return to the origins' and enact the national syndicalist and republican strands of the revolutionary interventionism and early Fascism of 1915–19. This was myth-making in the grand style, and to justify it Salò's propaganda evoked the legacy of Giuseppe Mazzini, D'Annunzio and Fiume.

Socialisation owed as much to the 'third way' corporatist rhetoric of the 1930s and of the Fascist New Order as to national syndicalism, at least in the proposals put together by the Republic's Ministry of Corporations. The principle of private property was still sacrosanct, but the state could regulate it in the context of a national economic plan and would take over or retain the running of essential national utilities and services. What the measure approved by the government in February 1944 proposed was a kind of socialisation of management, not capital, to create that collaborative and productivist 'community of producers'. The running of state and private firms was to be shared between an elected assembly of employees and shareholders, a management council of representatives of capital and labour and an executive director elected by the assembly or chosen by the government.

But the Republic could decide on anything and enact little to nothing.

Making 'labour . . . the foundation of the Social Republic'[3] in this abortive 'return to the origins' cut across the two unavoidable realities of the Republic's tenuous existence: German control. of Italy for the exploitation of its economy, and the worsening civil war between the Fascists and the Resistance. Hitler was mystified by the RSI's social policy but thought it irrelevant and innocuous. The German authorities on the ground intervened to nullify it. Hans Leyers, the head of the Italian arm of the German Ministry of Armaments and War Production, regarded socialisation as 'sabotage'[4] of the Italian industries working for the German war effort, and co-operated with the industrialists themselves to exclude or obstruct its implementation in key areas. By April 1945 perhaps 60–80 firms with about 130 000 employees had been 'socialised', mainly newspapers and publishers under the auspices of the Ministry of Popular Culture, which took the measure seriously. The decree of February 1945 for the socialisation of large industries was a dead letter, not only because of German-inspired procrastination by employers but also because most workers boycotted the council elections. Industrial workers had experience enough of the Fascist regime not to trust in this false dawn or twilight of labour reforms. The left-wing Resistance movements certainly warned them off, as they did employers. Fascism's attempt to redefine itself could not escape the taint of its past.

What was left of the 'return to the origins' was squadrism and the tone of fanaticism it conveyed, and a partial replay of some of the most important intra-Fascist disputes of the early 1920s. The PFR Secretary Alessandro Pavolini's report to the Verona congress of an alleged membership of 250 000 was greeted by cries of 'too many' from delegates who were the old squadrists and Militiamen responsible for the spontaneous reconstitution of some *fasci* in September and October. The question as to whether the PFR should be an élite squadrist party or a mass, all-talents party was soon lost in the RSI's understandable concern to attract whom it could.

Much the same outcome marked the divergent conceptions of the formation and recruitment of the Republic's army, the emergence of which as a proper fighting force on the German side Mussolini regarded as crucial to the RSI's independence and credibility. In light of the earlier events of 1943, the Germans were reluctant to allow this and refused to release interned Italian troops *en bloc* for a new Italian army. They trained four divisions in Germany drawn from internees, volunteers and conscripts, who were repatriated in the second half of 1944. These men were the core of what Rodolfo Graziani, the RSI's military commander and

Minister of Defence, had hoped would be a national apolitical army. In this he was opposed by Ricci, the MVSN commander who wanted to take up Mussolini's initial inclination to reorganise the armed forces around the Militia, a party-army. Again, the Republic got both kinds of force, out of its need to recruit whom it could. Ricci organised an armed police force of ex-policemen and ex-Militiamen, the Republican National Guard, some of whom then moved into the Black Brigades, formed by Pavolini in summer 1944 as the party-in-arms specifically for anti-partisan operations. These regular and hybrid forces existed alongside freelance criminal bands whose savage policing and anti-Resistance activity was covered by German or Fascist political protection.

In the circumstances of war and civil war the PFR could hardly avoid being a squadrist party in leadership and function. Only men of the committed old guard and the young fanatics were prepared to come out into the open when it cost something to declare oneself a Fascist, and there was need for violent repression of the Republic's enemies among their fellow Italians. Repression, in the end, was all there could be, with continuing popular discontent at wartime controls and shortages, the Resistance being fed by men evading the Republic's own coercive measures of conscription to the armed forces and labour service in Germany, and an escalating cycle of violence and counter-violence between Fascism and Resistance worsening from mid-1944. Significantly, only once did Mussolini leave the mundane bureaucratic chores of his office at Salò, a pattern of ordinary administration showing his own sense of resigned and depressed impotence, to address a public rally. This was not only an indication of the Germans' control of his movements, but also of the futility of trying to revive a popular rapport in favour of a man and a Republic which lacked standing and authority. Moving to Milan in April 1945, Mussolini was caught between partisan insurrections in the major northern cities and the German military's attempts to arrange a surrender with the advancing Allied forces. Fleeing north with a German military detachment, he was stopped, recognised and killed by partisans on 27–8 April 1945.

Fascism was dead as a functioning independent regime from late 1942. It is futile to argue retrospectively that Fascism would have survived but for the external factor of the Second World War. It might have done, but it would not have been Fascism. War was essential not incidental to Fascism. The Fascist movement emerged as an extreme and violent political response to a perceived national crisis, consequent on the social and political strains set up by the impact and outcome of the First World

War and expressed in what appeared to be socialist revolution. It became a new mass movement of the middle classes, united in a heterogeneous anti-socialist coalition with important organised sectional interests and members of liberal Italy's political, economic and military establishment. These probably inescapable compromising alliances with the old order were built into the system of power evolving by the late 1920s, corrupting the implementation of a new socio-economic corporative order which Fascism alleged was its distinctive and innovative contribution to managing the social conflicts of modern society.

What was really new was the 'totalitarian' state, Fascism's resolution of the national crisis which Fascists rooted in the weakness, inefficiency and divisiveness of parliamentary government, and the idea of the single mass party bridging the state to the population. The regime was built around the attempt to create through totalitarian mobilisation and control a national community and solidarity among a people notoriously divided by class and locality, which would progressively transcend the old order. The overriding aim of national unity was consciously linked to and a premise for territorial expansion and empire. War was means and end, the way of subverting both the existing internal and international order, effecting both conquest and 'fascistisation'.

This was Fascism's huge gamble, because wars can be lost as well as won. The great re-educative process of making Italians, based on organisation, propaganda and control, needed time. War was meant to accelerate things, but it destroyed any basis of rapport and support the regime had achieved, however imperfect and superficial this was. The lost war ruined the illusions and livelihood of the Italian middle classes, and detached the fellow-travelling conservative interests from the regime. This loss of popular consent, active, passive or lukewarm, was irretrievable in the period of the so-called Salò Republic, because everyone knew, Fascists, non-Fascists and anti-Fascists alike, that the Axis could never win the war. Throughout its short existence the Italian Social Republic was constantly and fruitlessly attempting to establish its legitimacy, in respect of the foreign powers occupying the country and the 'other' Italys located in the monarchical south and the anti-Fascist Resistance movements. The death of the Fascist regime was confirmed in the Social Republic's lack of credibility. Without any future prospects, Mussolini and the other Fascists of Salò were more concerned with the legacy of the past and putting the record straight. The Republic was seen as a kind of memorial to a Fascism which might have been.

Notes

1. THE POSTWAR CRISIS AND THE RISE OF FASCISM, 1919–29

1. R.A. Webster, *The Cross and the Fasces. Christian Democracy and Fascism in Italy* (Stanford, Calif.: Stanford University Press, 1960) p. 56.

2. Quoted in A. Tasca (pseud. A. Rossi), *Nascita e avvento del fascismo. L'Italia dal 1918 al 1922* (Florence: La Nuova Italia, 1963) p. 10. English version is *The Rise of Italian Fascism* (London: Methuen, 1938).

3. Socialist propaganda in 1917, quoted in E. Ragionieri, *Storia d'Italia*, vol. 4:3, *La storia politica e sociale* (Turin: Einaudi, 1976) p. 2031.

4. Quoted in Ragionieri, *La storia politica e sociale*, p. 2051.

5. Article in *Il Popolo d'Italia*, 15 December 1917, in E. and D. Susmel (eds), *Opera Omnia di Benito Mussolini*, vol. 10 (Florence: La Fenice, 1952) p. 141.

6. From the text of Mussolini's speech at the inaugural Milan meeting, March 1919, in C.F. Delzell (ed.), *Mediterranean Fascism, 1919–1945* (London: Macmillan, 1971) p. 9.

7. Mussolini, speaking of the 1919 movement, as quoted in E. Gentile, *Storia del Partito Fascista 1919–1922. Movimento e Milizia* (Bari: Laterza, 1989) p. 236.

8. From Mussolini's speech, March 1919, in Delzell, *Mediterranean Fascism*, p. 10.

9. C.S. Maier, *Recasting Bourgeois Europe. Stabilization in France, Germany and Italy in the Decade after World War 1* (Princeton, NJ: Princeton University Press, 1975) p. 128.

10. Quoted in P.P. Attore, 'Gli agrari bolognesi dal liberalismo al fascismo', in L. Casali (ed.), *Bologna 1920. Le origini del fascismo* (Bologna: Cappelli, 1982) p. 138.

11. R. Vivarelli, *Il dopoguerra in Italia e l'avvento del fascismo (1918–1922)*, vol. 1, *Dalla fine della guerra all'impresa di Fiume* (Naples: Mondadori, 1967) p. 552.

12. Quoted in Tasca, *Nascita e avvento del fascismo*, p. 78.

13. Quoted in R. De Felice, *Mussolini il fascista*, vol. 1, *La conquista del potere 1921–1925*, 3rd edn (Turin: Einaudi, 1966) p. 186.

14. All quotations from the PNF 1921 programme in Delzell, *Mediterranean Fascism*, pp. 27–37.

15. Quoted in P. Corner, *Fascism in Ferrara 1915–1925* (London: Oxford University Press, 1975) p. 209.

16. From Delzell, *Mediterranean Fascism*, p. 41.

17. From ibid., p. 40.

18. A. Lyttelton, *The Seizure of Power: Fascism in Italy 1919–1929* (London: Weidenfeld and Nicolson, 1973) p. 86.

2. BETWEEN 'NORMALISATION' AND 'REVOLUTION', 1922–5

1. The phrase was coined by Farinacci in October 1925 when he was Party Secretary. Quoted in A. Aquarone, *L'organizzazione dello state totalitario* (Turin: Einaudi, 1965) p. 63.

2. Mussolini said of his political opponents that he would 'pluck them like a chicken, feather by feather'. Quoted in D. Mack-Smith, *Mussolini* (London: Weidenfeld and Nicolson, 1982) p. 66.

190 ITALIAN FASCISM, 1919-1945

3. The words of the Liberal, Amendola, quoted in A. Lyttelton, *The Seizure of Power. Fascism in Italy* (London: Weidenfeld and Nicolson, 1982) p. 126.

4. From extracts of the speech in C.F. Delzell (ed.), *Mediterranean Fascism* (London: Macmillan, 1971) pp. 45-6.

5. Quoted in A. J. De Grand, *The Italian Nationalist Association and the Rise of Fascism in Italy* (Lincoln, Nebr. and London: University of Nebraska Press, 1978) pp. 155-6.

6. Quoted in P. Melograni, *Gli industriali e Mussolini. Rapporti fra Confindustria e Fascismo dal 1919 al 1929* (Milan: Longanesi, 1972) p. 45.

3.   THE CONSTRUCTION OF THE TOTALITARIAN STATE, 1925-9

1. E. and D. Susmel (eds), *Opera Omnia di Benito Mussolini*, vol. 21 (Florence: La Fenice, 1952) p. 362.

2. Gentile's speech of 8 March 1925, in G. Gentile, *Che cosa è il fascismo? Discorsi e polemiche* (Florence: Vallechi, 1925).

3. Mussolini's speech in Milan, 28 October 1925, in *Opera Omnia*, vol. 21, p. 425.

4. Article in Farinacci's newspaper, *Regime Fascista*, 31 August 1926.

5. From text in C.F. Delzell (ed.), *Mediterranean Fascism* (London: Macmillan, 1971) p. 65.

6. The circular is reproduced in A. Aquarone, *L'organizzazione dello stato totalitario* (Turin: Einaudi, 1965) pp. 485-8.

7. Both quotations from Mussolini's speech to PNF rally, 14 September 1929, in *Opera Omnia*, vol. 24, p. 141.

8. Quoted in B. Uva, 'Gli scioperi dei metallurgici italiani del marzo 1925', *Storia Contemporanea*, 1 (1970) p. 1028.

9. Archivio Centrale dello Stato (ACS), *Mostra della Rivoluzione Fascista* (MRF), Pt. 1, busta 9, 'Rapporto del Duce ai segretari federali (febbraio 1930)', 'Venezia Euganea'.

10. G. Miccoli, 'La chiesa e il fascismo', in G. Quazza (ed.), *Fascismo e società italiana* (Turin: Einaudi, 1973) p. 191.

11. *Opera Omnia*, vol. 22, pp. 37-8.

12. Mussolini's speech in Rome to a conference of FISA, 30 July 1925, in *Opera Omnia*, vol. 21, p. 377.

13. *Opera Omnia*, vol. 22, p. 384.

14. A. Lyttelton, *The Seizure of Power. Fascism in Italy* (London: Weidenfeld and Nicolson, 1982) p. 352.

4.   THE YEARS OF THE GREAT DEPRESSION, 1929-34

1. Mussolini's speech at Naples, 25 October 1931, in E. and D. Susmel (eds), *Opera Omnia di Benito Mussolini*, vol. 25 (Florence: La Fenice, 1952) p. 50.

2. Mussolini's speech to the Senate, 25 May 1929, in *Opera Omnia*, vol. 24, p. 101.

3. Quoted in A. Aquarone, *L'organizzazione dello stato totalitario* (Turin: Einaudi, 1965) p. 267.

4. As quoted in P. Morgan, 'Italian Fascist Social Welfare Policy, 1927-37', *Tuttitalia*, 4 (1991) p. 5.

5. ACS, *MRF*, Pt. 1, busta 9, 'Rapporto del Duce', 'Liguria'.

6. Taken from the text in P. Scoppola, *La Chiesa e il fascismo. Documenti e interpretazioni* (Bari: Laterza, 1971) p. 269.

7. From the text of the agreement in Scoppola, *La Chiesa e il fascismo*, p. 280.

8. Scorza's report to Mussolini, 11 July 1931, in ACS, *Segretaria particolare del Duce, carteggio riservato (1922–43)*, fascicolo 242/R, 'Direttorio del PNF', sottofascicolo 2, inserto A.

9. From text in C.F. Delzell, (ed.) *Mediterranean Fascism* (London: Macmillan, 1971) p. 127.

10. G. Salvemini, *Under the Axe of Fascism* (London: Gollancz, 1936) p. 114.

5. THE CREATION OF THE FASCIST EMPIRE, 1935-6

1. Mussolini's speech in Milan, 28 October 1925, in E. and D. Susmel (eds), *Opera Omnia di Benito Mussolini*, vol. 21 (Florence: La Fenice, 1952) pp. 423, 426.

2. Quoted in B. Vigezzi, *Politica estera e opinione pubblica in Italia dall'Unita ai giorni nostri. Orientamenti degli studi e prospettive della ricerca* (Milan: Jaca, 1991) p. 111.

3. Quoted in G. Candeloro, *Storia dell'Italia moderna*, vol. 9, *Il fascismo e le sue guerre* (Milan: Feltrinelli, 1981) p. 342.

4. Mussolini's speech in Rome, 9 May 1936, in *Opera Omnia*, vol. 27, p. 268.

5. Quoted in Candeloro, *Storia dell'Italia moderna*, vol. 9, p. 343.

6. THE AXIS CONNECTION AND THE 'FASCISTISATION' OF ITALIAN SOCIETY, 1936-40

1. From text in C.F. Delzell (ed.), *Mediterranean Fascism* (London: Macmillan, 1971) p. 201.

2. From the speech reproduced in R. De Felice, *Mussolini il Duce*, vol. 2, *Lo stato totalitario 1936–1940* (Turin: Einaudi, 1981) pp. 321–5.

3. Mussolini's speech to a rally of squadrists, 26 March 1939, in E. and D. Susmel (eds), *Opera Omnia di Benito Mussolini* (Florence: La Fenice, 1952) p. 251.

4. From text in De Felice, *Lo stato totalitario*, pp. 918–19.

5. Entry of 7 September 1939 in G.B. Guerri (ed.), *Giuseppe Bottai, Diario 1935–1944* (Milan: Rizzoli, 1982) p. 164.

6. From text of Charter in Delzell, *Mediterranean Fascism*, p. 149.

7. Reported in M. Gallo, *Mussolini's Italy. Twenty Years of the Fascist Era* (London: Abelard-Schuman, 1974) p. 281.

8. Entry of 10 July 1938, in R. De Felice (ed.), *G. Ciano. Diario 1937–1943* (Milan: Rizzoli, 1980) p. 156.

9. Mussolini's speech to the National Assembly of Corporations, 23 March 1936, in *Opera Omnia*, vol. 27, p. 244.

10. M. Donosti, *Mussolini e l'Europa. La politica estera fascista* (Rome: Leonardo, 1945) p. 166.

11. Mussolini's remarks to Ciano, entry of 29 January 1940, in *Diario*, p. 391.

12. From Mussolini's secret report to the king, quoted in B. Vigezzi, *Politica estera e opinione pubblica in Italia dall'Unita ai giorni nostri* (Milan: Jaca, 1991) p. 107.

7. FASCIST ITALY AT WAR, 1939-40

1. Mussolini's speech to the PNF Directorate, 26 May 1942, in E. and D. Susmel (eds), *Opera Omnia di Benito Mussolini*, vol. 31 (Florence: La Fenice, 1952) p. 73.

2. G.B. Guerri (ed.), *Rapporto al Duce: Il testo stenografico inedito dei colloqui tra i federali e Mussolini nel 1942* (Milan: Bompiani, 1978) p. 371.

EPILOGUE   THE ITALIAN SOCIAL REPUBLIC, 1943–5

1. Quoted in G. Bocca, *La repubblica di Mussolini*, 3rd edn (Bari: Laterza, 1977) p. 23.

2. Letter to Mussolini, 11 October 1943, from the ex-socialist and communist leader, Bombacci, who rallied to the regime in the 1930s and then to Salò, quoted in S. Setta, 'Potere economico e Repubblica Sociale Italiana', *Storia Contemporanea*, 8 (1977) p. 260.

3. From the text of the Verona Manifesto of November 1943 in R. De Felice (ed.), *Autobiografia del Fascismo. Antologia di testi fascisti 1919–1945* (Bergamo: Minerva Italica, 1978) p. 583.

4. Quoted in Bocca, *La repubblica di Mussolini*, p. 178.

Select Bibliography

The number of books and articles written on Fascism is endless. This book adds to the pile. Any bibliography is therefore necessarily selective, even idiosyncratic. This one broadly follows the structure of the book. Works are listed once under the period where they are most useful, but many of them are also relevant to the other periods. Good bibliographies can be found in G. Quazza *et al.*, *Storiografia e fascismo* (Milan: Franco Angeli, 1985) and in G. Candeloro, *Storia dell'Italia moderna*, vols 8–10 (Milan: Feltrinelli, 1978–84).

1. DOCUMENT COLLECTIONS AND COMMENTARIES

R. DE FELICE (ed.), *Autobiografia del fascismo: Antologia di testi fascisti 1919–1945* (Bergamo: Minerva Italica, 1978).

C.F. DELZELL (ed.), *Mediterranean Fascism 1919–1945* (London: Macmillan, 1971).

G.B. GUERRI (ed.), *Rapporto al Duce: Il testo stenografico inedito dei colloqui tra i federali e Mussolini nel 1942* (Milan: Bompiani, 1978).

A. LYTTELTON (ed.), *Italian Fascisms from Pareto to Gentile* (London: Cape, 1973).

P. SCOPPOLA (ed.), *La chiesa e il fascismo: Documenti e interpretazioni* (Bari: Laterza, 1971).

E. and D. SUSMEL (eds), *Opera Omnia di Benito Mussolini*, 36 vols (Florence: La Fenice, 1951–63).

2. BIOGRAPHIES AND MEMOIRS

G. BOTTAI, *Vent'anni e un giorno* (Milan: Garzanti, 1977).

F. CORDOVA (ed.), *Uomini e volti del fascismo* (Rome: Bulzoni, 1980).

R. DE FELICE (ed.), *G. Ciano. Diario 1937–1943* (Milan: Rizzoli, 1980).

G.B. GUERRI (ed.), *Giuseppe Bottai, Diario 1935–1944* (Milan: Rizzoli, 1982).

D. MACK-SMITH, *Mussolini* (London: Weidenfeld and Nicolson, 1982).

C.G. SEGRÈ, *Italo Balbo. A Fascist Life* (Berkeley, Calif.: University of California, 1987).

3. GENERAL WORKS

M. BLINKHORN, *Mussolini and Fascist Italy* (London: Methuen, 1984).

M. BLINKHORN (ed.), *Fascists and Conservatives: The Radical Right and the Establishment in 20th Century Europe* (London: Unwin Hyman, 1990).

R.J.B. BOSWORTH and S. ROMANO (eds), *La politica estera italiana 1860–1985* (Bologna: Il Mulino, 1991).

G. CANDELORO, *Il movimento cattolico in Italia*, 3rd edn (Rome: Editori Riuniti, 1974).

G. CANDELORO, *Storia dell'Italia moderna*, vols 8–10 (Milan: Feltrinelli, 1978, 1981 and 1984).

P.V. CANNISTRARO (ed.), *Historical Dictionary of Fascist Italy* (Westport and London: Greenwood Press, 1982).

G. CAROCCI, *Italian Fascism* (Harmondsworth: Pelican, 1975).

V. CASTRONOVO, *Storia d'Italia*, vol. 4:1, *La storia economica* (Turin: Einaudi, 1973).

M. CLARK, *Modern Italy 1871–1982* (London: Longman, 1984).

A.J. DE GRAND, *Italian Fascism: Its Origins and Development* (Lincoln, Nebr. and London: University of Nebraska Press, 1982).

C.J. LOWE and F. MARZARI, *Italian Foreign Policy 1870–1940* (London and Boston, Mass.: Routledge Kegan, 1975).

D. MACK-SMITH, *Italy and its Monarchy* (New Haven, Conn. and London: Yale University Press, 1989).

G. QUAZZA, *Resistenza e storia d'Italia* (Milan: Feltrinelli, 1976).

E. RAGIONIERI, *Storia d'Italia*, vol. 4:3, *La storia politica e sociale* (Turin: Einaudi, 1976).

L. SALVATORELLI and G. MIRA, *Storia d'Italia nel periodo fascista* (Turin: Einaudi, 1971).

E. SANTARELLI, *Storia del movimento e del regime fascista*, 2 vols (Rome: Editori Riuniti, 1967).

R. SARTI, *Fascism and the Industrial Leadership in Italy 1919–1940* (Los Angeles and London: University of California, Berkeley, Press, 1971).

L. SCHAPIRO, *Totalitarianism* (London: Macmillan, 1972).

C. SETON-WATSON, *Italy from Liberalism to Fascism 1870–1925* (London: Methuen, 1967).

Storia della società italiana, vols 21–2 (Milan: Teti, 1982–3).

A. TAMARO, *Venti anni di storia*, 3 vols (Rome: Volpe, 1971–5).

E.R. TANNENBAUM, *Fascism in Italy. Society and Culture 1922–45* (London: Allen Lane, 1973).

G. TONIOLO, *L'economia dell'Italia fascista* (Bari: Laterza, 1980).

G. TONIOLO (ed.), *L'economia italiana 1861–1940* (Bari: Laterza, 1973).

B. VIGEZZI, *Politica estera e opinione pubblica in Italia dall'Unità ai giorni nostri* (Milan: Jaca, 1991).

R.A. WEBSTER, *The Cross and the Fasces: Christian Democracy and Fascism in Italy* (Stanford, Calif.: Stanford University University Press, 1960).

E. GENTILE, 'The Problem of the Party in Italian Fascism', *Journal of Contemporary History*, 19 (1984).

E. GENTILE, 'Fascism in Italian Historiography: in Search of an Historical Identity', *Journal of Contemporary History*, 21 (1986).

MACGREGOR KNOX, 'Conquest, Foreign and Domestic, in Fascist Italy and Nazi Germany', *Journal of Modern History*, 56 (1984).

4. THE CONQUEST OF POWER, 1919–29

A. AQUARONE, *L'organizzazione dello stato totalitario* (Turin: Einaudi, 1965).

M. BERNABEI, *Fascismo e nazionalismo in Campania 1919–1925* (Rome: Edizioni di Storia e Letteratura, 1975).

A.L. CARDOZA, *Agrarian Elites and Italian Fascism. The Province of Bologna 1901–1926* (Princeton, NJ: Princeton University Press, 1982).

L. CASALI (ed.), *Bologna 1920. Le origini del fascismo* (Bologna: Cappelli, 1982).

S. COLARIZI, *Dopoguerra e fascismo in Puglia 1919–1926* (Bari: Laterza, 1971).

F. CORDOVA, *Le origini dei sindacati fascisti 1918–1926* (Bari: Laterza, 1974).

P. CORNER, *Fascism in Ferrara 1915–1925* (London: Oxford University Press, 1975).

R. DE FELICE, *Mussolini il rivoluzionario 1883–1920*, 3rd edn (Turin: Einaudi, 1965); *Mussolini il fascista*, 1: *La conquista del potere 1921–1925*, 2: *L'organizzazione dello stato fascista 1925–1929* (Turin: Einaudi, 1966 and 1968).

A.J. DE GRAND, *The Italian Nationalist Association and the Rise of Fascism in Italy* (Lincoln, Nebr. and London: University of Nebraska Press, 1978).

F.J. DEMERS, *Le origini del fascismo a Cremona* (Bari: Laterza, 1979).

G. DE ROSA, *Il Partito Popolare Italiano*, 3rd edn (Bari: Laterza, 1974).

C. DUGGAN, *Fascism and the Mafia* (New Haven, Conn.: Yale University Press, 1989).

E. GENTILE, *Le origini dell'ideologia fascista 1918–1925* (Bari: Laterza, 1975).

E. GENTILE, *Storia del Partito Fascista 1919–1922: Movimento e Milizia* (Bari: Laterza, 1989).

A. KELIKIAN, *Town and Country under Fascism: The Transformation of Brescia 1915–1926* (Oxford: Oxford University Press, 1986).

P. LAVEGLIA (ed.), *Mezzogiorno e fascismo: atti del convegno nazionale di studi promosso dalla regione Campania, 1975* (Naples: Edizioni Scientifiche Italiane, 1978).

A. LYTTELTON, 'Fascism and Violence in Postwar Italy: Political Strategy and Social Conflict', in W.J. MOMMSEN and G. HIRSCHFELD (eds), *Social Protest, Violence and Terror in 19th and 20th Century Europe* (London: Macmillan, 1982).

A. LYTTELTON, *The Seizure of Power. Fascism in Italy 1919–1929* (London: Weidenfeld and Nicolson, 1973).

C.S. MAIER, *Recasting Bourgeois Europe. Stabilization in France, Germany and Italy in the Decade after World War I* (Princeton, NJ: Princeton University Press, 1975).

P. MELOGRANI, *Gli industriali e Mussolini: Rapporti fra Confindustria e fascismo dal 1919 al 1929* (Milan: Longanesi, 1972).

F. PIVA, *Lotte contadine e origini del fascismo. Padova–Venezia: 1919–1922* (Venice: Marsilio, 1977).

G. SABBATUCCI, *I combattenti nel primo dopoguerra* (Bari: Laterza, 1974).

G. SABBATUCCI (ed.), *La crisi italiana del primo dopoguerra. La storia e la critica* (Bari: Laterza, 1976).

G. SALVEMINI, *Under the Axe of Fascism* (London: Gollancz, 1936).

F.M. SNOWDEN, *The Fascist Revolution in Tuscany 1919–1922* (Cambridge: Cambridge University Press, 1989).

F.M. SNOWDEN, *Violence and the Great Estates in the South of Italy: Apulia 1900–1922* (Cambridge: Cambridge University Press, 1986).

D.D. ROBERTS, *The Syndicalist Tradition and Italian Fascism* (Manchester: Manchester University Press, 1979).

A. TASCA (pseud. A. ROSSI), *Nascita e avvento del fascismo. L'Italia dal 1918 al 1922* (Florence: La Nuova Italia, 1963). English version, *The Rise of Italian Fascism 1918–1922* (London: Methuen, 1938).

N. TRANFAGLIA, *Dallo stato liberale al regime fascista. Problemi e ricerche* (Milan: Feltrinelli, 1973).

P. UNGARI, *Alfredo Rocco e l'ideologia giuridica del fascismo* (Brescia: Morcelliana, 1963).

R. VIVARELLI, *Il dopoguerra in Italia e l'avvento del fascismo 1918–1922*, vol. 1, *Dalla fine della guerra all'impresa di Fiume* (Naples: Mondadori, 1967).

R. VIVARELLI, *Il fallimento del liberalismo. Studi sulle origini del fascismo* (Bologna: Il Mulino, 1981).

J. PETERSON, 'Elettorato e base sociale del fascismo negli anni venti', *Studi Storici*, 16 (1975).

L. RAPONE, 'Il sindacalismo fascista: temi e problemi della ricerca storica', *Storia Contemporanea*, 4–5 (1982).

G. RUMI, 'Mussolini e il "programma" di San Sepolcro', *Movimento di Liberazione in Italia*, 71 (1963).

G. SAPELLI, 'Per la storia del sindacalismo fascista: tra controllo sociale e conflitto di classe', *Studi storici*, 19 (1978).

F.M. SNOWDEN, 'On the Social Origins of Agrarian Fascism in Italy', *Archives Européenes de Sociologie*, 13 (1972).

B. UVA, 'Gli scioperi dei metallurgici italiani del marzo 1925', *Storia Contemporanea*, 1 (1970).

5. THE FASCIST REGIME, 1929–36

A. AQUARONE and M. VERNASSA (eds), *Il regime fascista* (Bologna: Il Mulino, 1974).

G. CAROCCI, *La politica estera dell'Italia Fascista 1925–1928* (Bari: Laterza, 1969).

A. CASSELS, *Mussolini's Early Diplomacy* (Princeton, NJ: Princeton University Press, 1970).

S. CASSESE, *La formazione dell stato amministrativo* (Milan: Giuffré, 1974).

A. CENTO BULL, *Capitalismo e fascismo di fronte alla crisi: industria e società bergamasca, 1923–1937* (Bergamo: Il Filo di Aranna, 1983).

R. DE FELICE, *Mussolini il Duce*, 1: *Gli anni del consenso 1929–1936* (Turin: Einaudi, 1974).

A.J. DE GRAND, *Bottai e la cultura fascista* (Bari: Laterza, 1978).

V. DE GRAZIA, *The Culture of Consent: Mass Organization of Leisure in Fascist Italy* (Cambridge: Cambridge University Press, 1981).

G. GERMANI, 'The Political Socialization of Youth in Fascist Regimes', in S.P. HUNTINGTON and C.H. MOORE (eds), *Authoritarian Politics in Modern Society: The Dynamics of Established One-Party Systems* (New York: Basic Books, 1970).

T.H. KOON, *Believe, Obey, Fight. Political Socialization of Youth in Fascist Italy 1922–1943* (Chapel Hill, NC and London: University of North Carolina Press, 1985).

M.A. LEDEEN, *Universal Fascism. The Theory and Practice of the Fascist International 1928–36* (New York: Howard Fertig, 1972).

G. NENCI (ed.), *Politica e società in Italia dal Fascismo alla Resistenza: Problemi di storia nazionale e storia Umbra* (Bologna: Il Mulino, 1978).

M. PALLA, *Firenze nel regime fascista 1929–1934* (Florence: Olschki, 1978).

J. PETERSON, *Hitler e Mussolini: La difficile alleanza* (Bari: Laterza, 1975).

J.F. POLLARD, *The Vatican and Italian Fascism 1929–32: A Study in Conflict* (Cambridge, Cambridge University Press, 1985).

D. PRETI, *Economia e istituzioni nello stato fascista* (Rome: Editori Riuniti, 1980).

G. QUAZZA (ed.), *Fascismo e società italiana* (Turin: Einaudi, 1973).

G. QUAZZA et al., *Storiografia e fascismo* (Milan: Franco Angeli, 1985).

L. ROSENSTOCK-FRANCK, *L'économie corporative fasciste en doctrine et en fait. Ses origines historiques et son évolution* (Paris, 1934).

G. RUMI, *Alle origini della politica estera fascista 1918–1923* (Bari: Laterza, 1968).

G. SAPELLI (ed.), 'La classe operaia durante il fascismo', in *Annali della Fondazione G. Feltrinelli*, 20 (1979–80).

R. SARTI (ed.), *The Axe Within: Italian Fascism in Action* (New York: New Viewpoints, 1974).

D. THOMPSON, *State Control in Fascist Italy. Culture and Conformity 1925–1943* (Manchester: Manchester University Press, 1991).

P. TOGLIATTI, *Lezioni sul fascismo* (Rome: Editori Riuniti, 1976).

La Toscana nel regime fascista 1922–1939, 2 vols (Florence: Olschki, 1974).

N. TRANFAGLIA (ed.), *Fascismo e capitalismo* (Milan: Feltrinelli, 1976).

C. VALLAURI, *Le radici del corporativismo* (Rome: Bulzoni, 1971).

A. AQUARONE, 'Italy: the Crisis and the Corporative Economy', *Journal of Contemporary History*, 4 (1969).

A. AQUARONE, 'Violenza e consenso nel fascismo italiano', *Storia Contemporanea*, 10 (1979).

E. GENTILE, 'Fascism as Political Religion', *Journal of Contemporary History*, 25 (1990).

S. ROGARI, 'Azione Cattolica e fascismo', 1: 'Come la chiesa si difese da Mussolini', *Nuova Antologia*, 533 (1978).

6.   FASCIST EXPANSIONISM, 1936–1943

P.V. CANNISTRARO, *La fabbrica del consenso. Fascismo e mass media* (Bari: Laterza, 1975).

F. CATALANO, *L'economia italiana di guerra 1935–1943. La politica economica-finanziaria del fascismo dalla guerra di Etiopia alla caduta del regime* (Milan: INSMLI, 1969).

R. DE FELICE, *Mussolini il Duce*, 2: *Lo stato totalitario 1936–1940*; *Mussolini l'alleato 1940–1945*, 1: *L'Italia in guerra 1940–1943*, 2 vols (Turin: Einaudi, 1981 and 1990).

R. DE FELICE (ed.), *L'Italia fra tedeschi e alleati. La politica estera fascista e la seconda guerra mondiale* (Bologna: Il Mulino, 1973).

E. DI NOLFO, R.H. RAINERO and B. VIGEZZI (eds), *L'Italia e la politica di potenza in Europa 1938–1940* (Milan: Marzorati, 1986).

MACGREGOR KNOX, *Mussolini Unleashed 1939–1941. Politics and Strategy in Fascist Italy's Last War* (Cambridge: Cambridge University Press, 1982).

G. MAIONE, *L'imperialismo straccione. Classi sociali e finanza di guerra dall'impresa etiopica al conflitto mondiale 1935–1943* (Bologna: Il Mulino, 1979).

T.M. MAZZATOSTA, *Il regime fascista tra educazione e propaganda 1935–1943* (Bologna: Cappelli, 1978).

M. MICHAELIS, *Mussolini and the Jews. German–Italian Relations and the Jewish Question in Italy 1922–1945* (Oxford: Clarendon Press, 1978).

P. MORGAN, 'The Italian Fascist New Order in Europe', in M.L. SMITH and P.M.R. STIRK (eds), *Making the New Europe. European Unity and the Second World War* (London: Pinter, 1990).

Operai e contadini nella crisi italiana del 1943–1944 (Milan: Feltrinelli, 1974).

L. ROSENSTOCK-FRANCK, *Les étapes de l'économie fasciste italienne. Du corporatisme à l'économie de guerre* (Paris, 1939).

P.V. CANNISTRARO and E.D. WYNOT, 'On the Dynamics of Anti-Communism as a Function of Fascist Foreign Policy', *Il Politico*, 4 (1973).

A.J. DE GRAND, 'Cracks in the Facade: The Failure of Fascist Totalitarianism in Italy 1935–9' *European History Quarterly*, 21 (1991).

M. LEDEEN, 'The Evolution of Italian Fascist Anti-Semitism', *Jewish Social Studies*, 37 (1975).

A. LYTTELTON, J. PETERSON and G. SANTOMASSIMO, 'Il Mussolini di Renzo De Felice', *Passato e Presente*, 1 (1982).

S. ROGARI, 'Azione Cattolica e fascismo', 2: 'La crisi del 1938 e il distacco dal regime', *Nuova Antologia*, 534 (1978).

S. ROGARI, 'L'opinione pubblica in Toscana di fronte alla guerra 1939–1943', *Nuova Antologia*, 557 (1987).

D.C. WATT, 'The Rome–Berlin Axis. Myth and Reality', *Review of Politics*, 22 (1960).

7.   THE ITALIAN SOCIAL REPUBLIC, 1943–5

G. BOCCA, *La Repubblica di Mussolini* (Bari: Laterza, 1977).

F.W. DEAKIN, *The Brutal Friendship: Mussolini, Hitler and the Fall of Mussolini* (London: Weidenfeld and Nicolson, 1962).

S. SETTA, 'Potere economico e Repubblica Sociale Italiana', *Storia Contemporanea*, 8 (1977).

Index

Abruzzi, 16
Acerbo electoral law (1923), 65–6, 69, 71, 73
Action party, 183
Adriatic sea, 131, 132, 133, 184
Africa, empire in, 131, 132, 136, 137, 140, 142, 147, 148, 166, 167, 168, 175; *see also* empire and imperialism; Ethiopia, Mediterranean
Agnelli, Giovanni, 39, 76
'agrarian Fascism', 36, 39, 44, 45; *see also* Fascist movement; Fascist party
agricultural employers, 36, 38–9, 53; *see also* landowners
agriculture, Fascist policy in:
1919–22, 37–8, 68
1925–40, 101–4, 116
Second World War, 177–8
(see also *ammassi*, 'battle for grain', *bonifica integrale*, 'ruralism'
Albania, 133, 134, 168, 169, 174
Alliance of Labour (1922), 55
Allies
in First World War, 22, 28, 29, 131, 133
in Second World War, 157, 174, 175, 177, 178, 180, 183, 184, 185; *see also* Britain, France, United States of America
Amendola, Giovanni, 73, 74, 75, 78
ammassi, agricultural stockpiles, 178, 179
Ancient Rome, myth of, 112
Anarchists and anarchism, 23, 34, 55
Ancona, 23, 55
Ansaldo (steel firm), 22, 39

Anschluss, union of Austria with Germany, 140, 147, 148, 149, 160
anti-bourgeois campaign (1938–9), 154, 156, 158–62, 170
anti-Fascism, 75–6, 81, 120, 122, 161, 171, 178, 182, 183; *see also* Resistance
anti-semitism, 160–3, 175, 185; *see also* race and racism; Race Manifesto
anti-urbanisation, 102; *see also* demographic policies, 'ruralism'
Apulia, 23, 24, 25, 38, 55
Arditi ('Daring Ones'), 14, 15, 30
Arditi del Popoplo (anti-Fascist squads) (1921), 52
armistice (1943), 182
army and armed forces, 29, 34, 41, 57, 58, 65, 77, 94, 95, 97, 124, 140, 157, 158, 167, 176, 181, 182, 183, 186–7
Arpinati, Leandro, 35
Ascension Day, Mussolini's speech on (1927), 101–2
Associazione Nazionale dei Combattenti (ANC), National Servicemens Association, 15
Association of Social Defence (Bologna, 1920), 35
Austria (after 1919), 134, 135, 140, 148, 151; *see also Anschluss*
Austria-Hungary, 7, 8, 132, 133
autarky, 101, 128, 130, 165–8, 170, 177; *see also* economic policy
Avanti! (Socialist party newspaper), 8
Avellino, 73
'Aventine Secession' (1924–6), 75–6
Axis, Rome–Berlin, 147, 149, 150,

151, 152, 153, 154, 157, 158, 160, 161, 162, 165, 166, 167, 168, 169, 170, 171, 173, 174, 175, 177, 178, 180, 181, 182, 183, 184, 188

Badoglio, Pietro, 176, 181, 182, 183, 184
Balbo, Italo, 38, 44, 46, 52, 57, 157
Balilla, see *Opera Nazionale Balilla*
Balkans, 132, 133, 134, 135, 136, 139, 148, 169, 174, 175; *see also* Danubia, empire and imperialism
banking and banks, 82, 128–9
Bank of Italy, 129
Bari, 25, 35, 55
Baroncini, Gino, 44
Basilicata, 72, 73
'battle for grain', 98–9, 101, 103, 121; *see also* agriculture, 'ruralism'
'battle for the lira', *see* revaluation of the lira
Belgium, 135
Benedict XV, Pope (1914–22), 18
Beneduce, Alberto, 128
Benevento, 73
Bergson, Henri, 8
Bianchi, Michele, 15, 57
biennio rosso, 'Red Two Years' (1919–20), 21–8, 30, 31, 32, 33, 34, 35, 36, 42, 47, 53, 63, 76
Black Brigades, 187
Bocchini, Arturo, 86
Bologna, 15, 25, 26, 27, 34, 35, 37, 38, 44, 45, 53, 109
Bolzano, 53
bonifica integrale, comprehensive land reclamation, 102, 103; *see also* agriculture, 'ruralism'
Bonomi, Ivanoe, 43, 52, 53, 54, 184
Bottai, Giuseppe, 62, 90, 91, 123, 124, 125, 127, 154, 156, 181
braccianti, agricultural day-labourers, 24, 25, 36, 37, 38, 46, 52, 103
Brescia, 25, 26, 35, 45, 66, 84, 88
Britain, 7, 28, 98, 99, 131, 132, 133, 134, 135, 136, 138, 140, 142,

147, 148, 149, 150, 151, 152, 154, 160, 169, 171, 174; *see also* Allies

Calabria, 23
Caltanissetta, 85
Campania, 23, 71, 72
Caporetto, battle of (1917), 9, 10, 11
carabinieri, 111; *see also* police
Carrara, 39, 95
Catholic Action, 18, 89, 95, 96, 119–20, 121, 122, 164
catholics and catholic movement
    before and during First World War, 4–6, 7
    1919–22, 18, 19, 24, 25, 36, 54, 56
    1922–5, 62, 66, 82
    from 1925, 96, 109, 119, 162
    see also Catholic Action; *Confederazione Italiana del Lavoro*; church, catholic; 'clerico-moderate'; Vatican
catholic university, Milan, 122
Cavallero, Ugo, 176
Central Corporative Committee, 125–6; *see also* corporations and corporatism
Chamber of Deputies
    1870–1922, 7, 17
    1922–39, 66, 69, 75, 92, 150, 156, 157; *see also* parliament
Chamber of Fasces and Corporations, 156, 157, 182
Chambers of Labour, 67
Charter of Carnaro (1920), 29
Charter of Labour (1927), 90
church, catholic, 19, 20
    relations with liberal states, 4
    relations with Fascist state, 93, 95–7, 109–10, 120–2, 143, 163–5, 170, 181; *see also* Catholic Action, catholics and catholic movement, Vatican
Ciano, Galeazzo, 143, 148, 151, 154, 157, 158, 162, 169, 170, 181, 185
cinema, 115–16
civil service, 82

'clerico-moderate' 19, 20, 70
Colonies, Ministry of, 140
combattentismo, 'combatantism', 10, 12
*Comitato di Liberazione Nazionale per Alta
    Italia* (CLNAI), Committee of
    National Liberation of Northern
    Italy, 184
Commission for Autarky, 168
Communist party (France) (PCF), 152
Communist party (Italy), 27, 40, 55,
    74, 75, 76, 88, 122, 184
Conciliation, with catholic church
    (1929), *see* church, catholic
Concordat(s), 70
    1929, 96; *see also* church, catholic
Confederazione dell'Agricoltura
    (CONFAG), Confederation of
    Agriculture, 68
Confederazione dell'Industria Italiana
    (Confindustria), Italian
    Industrialists Confederation, 31,
    63, 68, 76–7, 88, 89, 90, 92, 93,
    97, 127, 142, 170, 181; *see also*
    industrialists and industry
Confederazione Generale del Lavoro (CGL),
    Socialist trade union
    confederation, 28, 31, 32, 69, 70,
    88, 89; *see also* Socialist party and
    socialist movement
Confederazione Italiana del Lavoro (CIL),
    catholic trade union
    confederation, 24, 89, 95, 96
*Confindustria, see Confederazione
    dell'Industria Italiana*
confino, internal exile, 122
Contarini, Salvatore, 133
Corfu, 133, 135, 137
Corgini, Ottavio, 63
Corporations, Ministry of, 90, 91, 100,
    124, 126, 127
    National Council of, 125–6
corporations and corporatism, 11–12,
    13, 34, 45, 48, 62, 67, 68, 89–90,
    91, 112, 120, 121, 125–30, 138,
    138, 141, 142, 156, 174, 182,
    185–6, 188; *see also* syndicalism
    and syndicates, Fascist

Corsica, 150
Council of Ministers (cabinet), 64, 65,
    76, 92, 156, 163
    Press Office of, 115
Cremona, 15, 25, 44, 45, 53, 54, 61,
    81
Critica Fascista, Bottai's Fascist journal,
    123
Croatia, 134, 175, 184
Cucco, Alfredo, 73, 85
Czechoslovakia, 132, 134, 151, 154,
    169

Dalmatia, 175
D'Annunzio, Gabriele, 14, 29, 30, 45,
    46, 131, 185
Danubia, 132, 133, 135, 174; *see also*
    Balkans
De Bono, Emilio, 77, 140, 157
demographic policies, 101–2, 114,
    121, 128, 138, 160, 162; *see also*
    'ruralism'
Depression, of 1930s, 91, 101, 107,
    108, 112, 122, 125, 127–9, 136,
    138–9, 141, 165, 179
De Vecchi, Cesare Maria, 157
diciannovismo, '1919-ism', 6, 10, 13, 15,
    16, 23, 30, 34
Dollfuss, Englebert, 140, 148
Dopolavoro, see Opera Nazionale Dopolavoro
Duce, 85, 94, 111, 123, 125; *see also*
    Mussolini, Benito

'Easter Accords' (1938), 149; *see also*
    foreign policy
economic policy, 48, 91, 97, 99–101,
    102–3, 166
    in agriculture, 98–9, 167
    in industry, 99, 167, 168
    in Depression, 127–30, 165
    in Second World War, 177–78; *see
    also* autarky, 'battle for grain',
    revaluation of the lira
Economy, Ministry of National, 114
education, *see* schools
Education, Ministry of National, 110,
    155, 156

Egypt, 135
elections, local (1920), 26, 34, 35
elections, parliamentary
  1913, 16
  1919, 3, 16, 21, 54
  1921, 16, 18, 32, 40, 41, 43
  1924, 71, 73, 74, 75
  1929, 97
  1934, 97; *see also* Acerbo electoral
    law, proportional
    representation
Emilia, 24, 27, 35, 37, 42, 44, 73, 78,
  81
empire and imperialism, 101, 102,
  104, 112, 130, 131, 140–4, 159,
  162, 177, 188; *see also* Adriatic sea,
  Africa, Balkans, Danubia,
  Ethiopia, foreign policy:
  Mediterranean
Ente Opere Assistenziali (EOA), Fascist
  party welfare organisation,
  112–14, 123
Ente Radio Rurale (ERR), Rural Radio
  Agency, 116
'equidistance', *see* foreign policy
Eritrea, 161, 175
Ethiopia, 140, 162, 175
  conquest of (1935–6), 121, 129, 136,
    138, 140–4, 147, 150, 152,
    155, 162, 168; *see also* Africa,
    empire and imperialism
'exceptional laws' (1925–6), 83
Exchange and Currency, Ministry of,
  166, 168

Facta, Luigi, 53, 54, 58
factories, occupation of the (1920),
  31–3, 34, 40
Farinacci, Roberto, 44, 53, 54, 61, 81,
  82, 84, 85, 88
fasci di azione rivoluzionaria,
  'revolutionary action groups'
  (1914–15), 8, 15
fasci di combattimento, 'combat groups', 6,
  13, 14, 29–30, 34, 35–9, 40, 48;
  see also Fascist movement and
  Fascist party

Fascist movement (1919–21), 13, 14,
  15, 30, 34
Fascist party, *Partito Nazionale Fascista*
  (PNF) (1921–43)
  1921–2, 15, 43–4, 45, 46–50, 51,
    52–3, 55–6, 57
  1922–6, 60, 61, 62, 63, 64, 65, 67,
    69, 71, 72, 73, 74, 75, 76, 77,
    78, 79, 80, 81, 82, 84
  1926–40, 85–6, 87, 88, 90, 93, 94,
    97, 99–101, 107, 108–9,
    110–16, 118–19, 120, 122,
    123, 124, 126, 128, 137, 138,
    154, 155–6, 158, 163, 164, 188
  1940–3, 179–80, 182, 185
Fascist regime, Chapters 3–6
Federazione Italiana Operai Metallurgici
  (FIOM), metalworkers trade
  union, 28, 31, 88
Federazione Italiana Sindacati Agricoltori
  (FISA), Fascist union of farmers,
  67, 68
Federterra, socialist agricultural union,
  24, 25, 26, 27, 36, 37
Federzoni, Luigi, 77, 82
Ferrara, 25, 35, 36, 37, 38, 44, 52, 73
Fiat, car firm, 22, 76, 167
fiduciari di fabbrica, Fascist factory
  agents, 88, 92, 159; *see also*
  syndicalism and syndicates,
  Fascist
Finance, Ministry of, 128
Finsider, steel combine, 167, 168
Finzi, Aldo, 77
First World War
  Italian entry into, 7, 133
  internal developments during, 9–10
  consequences of, 188
Fiume, 14, 28, 29, 30, 45, 131, 185
Fiume legionaries, 50
Florence, 15, 50, 63, 83, 84, 109
Foggia, 25
Foreign Affairs
  Minister of, 139, 148
  Ministry of, 124, 132, 133
foreign policy
  liberal, 132–3, 136

foreign policy (*Cont.*)
 Fascist, 130, 131–6, 138–40, 142,
  144, 147–54, 165–6, 169–70,
  171–2; *see also* Axis,
  Rome–Berlin
Four Power Pact, 135, 139–40, 147
France, 7, 28, 121, 131, 133, 135, 138,
  140, 141, 142, 147, 152, 160,
  161, 169, 171, 172, 175
 conflict with, 132, 133, 134, 135,
  148, 149, 150, 151, 152, 153,
  154, 160, 174
Franco, Francisco, 148, 153
Freemasonry and Freemasons, 82, 83,
  161
Futurists, 14, 15, 16, 34

General Confederation of Labour
  (CGL), *see Confederazione Generale del
  Lavoro*
Genoa, 31, 55
Gentile, Giovanni, 79–80, 96
'Gentlemen's Agreement' (1937), 149;
  see also foreign policy
Gerarchia, Mussolini's political journal,
  172
Germany, 7, 125, 132, 133, 135
 and interwar diplomacy, 139, 140,
  147, 148, 149, 151, 152, 153,
  154, 158, 159, 160, 166, 168,
  169, 170, 171
 and Second World War, 172, 173,
  175, 177, 180, 182
 and occupation of Italy (1943–5),
  182, 183, 184, 185, 186, 187;
  see also Axis, Rome–Berlin
Giampaoli, Mario, 85
Giolitti, Giovanni, 5–6, 7, 18, 20, 21,
  28, 30, 31, 33, 39, 40–3, 51, 52,
  54, 74, 78
Gioventù Italiana del Littorio (GIL), Fascist
  party youth organisation, 155,
  156, 179
Gioventù Universitaria Fascista (GUF),
  Fascist university students'
  organisation, 110–11, 118, 159
Giuriati, Giovanni, 108, 121

Gramsci, Antonio, 27, 28
Grand Council, Fascist, 64, 67, 77, 82,
  84, 92, 93, 94, 125, 150, 156,
  162, 163, 181, 182, 185
Grandi, Dino, 44, 45, 46, 124, 139,
  157, 181, 182
Graziani, Rodolfo, 187
Greece, 133, 174–5
gruppi di competenza, 'technical study
  groups', 49, 51, 62

Head of Government, 85, 92, 93–4,
  126, 127, 157, 176, 181
Hitler, Adolf, 139, 140, 148, 150, 151,
  157, 161, 169, 171, 174, 175,
  176, 180, 184, 186
Hoare–Laval agreement (1935), 142
Horthy, Admiral Nicholas, 135
Hungary, 134, 135, 166

Ilva, steel firm, 22, 39
imperialism, *see* empire
industrial workers
 in First World War, 9
 in *biennio rosso*, 23, 27–8, 31–2
 and Fascism, 40, 46, 101, 115,
  117–18, 122, 128
 in Second World War, 177, 178, 186
industrialists and industry
 during *biennio rosso*, 23, 27, 28, 31–2
 and Fascism (1919–22), 39–40, 47
 under Fascism (1922–40), 82, 88,
  89, 92, 99, 115, 127–8, 141,
  168
 in Second World War, 176–7, 181,
  182, 186; *see also Confederazione
  dell'Industria Italiana*
inquadramento 'totalitarian
  regimentation', 107–8
Institute of Foreign Exchange, 128
Institute for Industrial Reconstruction
  (IRI), 129, 167, 168
Interior, Ministry of, 58, 77, 82, 85–6,
  87, 95
international fascism, 125
Intersyndical committees, of the PNF,
  100

interventionism and interventionists, 7, 8, 12, 13, 14, 15, 16, 45, 131, 185
'intransigents', of the PNF (1922–5), 61, 62, 77, 78, 79, 80, 81, 84, 85
Iron Guard, Rumanian fascist movement, 125
Italian Confederation of Labour, see Confederazione Italiana del Lavoro (CIL)
Italian Industrialists Confederation, see Confederazione dell'Industria Italiana
Italian Social Republic, see Repubblica Sociale Italiana (RSI)

Judiciary and legal system, 83
Jung, Guido, 128
'Justice and Liberty', anti-Fascist movement, 122
Justice, Ministry of, 81, 124

king, see monarchy

labourers, agricultural day-, see braccianti
land, occupations of (1919–20), 10, 23–4, 31
land reclamation, see bonifica integrale
landowners, 22, 24, 31, 36, 37, 68, 86, 103; see also agriculture
Lateran agreements (1929), 95–6, 97, 109; see also church, catholic
latifundia, large estates, 5, 23, 99
Lazio, 23
League of Nations, 132, 133, 135, 139, 140, 148
  sanctions against Italy (1935–6), 142–3, 147, 161, 162, 165
Le Bon, Gustave, 8
Leghorn, 35, 55
Leo XIII, Pope (1878–1903), 120
Leyers, Hans, 186
liberals
  1870–1918, 3–4
  1918–22, 16–17, 18, 20, 21, 30, 40, 42, 43, 47, 51, 54, 56, 57, 58, 59, 60
  1922–5, 62, 63, 66, 70, 72, 73, 74,
75, 78
Libya, 134, 175, 180
Libyan War (1911–12), 6
Liguria, 23, 24, 39, 73, 81, 184
Lipani, Damiano, 85
listone, 'big list' (1924 elections), 71, 73, 74, 78
littoriali, Fascist student games, 111
Ljubljana, 184
local government, see elections, local; Podestà
Locarno agreement (1925), 135, 148; see also foreign policy
Lombardy, 19, 24, 35, 37, 39, 73, 181
London, treaty of (1915), 7, 28, 133
Lucca, 110
LUCE, film agency, 116

Macedonia, 134
mafia and mafiosi, 73
Malatesta, Errico, 34
Mantua, 25
Maraviglia, Maurizio, 158
March on Rome, the (1922), 57–9, 61, 66, 67, 72, 76
Marche, 23
Marinelli, Giovanni, 77
Marsich, Pietro, 29, 45, 46
Marx, Karl and Marxism, 8, 9, 11
Matteotti, Giacomo, 60, 75, 78
Matteotti crisis (1924), 65, 75–8, 81, 88, 94, 97, 182
Mazzini, Giuseppe, 45, 185
Mediterranean, 131, 132, 133, 134, 137, 147, 148, 149, 150, 151, 153, 154, 173, 174, 180; see also empire and imperialism
mezzadri and mezzadria, sharecroppers and sharecropping, 24, 25, 26, 37, 38, 47, 103
Middle East, 132, 134
Miglioli, Guido, 19, 53, 54
Milan, 13, 14, 15, 16, 31, 55, 85, 117, 187
Militia, Fascist (MVSN), 61, 65, 67, 69, 76, 77, 78, 81, 86, 111, 153, 158, 182, 186, 187

Misuri, Alfredo, 63
Molise, 16
monarchy, 7, 48
    and rise of Fascism (1919–22), 54,
        57, 60
    and Fascist government (1922–5),
        63, 64, 65, 76, 77, 81
    in Fascist regime (1925–43), 92, 93,
        94–5, 97, 132, 143, 157–8,
        170, 171, 172
    and fall of Mussolini, 181, 182
    after fall of Mussolini, 183, 184, 185,
        188
Montecatini, chemical firm, 167
Montreux conference (1934), 125
Mori, Cesare, 53
Munich conference (1938), 154, 159,
    169
Mussolini, Benito
    as a Socialist, 8–9
    during First World War, 8, 11, 12
    as a Fascist (1919–22), 13–15, 29,
        30, 33, 36, 39–46, 51–9
    as Prime Minister (1922–5), 60–88
    as dictator (1925–40), 89–172
    in Second World War (1940–5),
        173–88
Muti, Ettore, 179

Naples, 35, 57
National Bloc (1921 elections), 40, 41,
    42, 43, 56
Nationalist Association and
    Nationalists, 8, 12, 15, 62, 63, 71,
    72, 73, 80, 81, 131, 132, 137
Nazis and Nazism, 125, 135, 139, 160,
    161, 163, 173, 184
Near East, 131
Neurath, Konstantin Von, 148
New Order, Fascist in Second World
    War, 173–4, 175, 185
Nice, 150
Nietzsche, Friedrich, 8
Nitti, Francesco, 17, 20, 28, 29, 30, 73,
    74
non abbiamo bisogno, papal encyclical
    (1931), 109, 120

'non-belligerency' (1939–40), 150,
    171, 173
non-expedit (1874), 4, 18; see also church,
    catholic
'normalisation' (1922–4), 61, 62, 63,
    64, 65, 66, 75, 77, 78

occupation of the factories, see
    factories, occupation of; of the
    land, see land, occupations of
Olivetti, Gino, 39
Opera Nazionale Balilla (ONB), National
    Balilla Organisation, 95, 110,
    118, 119, 121, 155
Opera Nazionale Dopolavoro (OND),
    National Afterwork Organisation,
    114–16, 117–18, 119
Opera per la Vigilanza e la Repressione
    Antifascista (OVRA), secret police,
    87
Ordine Nuovo, l', communist newspaper,
    27
Orlando, Vittorio Emanuele, 28

Pact of Pacification (1921), 43, 45, 46,
    52
'Pact of Steel', Italian–German
    alliance (1939), 153, 169, 170; see
    also Axis, Rome–Berlin; foreign
    policy
Padovani, Aurelio, 71, 74
Padua, 15, 25, 38, 42, 45, 113
Paglia–Caldo agreement (1920), 26, 34
Palazzo Chigi agreement (1923), 68, 88
Palazzo Vidoni agreement (1925), 68,
    88
Palermo, 73, 85
'parallel war' (1940–1), 171, 173–4
parliament
    before First World War, 3–5
    during First World War, 7–8
    1919–22, 17–19, 21, 30, 56, 57,
        58–9, 188
    1922–5, 60, 62, 63, 65, 66, 69, 75,
        76
    1925–43, 92, 94, 182; see also
        Chamber of Deputies, Senate

Parma, 66
Partito Nazionale Fascista (PNF), *see*
    Fascist party
Partito Socialista Italiano (PSI), *see*
    Socialist party
Pavolini, Alessandro, 186, 187
peasant landlords and proprietors, 37,
    47, 103; *see also* agriculture,
    landowners, *mezzadri*
Perrone-Compagni, Dino, 63
Perugia, 63
Pesarò speech (1926), 99; *see also*
    revaluation of the lira
Piedmont, 23, 28, 39, 44, 73, 74, 181
Pius IX, Pope (1846–78), 4
Pius IX, Pope (1922–39), 70, 76, 96,
    109, 120, 121, 161, 164–5; *see also*
    church, catholic
Podestà, Fascist local government
    official, 85–6
Poland, 132, 170
police
    1919–25, 41–2, 50, 52, 55, 56, 61,
        82
    1925–43, 83, 86–7, 102, 122, 123,
        164
Po valley, 24, 25, 26, 35, 36, 37, 38,
    41, 42, 48, 67, 68
Popolari, *see* Popular party
Popolo d'Italia, Il (Mussolini's
    newspaper), 11, 12, 39
Popular Culture, Ministry of, 155, 161,
    186
Popular Fronts, 121, 152, 153, 161
Popular party (PPI)
    1919–22, 16, 17, 18, 19, 20, 21, 24,
        30, 40, 47, 53, 54
    1922–6, 66, 70, 71, 73, 75, 76, 95,
        96
    after 1926 (ex-PPI), 120, 121
    see also church, catholic; Vatican
Posts and Telegraphs, Ministry of, 72
prefects
    in the liberal state, 4
    and the Fascist movement
        (1919–22), 41–2, 50, 52, 55,
        56, 58, 67

and the Fascist government
    (1922–5), 64, 68, 72–3, 82
in the Fascist regime, 83, 84, 85–7,
    102
Press and Propaganda, Ministry of,
    115, 143, 155; *see also* Popular
    Culture, Ministry of
'productivism', 12, 13, 34, 37, 48, 49,
    67, 68, 76, 91, 92, 126, 127, 138,
    185
proportional representation, 3, 17, 18,
    19, 20, 66
Public Works, Ministry of, 72

Quadragesimo Anno, papal encyclical
    (1931), 120
race and racism, 156, 160–3, 165; *see
    also* anti-semitism, Race
    Manifesto
Race Manifesto (1938), 160–1
Radicals, 8, 15
radio, 115, 116, 143
Rahn, Rudolf, 184
Rapallo, treaty of (1920), 30
ras, local Fascist boss, 49, 51, 55, 57,
    61, 62, 65, 66, 79, 88, 95
'Red Week' (1914), 6, 23
Reggio Emilia, 63
Repubblica Sociale Italiana (RSI), Italian
    Social Republic (1943–5), 180,
    184–7, 188
Republican Fascist Party (PFR), 185,
    186, 187
Republican National Guard, 187
Republicans, 8, 15, 34, 38, 48, 55, 74,
    75
Resistance, the anti-Fascist, 183, 184,
    185, 186, 187, 188; *see also*
    anti-Fascism
revaluation of the lira (1926–7), 91–2,
    98–101, 102, 103, 107, 108, 114,
    127, 136, 168
'revisionists', in the Fascist party
    (1922–4), 62
revolutionary syndicalism and
    revolutionary syndicalists, 8, 11,
    12, 15, 27, 29, 36, 45, 48, 126

Rhineland, German reoccupation of (1936), 148
Ribbentrop, Joachim von, 151, 169
Ricci, Renato, 39, 95, 110, 187
Rimini, 184
Rocca, Massimo, 62, 75
Rocco, Alfredo, 80, 83, 89, 90, 91, 93, 97, 124
Romagna, 42
Rome, 184
Rommel, Erwin, 175
Rossi, Cesare, 15, 77, 78
Rossoni, Edmondo, 67, 88, 90, 126
Rovigo, 25
Rumania, 132, 174
'ruralism', 101–4, 119, 121, 138; *see also* agriculture, *bonifica integrale*, demographic policies
Russia, 125, 152, 153, 171, 174, 175, 180

Salandra, Antonio, 7, 28, 54, 58, 63, 66, 75, 78
Salerno, 73
Salò Republic, *see Repubblica Sociale Italiana*
Sardinia, 16, 23
Savoy, 15
School Charter (1939), 156
schools
  in Fascist regime, 110, 116, 118, 155–6; *see also Opera Nazionale Balilla*, teachers
  religion in, 70, 96
Schnuschnigg, Kurt Von, 148
Scorza, Carlo, 110, 121, 123, 180
Second World War, 93, 172, 173–80, 187
Senate, 92, 156, 157
sharecroppers and sharecropping, *see under mezzadri*
Sicily, 23, 25, 73, 74, 81, 85
Siena, 27, 45
Slovenia, 175
Social party (PSI) and socialist movement
  before First World War, 4–6

during First World War, 7, 8, 9, 10, 11
1919–22, 16–56, 188
1922–6, 70, 74, 75, 76, 86, 88, 89
and anti-Fascism, **1926–43**, 122
and Resistance, **1943–5**, 183
Social Reformists, 8
Somalia, 135, 175
South Tyrol, 53, 134, 151, 184
Southern Italy
  politics in, **1870–1922**, 3–6, 15, 16, 17, 21, 23–4, 35
  politics in, **1922–5**, 71–4
  Fascism in, **1925–43**, 103, 118–19, 141
  1943–5, 183, 188
Sorel, Georges, 8
Soviet Union, *see* Russia
Spain, 121, 153, 161, 167
Spanish Civil War (1936–9), 12, 148, 149, 153, 161, 168
Special Tribunal for the Defence of the State, 83, 182, 185
sport, 87, 109, 110, 115, 118, 120, 155
squadrism and squads, Fascist, 14–15, 30, 34–5, 36–7, 38, 40, 41, 42, 44, 45, 46, 49, 50–1, 52, 53, 55, 57, 58, 61, 63, 65, 66, 68, 70, 75, 77, 79, 81, 82, 84, 85, 98, 111, 158–9, 180, 186, 187
State, the Fascist, *see* Fascist regime, 'totalitarian'
Starace, Achille, 108, 109, 110, 111, 113, 116, 155, 158
Stresemann, Gustav, 151
students, 111
Sturzo, Luigi, 18, 20, 40, 70
Suvich, Fulvio, 166
Switzerland, 171
syndicalism and syndicates, Fascist, 61, 67, 68, 69, 79, 87, 89, 97, 99–100, 107, 113, 120, 126, 128, 159, 185
  in agriculture, 36, 37–8, 44, 45, 48
  in industry, 40, 61, 67, 68, 88, 89, 91, 92, 115, 116–17; *see also* corporations

teachers, 47, 110
tenant farmers, 24, 26, 37, 47, 103
'totalitarian', 'totalitarian' state,
    'totalitarianism', 79–81, 82, 84,
    87, 89, 95, 96, 97, 98, 108, 109,
    113, 115, 116, 119, 120, 123,
    124, 127, 136, 137–8, 143–4,
    152, 154, 155, 159, 160, 161,
    163, 173, 174, 188
trade unions
    catholic, *see Confederazione Italiana del
        Lavoro*
    socialist, *see Confederazione Generale del
        Lavoro, Federterra, Federazione
        Italiana Operai Metallurgici*
    Fascist, *see* syndicalism
trasformismo, 'transformism', 4–6,
    21, 33, 41, 43, 73, 74, 77,
    119
Trento, 53
Treviso, 46
Trieste, 34
trincerocrazia, 'trenchocracy', 12
Triple Alliance, 7, 133
Tunisia, 150
Turati, Augusto, 44–5, 66, 84, 87, 88,
    99, 107, 108, 111, 114
Turin, 9, 23, 27, 31, 66
Tuscany, 23, 24, 27, 35, 38, 39, 41, 42,
    44, 73, 78, 81, 86

Udine, 57
Umbria, 24
United States of America (USA), 22,
    28, 29, 98, 99, 136, 138, 139,
    166, 181; *see also* Allies
'universal' fascism, *see* international
    fascism
universities, *see Gioventù Universitaria
    Fascista*, students
Ustasha movement, Croatia, 134

Vatican, 18, 19, 20
    and Fascist government, **1922–6**,
        70–1
    and Fascist regime, 95, 96, 121, 122,
        164, 165, 171, 181; *see also*
        church, catholic
Venetia, 19, 24, 35, 37, 44, 45, 53, 73,
    184
Venezia Giulia, 34, 81
Venice, 15
Verona, 185, 186
Versailles Peace Conference and
    Treaty, 28, 29, 131, 132, 139,
    140, 148, 150
Victor Emmanuel III, king (1900–46),
    see monarchy
Visocchi decree (1919), 31
Volta conference (1932), 125

Weimar Republic, Germany, 135
welfare, 87, 112–14, 118, 123, 179; *see
    also Ente Opere Assistenziali*
Wilson, Woodrow, 29
Women's *fasci*, 114, 179
women's Fascist organisations, 118
Wolff, Karl, 184

Young Fascists, 110–11, 120, 155
youth
    catholic organisations, 95, 111, 120,
        121
    Fascist organisations, 87, 95, 108,
        109–11, 118, 123–4, 155–6; *see
        also Gioventù Italiana del Littorio,
        Gioventù Universitaria Fascista,
        Opera Nazionale Balilla*, schools
Yugoslavia, 132
    conflict with, 134, 175

Zara, 184
Zionism, 134, 162